# Agent 146

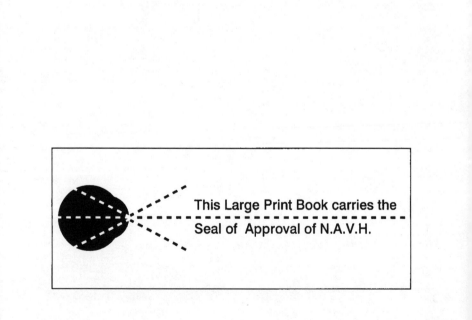

This Large Print Book carries the
Seal of Approval of N.A.V.H.

# Agent 146

## The True Story Of A Nazi Spy
## In America

## Erich Gimpel

## Foreword by Charles Whiting

**Thorndike Press • Waterville, Maine**

Published in 2003 by arrangement with
St. Martin's Press, LLC.

Thorndike Press® Large Print American History Series.

The tree indicium is a trademark of Thorndike Press.

The text of this Large Print edition is unabridged.
Other aspects of the book may vary from the original edition.

Set in 16 pt. Plantin by Myrna S. Raven.

Printed in the United States on permanent paper.

**Library of Congress Cataloging-in-Publication Data**

Gimpel, Erich, 1910–
    [Spion für Deutschland. English]
    Agent 146 : the true story of a Nazi spy in America /
Erich Gimpel ; foreword by Charles Whiting.
        p. cm.
    "Published in Great Britain in 1957 as Spy for Germany"
— Verso t.p.
    ISBN 0-7862-5369-X (lg. print : hc : alk. paper)
    1. Gimpel, Erich, 1910–  2. Spies — Germany —
Biography.  3. World War, 1939–1945 — Secret service —
Germany.  4. World War, 1939–1945 — Secret service —
United States.  5. Espionage, German — United States —
History — 20th century.  I. Title.
D810.S8G4513 2003
940.54′8743′092—dc21
    [B]                                          2003047376

# Agent 146

# CONTENTS

# FOREWORD

## THE ENEMY WITHIN

By 1944, "Father Christmas," as the head of the *Abwehr*, the German secret service, was known, due to his shock of white hair and benign appearance, had been sending his agents and saboteurs to the United States for six years or more. The early ones had been very successful. They had entered a peacetime America totally unprepared for the "war in the shadows." They had stolen the plans of the Norden bombsight, had organized a peaceful pro-German, anti-British oil cartel, and had infiltrated potential war plants and port installations along the whole East Coast.

But by the time "Father Christmas," or, to give him a real name, Admiral Canaris, had been thrown out of office and sent to a concentration camp, his operations in the States were at a virtual standstill.

In early 1945, however, the S.S.'s own secret service, the S.D., led by cunning, scar-faced ex-lawyer General Schellenberg had more drastic plans for an offensive against far off *Amerika.* They included launching the new German "revenge weapons," the V-1 and V-2, against New York from U-boats and a new sabotage/spy operation against key U.S. installations.

The latter were to be carried out at the request of the hard-pressed Japanese. For more than a year and a half, Japan had been trying to retaliate against the United States for the increasing destruction of their cities. Balloons, launched from Japanese submarines off the West Coast, had been designed to act as incendiaries when they landed on American soil. But these attempts had basically failed. There had been a few large fires in the northwest and exactly five civilian fatalities. These had been sad, but insignificant in Japanese eyes in comparison to the thousands of civilian casualties they had suffered in their native land.

But now the S.S., a much more ruthless force, was in charge of the anti-American operation. Although Schellenberg was very experienced in such matters (he had personally kidnapped the two heads of the British M.I.6 on the Continent in 1939 and a year later he had come within a hairsbreadth of seducing the Duke of Windsor, ex-King Edward VIII, into the

German camp), his subordinates were not, and their choice of the two agents who would carry out the first two-year mission against the United States (code-named "Operation Magpie") was poor from the start.

The first agent-to-be was German-born, thirty-four-year-old Erich Gimpel. Gimpel had been recruited into German Intelligence in 1935 in Peru, where he was asked to spy on shipping and cargoes leaving that South American country for Anglo-French ports. After Pearl Harbor, when Peru sided with the States, he repatriated to Germany in August 1942. After working there as an *Abwehr* courier, he was ordered to attend formal espionage training at S.S. schools in France and Holland.

Here using the cover name of Wilhelm Coller, he met his fellow agent-to-be William C. Colepaugh, then age twenty-six. It was going to be an unlucky friendship for Gimpel. Colepaugh was a native American. Born in Niantic, Connecticut, he had attended Admiral Farragut Academy and M.I.T., where he had studied naval engineering. In October 1942, Colepaugh joined the U.S. Naval Reserve. A year later he had been discharged "for the good of the service." This was perhaps because the

F.B.I. had begun investigating him for alleged Nazi sympathies. What the F.B.I. didn't know was that Colepaugh was more than sympathetic. In 1941 he had sailed on a British ship as an *Abwehr* spy to report on British convoy routes and tactics between the States and Scotland. But by the time the F.B.I. had discovered they had a real traitor on their hands, Colepaugh had disappeared. He had hired himself out as an ordinary seaman on the Swedish ship the *Gripsholm*, the same vessel that had taken Gimpel back to Germany two years before.

Thus the two men, Gimpel and Colepaugh, prepared for their mission throughout the summer of 1944 with the Western Allies already marching on Germany. By the time the two agents were ready to go, American troops would have already penetrated the Reich. Were they being sent on what they call in Germany a *Himmelfahrtskommando* (an Ascension Day commando, i.e., a suicide mission), they must have asked themselves. But as we know from recent tragic events in the United States, fanatics, mostly young, can always be found to risk their own lives in such desperate ventures.

Their mission was carefully worked out and far-reaching. From the States,

Colepaugh and Gimpel were to report on what they had found out about American missiles, jet planes, shipbuilding, and possible atomic bomb developments. On October 6, they sailed on the U-1230 for the States. More than a month later, after the U-boat had already sunk some U.S. shipping, they were set ashore on an isolated beach on Frenchman Bay, near Bar Harbor, Maine.

Gimpel's account is exciting, eloquent, and perhaps a little sad at the end when he realizes just how duped and abandoned to his fate he was when the two of them set off through that raging Maine snowstorm in the hope they might find some refuge for their undertaking, only to find that Colepaugh would turn traitor yet again and betray him to his enemies, the F.B.I.

But Gimpel's story is more than that. It is a reminder and a warning that in the times in which we live we must be constantly on our guard. After the events of September 11, it is a salutary warning. For it tells us we must be permanently vigilant, not only against the enemy from without, but also for the one within.

Charles Whiting
*Fall 2002*

# INTRODUCTION

Spies normally keep silence. But I am going to speak. I have left the service for ever. I am going to write of all the trickery, all the low cunning; otherwise nothing will ever be told of this devil's game.

A spy has feelings like any other man. As you will see from my story, he falls in love, gives way to the same passions, has moments of black despair and great jubilation. But, unlike other men, he walks hand in hand with fear. It rules his every action, injects itself into his every thought. He has always to be on his guard, always suspicious, never himself. One error of judgment can lead him to the scaffold. It was indeed a failure to assess the weakness in the character of my companion that led me almost to the hangman's noose at Fort Jay on April 11th, 1945.

I recall the scene vividly as I write. It was seven o'clock in the morning. Officially I did not know that on the 15th of April, that is to say in ninety-six hours time, between five and seven in the morning, the hangman was to place the rope around my neck. Thirteen steps and thirteen knots as the death protocol demanded. The prisoner is usually told only twenty-four hours before execution in America, for the State is dutybound not to tell the prisoner until one day before the end. But a sympathetic warder told me three days before the appointed time.

Pause now, in your reading, and imagine yourself in a similar situation. . . .

At first the time passes quite slowly but as the end draws near it passes much too quickly; much, much too quickly. You feel as if you want to hold time back by force. You want to pummel on the walls with your fists, break the iron bars, laugh and cry. A false, rough travesty of a laugh. No laugh at all in fact, but a whimper.

I had four days. Too little for living; too long for dying. The warder brought me coffee and white bread. I was not to want for anything. I even enjoyed something akin to sympathy. Usually only murderers are hanged, but in wartime standards shift.

"Listen, Gimpel," said the warder. "You know what is going to happen, don't you? There's not much hope for you now. Wouldn't you like to have a word with the chaplain? I can arrange it for you."

"I don't want to see any chaplain," I replied. I imagined that a man in a black soutane would come into the cell, say a few words to me in a soft parsonic voice and then tell his friends all about me over a cup of coffee. The shadow of death, that is how the man in black would appear to me, the last stage of civilisation before the hangman's rope.

"He's not actually a priest," explained the warder. "He's a captain, an Army officer. He just has a cross on his cap and his shoulder flashes. He's an awfully nice chap. Have a word with him. It can't do any harm, anyway."

He came. He greeted me as casually as was possible in the circumstances. He gave me his hand and looked me straight in the eyes. What sort of chaplain was this? How free and easy he was, how comradely! He seated himself on my bench and we smoked a cigarette together. He crossed his legs and smiled at me. Not an embarrassed smile, not like the smile of the many other high-ranking officers who had been visiting me every day. We smoked in silence.

"Have no fear," he said. "I'm not going to preach you a sermon. Sermons are no good, and anyhow a sermon wouldn't be of much use to you now." He nodded and smiled at me again. Then he leant back against the wall.

"Read the Old Testament," he said. "There you have got everything you want, sex and crime, war and peace. There is no more exciting story than the Bible."

"I haven't read the Bible for a long time," I replied.

"That's a pity," he replied. "I'll come again in the morning. That is, if it's all right with you."

He went. There were it seemed just three more days of life left to me. How I escaped the scaffold you shall read in my story, which I now present to you.

# CHAPTER 1

## MY CAREER AS A SPY BEGINS

My story, the story of Agent 146 of the German M.I., later taken over by Reich Security, began in 1935, two days after my twenty-fifth birthday. In Berlin. I was a radio engineer. There was at the time much military training and "toughening up" going on in Germany. I had an offer to go to Peru. A German firm there was looking for a young man for their radio department and they decided on me. But I had to get the formal consent of my District Military Command.

I knew next to nothing about South America. All I knew was that it had a hot climate, that coffee grew there and that it was renowned for wide-eyed, fabulously dressed women who drove about in expensive cars and frequented sophisticated clubs.

"Are you a Jew?" asked the captain at the District Military Command when I applied to him for formal consent.

"No."

"Well, why do you want to leave the country?"

"For professional reasons. I want to learn Spanish and English. And, of course, I shall be very well paid there."

The captain obviously relished his authority. He walked thoughtfully up and down, nodding his head.

"Very well then," he said. "I have confidence in you. You may go on two conditions. You must, first, swear on oath that you will never relinquish your German citizenship."

"And the second condition, Captain?"

"You must report to the German Legation in Lima immediately on arrival."

"Very well."

The Foreign Exchange authorities allowed me ten marks pocket money for the voyage, and my passage was paid for by Messrs. Burger, Import and Export, Lima, Peru. I travelled via Paris into Normandy and at La Rochelle went on board s.s. *Orbita*. Little did I realise that never again in my life was I to travel so happily and so free of care.

Lima had everything that my imagination had promised. My employer placed at my disposal a room in his villa, which was situated among the olive groves of the San Isidro quarter. In the mornings I got up, took the firm's Chrysler, drove in bathing trunks to the country club for a swim, then breakfasted on the terrace. Then between nine and eleven I did my day's work. I earned 300 dollars a month, but my expenditure was practically nil, as I was entertained everywhere. I learned Spanish and did my best to become a *caballero*. I learned how to tie a black bow-tie, and how to kiss the ladies.

I was in no great hurry to report to the German Legation. In South America there is so much time that one never has time for anything. But it had to be done. I discovered that the German Diplomatic Mission had settled itself in a beautiful villa in the Mira Flores quarter, and when I called there I was referred to an attaché whose name began with G, and whom I will here call Gringer.

Like everyone else in Lima, the diplomat wore a snow-white suit. He looked me over without any special interest. At first he said very little and behaved as if talking was an effort. He seemed to me like an uncle who had sown his wild oats long since and had now reformed. We drank *pisco*, the colourless South American gin.

"What are you by profession?" Gringer asked me.

"Radio engineer."

"*Bueno!* That's a good profession. Do you happen to play skat?"

"I like it very much," I answered.

"Chess?"

"Yes; I play chess too, Herr Attaché."

"Please call me Gringer. We're abroad now. Titles don't count in this country; only bank accounts."

I had plenty of opportunity later of observing the man who this evening sat facing me. He was not the sort of person one dislikes at first sight. He was rather a type to make one smile; his exaggerated chivalry with the ladies and his attempts to make an impression with his appearance did not seem to suit his age. We kept our distance. Once we played skat together for two days and a night. He lost with good grace.

Then he went to Germany. A few months before the outbreak of war he returned and telephoned me. It was urgent, he said. The room in which he received me was furnished with dark period furniture. An electric fan hummed below the portrait of Hitler. We sat relaxed facing each other. Gringer did not let me out of his eyes.

"There's going to be a war," he said, "and I don't know what will happen to us here. It's our duty to be prepared. Every German is a soldier and must do his duty wherever he may be." He nodded his head with each word, as if in self-approval. Words like this could be heard any day in Lima. The German colony was giving nationalism an airing, and so were the French and English colonies for that matter.

"Would you like another drink?" asked Gringer. I nodded. It was said that drink helped to combat the heat. Well, I certainly never suffered from the heat. My own car was waiting for me outside, a Super Six — I had several thousand dollars in the bank — and every day I was at a different party. My only worry was that I might be missing something.

As I now look back on this time it seems to me so unreal that I begin to wonder whether I ever really lived through it. In Lima I never missed a party. In Atlanta Prison some time later I missed eleven years of my life. . . .

"If you were in Germany now you would have been in the Army for some time," Gringer continued, "but I'd rather you were here. A front is taking shape here too, and I know I can count on you."

"Of course," I said.

"You circulate a good deal. You're *persona grata* everywhere. That is excellent. Well, from now on your social relationships will be put into the service of your Fatherland."

He got to his feet and paced up and down the room. "Here it comes," I thought. "German in block capitals." I realised that I was in the company of a fanatic.

"For us all! You are working for Germany, man, and don't forget it!"

I drank up and he at once filled my glass again.

"You've got a Navy complex, haven't you?"

"Yes; I should like to have been a sailor."

"Fine. From now onwards I want to know what ships come into port here. The names of their captains. How many in the crews, what their cargoes are. In short, there is nothing that does not interest me. Can you give me that information?"

"There's nothing in it," I replied. "It's no secret. The only thing that puzzles me is what use it is going to be to you."

He laughed. I got the impression that he was having a little game of spy on his own. Little Gringer was seeing himself as no end of a fine fellow. I was amused that he

23

should be wanting to make an agent of me. I certainly had nothing against it.

Everything was sport in Lima — car-driving, politics, drinking, women. As long as it didn't take up too much of my time . . . for here in Lima, the Rio of the west coast, one had a whole host of social obligations. He gave me his hand, it was sticky.

"Tomorrow there is a ball in aid of our Winter Relief," he said. "You can start straightaway there and prove yourself. According to my information the Texter family will be there . . . you know who they are . . . I want you to make friends with Evelyn Texter. See if you can do that, and see to it that you are invited by the family to stay the week-end. I will tell you the rest later."

I was glad to get away from him at last. I did not take him seriously. I did not take myself seriously either, but I found my mission quite attractive. Why not? Spying was preferable to square-bashing.

That was how my career as a spy began. I never really wanted to be one. I began as a dilettante, as an amateur with some contempt for my task, a task which eventually was to knock all the contempt out of me. They were indeed ridiculously unimportant commissions with which my career began, but in later chapters you will discover what perilous adventures were to follow.

Every ticket for the Winter Relief ball in Lima was sold. It took place in a German school, very much tricked up for the occasion. Practically the entire Diplomatic Corps put in a perspiring presence to contribute to the end that no one in Germany should feel the cold. In one of the pauses between dances I struggled through to the buffet. I had caught sight of Miss Texter.

She stood beside me, wearing a yellow evening dress, and certainly made my task seem quite inviting. She was tall and slim with green vivacious eyes which looked out upon the world straightly and openly. We smiled at each other. We were both holding our plates in our hand. Evelyn Texter put hers down and pointed to the dance floor. I nodded.

"That was a nice little bit of pantomime, wasn't it?" she said. She spoke pure Oxford English. "Are you one of the Winter Relief people?"

"No."

I introduced myself. We walked together on to the terrace. The dance had come to an end before it had properly begun for us. I twisted a glass between my fingers. She noticed this and took it away from me.

"And now, what can I do for you?" Evelyn asked.

"Oh," I answered, "how would you like a little stroll along the shore? You're not afraid of me, are you?"

"I'm never afraid of fair men," she answered. "I find that the trouble with them mostly is lack of spirit."

"Well, that makes them reliable in a sense, anyhow," I said.

Our first conversation was no more profound than this.

We were both young. Perhaps my life would have taken a different course if it had not been for Gringer. Three days later I received an invitation from Evelyn's father, who was director of a group of English-American shipping lines.

I was soon dropping in and out of the Texters' house like one of the family, although my relationship was in no way formalised. I had almost forgotten the original purpose of the first meeting. Evelyn and I flirted with varying degrees of finesse; life was fun and neither of us took it very seriously. I learned to speak English, to think English and to acquire English manners. I completely lost my accent. Without realising it, in the Texters' home I laid the foundations of a career which was to lead me down into hell. . . .

War broke out and the game became serious. If Germans and Englishmen met in a bar it would develop into a row. The war of the battlefields was carried over into the dance halls. Close friends ceased to be on speaking terms. But there were exceptions, and one of these was the Texter family. I was still a friend of the family, a false friend. . . .

I had a short-wave transmitter in my room. My reports went to Chile, and from there were passed on direct to German U-boats. The sailors with whom I went drinking one night might find their ship under assault two days later.

The German colony were all out for victory and I was with them. Every scruple was drowned in waves of patriotic enthusiasm. Poland was overrun, France fell. The German colony celebrated victory with Latin-American fervour, and meanwhile the Morse signals tapped on. . . .

I learned to distinguish the significant from the irrelevant. I became familiar with cargo ships and warships of every kind. The Allied warships' every movement was reported by me. The sailors took me for an American and, standing at the bar, foolishly forgot what they had been taught about holding their tongues.

The *Leipzig*, under Captain Schultz, had been surprised by the war while on the high seas. It had cars and refrigerators on board and had immediately taken shelter in the harbour of Guayaquil (Ecuador). Then the crew began to run short of food. Needless to say the position of the ship had long since been known to the British. One night the *Leipzig* started on a dramatic race with the cruiser *Despatch*. The *Leipzig* came from the north, the *Despatch* from the south. Both were equidistant from the harbour of Lima.

Captain Schultz succeeded in eluding the *Despatch*. For days on end the newspapers followed the *Leipzig*'s course. There were giant headlines and people were betting on the outcome. Then came the final spurt. Both ships were shaping a direct course towards Lima. They were still a few miles from the harbour. Everyone took a day off to see the final phase. Close behind each other *Leipzig* and *Despatch* sailed in. The *Leipzig* won by a few feet. Germans and Peruvians celebrated the victory, a victory to which I had contributed with my messages.

I was doing well. The American Secretary of State, Cordell Hull, came to Lima for confidential talks with members of the Peruvian Government. I discovered the subject of their deliberations and reported it to Germany. Shortly after that — as predicted by me — diplomatic relations between Peru and Germany were broken off. Gringer packed his trunks. I stayed on. An experimental Fortress four-engined bomber landed on the airfield at Lima. I made it my business to discover all its technical details, the nature of its armament and its operational radius, and reported via Chile to Berlin. Some months later whole swarms of Fortress bombers appeared in the night sky over Germany. It wasn't a game any longer. It was war in earnest now, war which increased in severity with every day that passed.

"How's the war?" Evelyn asked me one day. She was wearing blue shorts and a white pullover.

"I snap my fingers at the war," I answered.

"So do I," she said. "But Father's getting more and more nervy every day. He's expecting a transport, and then he's working on those wretched proposals for improving the convoy system."

"Are you talking to the enemy again?"

Evelyn's mother had arrived on the scene, and welcomed me warmly.

That same evening I reported on the new convoy system, the recently developed answer to the magnetic mine, the expected transport and a host of other things. I sat at the Morse keyboard and thought of Evelyn. "The end justifies the means," I reasoned. "But the end is war. To hell with it!"

For two days I pondered on how I could get into Ward 2 of the British-American hospital as a patient. There was a sailor there from the *Despatch*. The cruiser had captured the German cargo ship *Dortmund*, and contrary to the normal course of marine warfare the ship had fallen into the hands of the British intact. What we wanted to find out was why it had not been scuttled.

I went to a German doctor and asked him to show me how I could simulate a case of nephritis. He was quite intrigued with the idea and gave me the tips I needed.

I returned home. I had arranged to meet someone or other at a German club that evening — I can't remember now the details of the appointment — and went to take a shower before changing. I was just drying myself when the door bell rang furiously.

An officer of the Peruvian Criminal Police had called to see me. He was accompanied by an expert from the State telegraph service. Both men greeted me politely. I offered them a *pisco* and they accepted. I concealed my nervousness as well as I could for I realised, of course, that they would want to search my home and that as a result I would be deported.

"You have been reported to us, Señor," said the detective. "You are under suspicion of operating a secret transmitter. We must take a look around here. *Con su permiso, Señor.*"

My mind worked feverishly. I couldn't think what to do. I was a beginner, a bloody beginner. I was still a long way from being Agent 146 of the German War Department. I still had ordinary human feelings. I still had to battle with my racing pulse. Later I was to learn iron control. Later, much later, I talked in Leavenworth prison to German prisoners-of-war, condemned to death for insubordination, five minutes before their execution — and could remain quite calm. I watched them as they went to die and I remained fully self-possessed. . . . But that time in my

31

room in Lima I was frightened as the two men suddenly stood up.

"With your permission, Señor?" And they began a systematic search. I was in a cold sweat. "Now," I thought, "I'm right in the cart."

# CHAPTER 2

## FIGHTING A WAR IN DINNER JACKETS

It was impossible to deny it. The Peruvian Police Inspector was gesticulating wildly, his brow gleaming with sweat. The corner of an outsize pocket-handkerchief hung from his breast pocket. Should I try to bribe him? There were two possibilities. Either he would take the thousand sol which I had at hand and go, or he would take them — and stay.

The expert of the State telegraph service was indicating an apparatus he had found in my room, and the Inspector was asking:

"Señor, what is this?"

"A transmitter," I replied.

"And what do you do with it?"

"Transmit."

"Too bad. I shall have to take you along with me."

Evidently he had been surprised by the frankness of my replies and could not understand why I should have spoken like this. He looked worried, shook his head and cursed quietly to himself. It seemed to me that he was taking the search far less seriously than I was.

"I work for several mining companies," I explained. "I am a radio engineer. Many of the firms I work for have their own transmitters. By special concession. You can check up on that any time you like. If anything goes wrong with one of their sets they bring it to me. That's how I earn my living." The officer of the law continued to shake his head. I explained the matter to him a second time.

"What firm were you working for yesterday at three o'clock?"

"I think it was the Fernandini Iron Company."

"So you didn't transmit any military information?"

"No," I answered. "I don't know a thing about military affairs. I never was a soldier."

"So you're not a spy?" he pursued.

"Certainly not."

He came up to me, smiled happily and clapped his hand on my shoulder. He was glad that I was not going to make any more work for him. We drank a few more glasses of *pisco* together. Then he went, and I never saw him again.

On the following morning I presented

myself at the British-American hospital. I wanted to get at the sick man from the *Despatch.* I said I was Dutch, hoping meanwhile that there were no real Dutchmen in the hospital. I was lucky. The hospital doctor examined me. I complained of pains in the kidney regions and he diagnosed some trouble with the gall bladder.

I lay in bed and was put on a diet. Apart from me there were five men in the ward. We were soon friends and made up such a good poker table that I could almost have forgotten my mission. The sailor — he was called Johnny, I won't mention his surname — lay in the bed next but one to me. The doctors had removed his appendix and forbidden him to drink. He was a cheery fellow with a hearty appetite and much preferred reminiscing about his girls than talking about the war. But after three days I got him to the point.

"What ship were you on, Johnny?" I asked him.

"The *Despatch.*"

"What's that, a minesweeper?"

He roared with laughter.

"It's time you joined the Navy, my boy," he replied. "No, it's a cruiser. An old tub with new guns."

"Have the guns been fired yet?"

"Oh yes," he answered. "D'you think we get our extra war rations for nothing?"

"But none of you have got any medals yet?" I encouraged him to go on talking.

"Oh yes," he said, "the Captain's got one. The Captain's always the last to leave the sinking ship and the first to get the new war medals."

"Well, what did you do for it?"

"We caught the *Dortmund*, a German freighter, and took her home in one piece."

"How did you manage that?"

"Well, things like that do happen sometimes, you know. We'd got quite close to the *Dortmund*, and as we stopped her, her officers had the valves opened ready for scuttling. On the port side everything went according to plan, but something went wrong to starboard. We boarded the *Dortmund* like lightning, closed the valves again and pumped the water out."

I had found out what I wanted to, so I made a quick recovery and had myself discharged. So there had been no sabotage on the *Dortmund* and the British were not using some new system or secret weapon to stop captured ships from scuttling themselves.

I radioed the story to Chile.

My days in Lima were numbered but I did not know it. We were fighting our war in dinner jackets and with cocktail glasses in our hands. We drank to the Fatherland, had an occasional scuffle with an Englishman and for the rest conducted ourselves just as our enemies did. Five German ships, the *München*, *Leipzig*, *Hermontis*, *Monserrate* and *Rakotis* were unable to leave harbour and lay at the quayside. I received instructions to sell them discreetly at knock-out prices. I looked round for someone who might be interested and found him.

Mr. Texter was anxious to seize the opportunity.

"What do you want for them?" he asked.

"Oh, they're quite cheap," I answered. "Five times one million dollars. That's five million."

"Agreed," said Texter. "But I must just telephone my company in New York." A few days later he telephoned me.

"Everything's in order," he said.

"And when can I collect the money?"

"When the war's over," answered Texter. "Meanwhile you'll get a cheque."

The sale had gone wrong. When America entered the war the ships were seized, but up to that time the crews had a good time. It was a matter of honour that the German colony in Lima should entertain them fittingly, and in the evenings we went from one bar to another. Nearly everyone else moved out when they saw us coming. In the Crocodile Bar I had some typical beginner's luck. I happened upon a scuffle between some English and Americans and I got two Americans out of it. One of them was short and the other was a big chap. Both wore uniforms which had seen their best days. The Americans had insulted King George and that was how it had started. This was as good a way as any to start a row if you felt like it.

One of the two officers was called B. He was a Colonel in the U.S. Army. His companion introduced himself as Major G. They were heading the American Military Mission in Peru. From then onwards we sat there, nearly every day, playing heads-or-tails and discussing military matters between whiles.

"Another four weeks," said Major G. when the Russian campaign had begun, "and Russia will be smashed."

"And then?" I asked.

"And then it'll be the Tommies' turn."

"And then?"

"Then you'll have won your damn war," he said.

B. and G. gave me some interesting details about the inadequate equipment of the American Army, about their mobilisation possibilities and about the production of modern weapons. After nights drinking with them I would sit at the Morse keys and report everything indiscriminately, true and false, important and unimportant.

War with America broke out. We remained friends but the two Yankees were by no means as dumb as I had hoped. They became suspicious and started keeping an eye on me. One day two Peruvians stopped me right in town.

"Are you Señor Gimpel?"

"Yes," I said. What did they want?

"I must ask you to come to the Prefecture with me."

"After dinner," I said.

"I'm afraid not," said one of the officials. "It is very urgent. I have a warrant for your arrest."

When I was taken to the four-storeyed Remand Prison of the 6th Commissariat, a friendly warder said to me: "Get up as high as you can, Señor. You will know why tonight."

The cell contained nothing but a pile of old newspapers. My neighbour was a Frenchman who had been arrested on a smuggling charge. He was delighted to see me. His knowledge of prisons the world over certainly did not come out of books. As a welcome he made me a can of coffee. He showed me how with the help of a newspaper you could make coffee without making smoke. His trick was very useful to me later on. It was one of the few I knew which I did not learn at the Espionage School in Hamburg a few months later.

It was a full house, full of people and full of life-stories. They had left me my watch and my money and had given me the tip about getting on to the fourth floor. The architect of the Remand Prison had evidently overlooked the need for some sort of sanitary installation. The cell doors served as w.c.'s and canalisation was provided only by the natural gradient from floor to floor. Early in the mornings it was washed down with water. I was not allowed to speak to anyone. No lawyer came to me. I learned that I had been arrested as a spy at the request of the American Government.

Three days later I went aboard the s.s. *Shawnee*. Texas Rangers in olive-green uniforms and outsize sombreros greeted me and the other deportees. Each had two pistols in his holster and now and again fired a few shots to pass the time. We were allowed to move freely about the ship and were well treated and well cared for. We sailed close to the coast. On the west coast of South America there was no danger from U-boats. As we passed through the locks on the Panama Canal we had to go below deck, so that we should not see the military installations there and later pass on information about them.

In the Gulf of Mexico we saw dozens of burning tankers. German U-boats had shot them to ribbons. American U-boat chasers were running a zig-zag course and firing depth charges. We stood at the ship's rail feeling thrilled. We all believed in victory. We were 'Lima Germans.'

In the New Orleans docks, numerous ships which had been damaged in combat were being repaired. I decided that the Atlantic must be alive with German torpedoes.

Here in New Orleans we were loaded on to the railway and taken to the Kennedy Interment camp near San Antonio. Apart from our freedom, we got everything there we wanted. After seven weeks I was summoned to the presence of the Camp Commandant. He was a man of medium build and his name was Hudson. A pretty girl of round about twenty sat near him; she wore a sweater with the name 'Betsy' embroidered across it. She had a paper in front of her and took down our conversation in shorthand.

"Sit down," said the captain as he gave me a cigarette. "You can return to Germany as an exchange if you wish. Your name is on the list of internees requested by Germany."

"I'm glad to know that," I replied.

"You need not go back to Germany if you do not want to. The agreement explicitly provides for the right of refusal. You can stay here in America, work here and become an American citizen. In that event you would be released tomorrow."

Betsy looked at me with big eyes. I smiled at her.

"Would you let me take you out if I stayed here?" I asked.

"Perhaps," she replied.

"That's not good enough for me."

I went up to the officer.

"Many thanks for the offer, Captain," I said, "but don't trouble any more. I'm going back, of course."

He gave me his hand. He would have done exactly the same if he had been in my place. . . .

On the sides of the ship which brought us back to Europe the word *Diplomat* was painted in huge letters. It sailed under the Swedish flag and was called the *Drottningholm*. Once outside the three-mile zone we were free. There were also many private passengers on board. The guests fell into two groups: those who were afraid of U-boats and drifting mines and those who were not. We were asked to assist the crew on look-out duty. Wrapped in heavy rugs we sat on deck and showed off our fearlessness. Once a mine floated right up to us and we avoided it at the last moment. It would have been an easy matter to make the mine harmless but we were of course on a neutral ship and to explode a mine was, according to the rules of the game, to participate in the war. The mine travelled on to who knows where. . . .

Our ship crawled across the ocean. For security reasons it could not do more than three knots. We met convoys, U-boats and aircraft. Near the Faroes we were stopped by a British cruiser. A very polite British officer came on board and inspected our papers. Then for "security reasons" he requested that all newspapers should be thrown overboard. It was one of those senseless measures which war conditions produce by the score.

On the *Drottningholm* fate offered me a last chance. I got to know Karen, Karen S. She was a Swede. I am trying to recall what she looked like as I write, but I cannot bring her face to mind, although I can still remember every detail of our meeting. We soon became friends. It was one of those affairs which begins lightly and ends in deadly earnest. We formed a team for mine-watching. Women could take part in this too, if they wished. For Karen I abandoned my games of skat and my military and political conversations. We laughed and walked up and down on deck, flirted and kissed. The war could take care of itself.

But even at three knots we were gradually getting nearer to Europe. Karen was sad.

"We will soon have to say good-bye," she said.

"Yes," I replied.

"I don't want to, Erich."

"Nor do I."

"Isn't there any way we can stay together?"

"No," I replied. "It's not possible just now, I must get back to Germany. They're waiting for me."

"It's this wretched war," she said. "War, war, nothing but war! Do we have to sacrifice everything to it?"

"We must go through with it," I answered.

"Come with me to Stockholm. My father's in business in a fairly big way. I'm his only daughter — and my family would like you. Sweden is a neutral country . . . come on, stay with me."

We walked up and down together. I remained adamant. The devil had already got me by the collar. I was on the way back from America, on the way back from a country whose language I spoke, whose customs I was familiar with and whose people I knew. I did not then know in what circumstances I was to land again in America two years later.

"When the war is over," I told Karen, "I'll come again. I'll have your address in my pocket as long as the war lasts. I'll get to know your father. After all, we're still young and one day you and I will laugh about all this. Don't cry. I'm always lucky. People like me always come out on top. You don't know why I have to go back to

45

Germany. You have to be a man to understand that — and thank heavens, you're
not a man!"

I kissed her. A sailor who had been
watching us smiled. We were heading for
Göteborg and Göteborg meant good-bye.

I got into the train, crossed the ferry
from Helsingborg to Helsingor and travelled via Copenhagen and Warnemünde to
Stettin. We travelled first-class. We were all
people with a special value to the German
Reich. For each one of us an American of
equal value had been exchanged.

I was met in Stettin. A man in civilian
clothes came up to me.

"Herr Gimpel?" he said. "Welcome
home! We've been waiting for you."

We shook hands.

"I've money for you, papers and ration
cards. Go to your relatives and take a good
rest. There's no hurry. Stay as long as you
like."

"Many thanks. And then?"

"Note this address: Berlin, Tirpitzufer
80. Repeat!"

"Berlin, Tirpitzufer 80," I said. I knew
this was the headquarters of the German
Secret Service.

We parted. I had become a member of
the Secret Service. For the last time the

war gave me a few weeks' leave. Then I went back. Into the craziest school in the world. The German M.I. School for secret agents. The amateur was to become an expert.

# CHAPTER 3

## TRAINING AS A SPY IN GERMANY

My mind was a blank as I walked the long, aggressively clean corridors in the four-storeyed building of Tirpitzufer 80, distinguished by no official marking outside. The building was too old to rank as a modern structure and too new to look old-fashioned. It smelt of turpentine. In this building Canaris had his office. To the right of the main entrance a guard-room had been installed, then up a few steps and you came to the doorkeeper's desk. I gave my name.

"One moment please," the man said. He had been expecting me although I had not been told to come on any particular day. He picked up the telephone, and two minutes later someone came for me. A man in civilian clothes introduced himself rather hastily and led me silently through the building.

On the third floor we turned to the right. It was very quiet in the 'fox-hole' as the headquarters of the German M.I. were called. My companion knocked on a door.

I walked in. A colonel, tall and slim, in a well-cut Army uniform came towards me and shook hands.

"Colonel Schade," he introduced himself. He took a good look at me.

I was surprised to find he was in uniform. I was above all surprised to find how peaceful, how normal the 'fox-hole' seemed to be. The Colonel offered me a cigarette. He had long, white, very well-cared-for hands.

"I know you already," he smiled. "You have been highly commended to me by the former German Embassy in Peru." He offered me a light. "You're looking very well," he continued. "It's quite clear that you've got better times behind you than ahead of you." We chatted about America. It was an entertaining hour. Colonel Schade was head of the American division. He was greatly interested in the general feeling in the United States. He was courteous and urbane. He thought quickly and talked slowly in cultivated high German.

"Actually you should now report for military service," said Colonel Schade, "but perhaps I know of something else for you. I believe that with your experience abroad you could be of greater use to us in another sphere. Of course we shan't compel you."

49

"I shall be very pleased to help you if I can," I replied.

"Then we shall take you in hand," he went on. "You are now called Jakob Springer, and you are going to Hamburg. You must say nothing about this to anyone. You must go to the Four-Seasons Hotel. That is all. You will never come here again, at any rate not through the main entrance. We have never seen each other, but I don't need to tell you that. Mark carefully the way by which you will now leave this building."

We shook hands. My silent companion came with me once more, and in front of the porter's desk we turned off into the opposite direction, crossed a yard, went through a hall, across a backyard, and then through a tenement building. I was then standing on the street that ran parallel with the Tirpitzufer. I took the train to Hamburg.

I breakfasted in the Four-Seasons Hotel. The sun was shining on the river and I was just thinking how strange it was that one could live so comfortably in Germany in the midst of the war, when a man came up to me.

"Are you Herr Springer?" he asked.

"Yes."

"My name is Jürgensen," he said. He was unobtrusive in every way. His face, his bearing, his manner of speaking were all thoroughly middle-class.

"Go today to Mönckeberg Strasse." He gave me a number which I have since forgotten. "You will find there on the first floor an import and export firm. Give two short rings and one long one." He pushed a photograph across the table. "Take a good look and get that face well into your mind. Report to this man. Just give him your name."

"Right," I answered.

I went on foot. At that time Hamburg had been only slightly damaged by air attack and no one there had any idea of the fate which lay in store. Girls were walking about in gay summer dresses. They looked chic, and they smiled at you if they felt like it. There were few men about, at least at this time of the day. The barracks did not empty until six o'clock in the evening.

A fair, virile-looking civilian of about thirty received me in Mönckeberg Strasse. We went into an adjoining room. He pointed to a Morse apparatus.

"Let me see what you can do."

"Much too slow," he said when I had reproduced the first test piece. He was called

Heinz, and he lived as men usually live during an interval between two spells of service at the front. He carried a heap of girls' photographs in his pocket and always looked as if he hadn't had enough sleep. Within a few days we were on intimate terms and spent our nights on the tiles together.

I don't know when I first noticed the man who was following my every movement. It was the fact that he always wore the same suit that put me on my guard. Either he was a beginner or he was going out of his way to look like a beginner. When I felt sure I was being watched I went to Jürgensen. (This, of course, was not his real name.)

"I'm being shadowed," I said. "I'm not anxious, but it's beginning to get on my nerves a bit."

Jürgensen smiled. "You're seeing things," he said. "Show me your shadow."

I left the hotel foyer to look for him, but he had disappeared.

"You see?" said Jürgensen.

"I'll show you the man," I replied and took my mentor back with me to Mönckeberg Strasse. We went up to the fourth floor and sat there for ten minutes. Then I made to leave the house. In the hall stood my watch-dog, still wearing the same suit. Jürgensen smiled.

"I'll call it off now," he said. "It was a little test we always put new men through. If you had not noticed that you were being shadowed you could have come and collected your ticket to the eastern front in the course of a few days. The next thing we will practice is how to shake off a pursuer. Now pay attention to what I am going to tell you.

"Supposing you take a taxi. You must never give an address as you get in. You must change taxis three times. From today onwards you must never go to your destination direct. You must get out at least three blocks before and complete the journey on foot. Always take your time. If you don't give yourself enough time you'll lose your head one of these days one way or the other, and it's a poor look-out without a head."

"It must be," I said.

"Now let us imagine that you go into the street," continued Jürgensen, "and become suspicious that someone is following you. You must never turn round. You must never stand still. You must never change your direction. You must give absolutely no sign that you have become suspicious.

You must neither slow down your pace nor quicken it. And of course you will want to see the man. How are you going to do it?"

"Don't ask me," I replied.

"You stop in front of a shop window. You look at the window display. Resist any temptation to squint to the right and be equally careful not to look to the left. You are interested only in hats and coats. Then comes your moment. The man must pass you. Look carefully into the glass. His face will be mirrored there. You have only a second's time. Mentally photograph him but take no notice of him. Ah well, you'll soon learn how to do it. . . ."

I certainly learned how to conduct myself when in danger. How to swallow back the shock, the fear, the horror of it all. How the mind can work feverishly while the hands remain still — quite still. How the eyes can look quite unconcerned as if one were thinking about a rendezvous which had misfired or an unpaid gas account, or what to choose from the menu. It was good that I had learned how to conduct myself when in danger, but I was to realise this only years later — in America. . . .

For three weeks I tapped out Morse signals in Hamburg under Heinz's direction. I was too slow. I had to learn to do it more quickly. Much more quickly. In the odd import-export firm in the Mönckeberg Strasse I met practically no one. It also ran quite a normal business and I was, so to speak, only a member of the secret sub-section, Springer, the private pupil. Shortly before the end of my radio training I had to transmit a long text three times over, one after the other, the meaning of which remained incomprehensible to me.

"Now we have your hand-writing," said Heinz.

"How do you mean?"

"Every operator has a quite individual style of Morse transmission," my teacher explained. "With one the pauses are longer, another may give the dots rather too abruptly or make the dashes a trifle too long. Every individual 'hand-writing' is re-corded on wax discs. We have specialists who, when they have compared them, can say at once if it was actually our man at the transmitter or whether it was someone else."

Without realising it, I had undergone the wax disc test, which is international prac-tice. More than eighty per cent of all agents sent abroad were caught and in practically every case the opposing secret service tried to make capital out of the capture. They continued to use the apparatus which had been seized and to transmit bogus messages. In Germany these messages were received and compared with the recordings. If they did not coincide exactly with the original "handwriting" one was put on one's guard.

The Hamburg M.I. School for secret agents was scattered all over the town and one never saw a fellow pupil. I was sent to a radio repair works near what was then called the Adolph Hitler Platz. I learned how a transmitter was made. Then I went to the cipher department in Baumwall. At a chemist's in the Rödingsmarkt, I learned to write with invisible ink. The man who taught me the process had invented the ink himself. He was a qualified chemist and was very proud of his discovery, which was, however, to be superseded later by a preparation of I. G. Farben. The invisible ink was a colourless fluid. One wrote with a toothpick around the point of which a tiny wisp of cotton wool was wound so that the paper should not be scratched. The writing became visible when a warm iron was passed over the paper.

In the photographic department of the school for secret agents I was initiated into dot photography. One could photograph a whole page of manuscript in such a way that it appeared as only a tiny dot. Dots of this kind were introduced into normal letters, and many pieces of information crossed the frontiers until the F.B.I. at last discovered the trick.

After my training in Hamburg, which lasted for several months, I did a few weeks' practical service in naval radio.

After that I had to go through other naval departments. Then the Reich Air Ministry took me in hand. The overriding interest at the time was radar. I was shown aircraft types of every kind. I picked things up quickly and enjoyed my strange schooling. Everyone with whom I was put in touch to receive the final polish for my later activity abroad, had learned to hold his tongue. No one asked me where I came from or where I wanted to go. I was asked absolutely nothing, and I soon learned to keep my own mouth shut. I was not allowed to keep one single written note. My memory was systematically trained. I learned how to store important information in my head. Even the code had to be memorised, and retained only in the head. The greatest effort, the most severe strain and the most difficult task demanded of the spy is the struggle with his own memory.

In Berlin, I received my practical training: shooting, boxing, ju-jitsu, running. In the Alexander Platz, Berlin, I was further trained to high school standards in smuggling, stealing, lying, cheating and similar arts.

Herr Krause, Commissioner of the Berlin Criminal Police, had a quite unusual method of teaching and it was his contribution to initiate me into the art of evading capture. He took me every day through his office in the Alexander Platz to demonstrate his points with practical examples. I can still remember Benno. He weighed nearly three hundredweight, had a fat, red, good-humoured-looking face and something about him which radiated friendliness. Benno was a bank robber.

He sat on a chair in the interrogation room and groaned.

"Good day, Benno," said Krause, bringing me forward. "Now give the gentleman your hand nicely and tell him why they caught you."

"Because I was a fool," said Benno.

"That's right," said the Commissioner. "And why were you a fool?"

"Because I didn't keep my mouth shut."

"And why didn't you keep your mouth shut?"

"Because I was drunk."

"And why were you drunk?"

"Because of a woman."

"You see," said the Commissioner, and turned to me again. "There you have a story from real life." He took my arm and walked along the corridor with me. "Here you have practically everything there is to be learned," he continued. "It's really quite simple. First, keep your mouth shut. Secondly, keep away from drink, and thirdly, keep away from women. If all criminals observed these rules, we policemen would have to be better paid because there would be much more need for us."

We went to a little pub together, just by Exchange station, which the spivs and gaol birds used as a meeting place when they had not been picked up for national service — fences, pickpockets and similar types. The Commissioner knew them all, greeted them intimately and was similarly received by them.

He told me each one's story, sharing with me quite freely all the police force's inside knowledge of their methods. He did not know the real purpose of my presence there; as far as he was concerned I was a sort of lawyer who had completed his theoretical training and was now taking the usual practical instruction. He was very amusing and I enjoyed his company.

But I enjoyed even more the company of Ingrid, whom I had met during my training. She was dark, petite and elegant. She liked to drink and dance and we often went out together. I could hardly wait till the evenings came round. I never dreamt that Ingrid was to give me one of the worst shocks of my life.

My training was nearly complete when Jürgensen once more appeared on the scene.

"You have been a model student," he said, "and now you must put what you have learned into practice."

"Splendid!" I said. "When do we start?"

"At once," he replied.

"And what have I got to do?"

"You are to go to Holland," he replied. "There is a city in Holland called The Hague, a very lovely city. It is occupied by our forces."

"I know that," I said.

"Good. Go there and see what you can bring back. Anything of military interest. The name of the Commandant, how many troops are stationed there, what armaments they have. This is only a test piece."

"And what if I'm caught?"

"Then it will be just too bad."

"And how do I get through?"

"Just as you please," answered Jürgensen. "I would say with a special plane and a parachute. Just tell me tomorrow what you need, what sort of uniform, how much money and what papers. Then get on with it and radio three days later what's happening. If you are not caught at the job you are all right and the people there are dunderheads. Well, off you go. Enjoy yourself!"

He was quite serious. I soon realised that. It was serious for me too, though I must admit that I approached the adventure with a certain feeling of pleasurable anticipation. I had not given a thought as to whether my training had been for the good or the bad. I left one day later. Agent 146 of the German M.I. had reached the first station of his Via Dolorosa.

I sat in the Berlin–The Hague train, travelling second-class, of course. I had given myself some everyday German name. According to the papers I carried I was going to Holland on business, something to do with secret installations. The journey out was paid for by the German War Department. For my return I had to rely on good luck.

Apart from a service passport I had a whole bundle of Dutch guilders. My task was to find out all about the German occupying forces in the Dutch capital within three days and to radio the information to Berlin. I had a two-fold aspiration: I wanted to do it in two days, and I wanted to get by without spending any money. It was only a test assignment; a quite innocuous affair. Shortly beforehand one of our men had come to grief in Bordeaux on a similar mission. Either he had raised his hands too late, or the military policeman's gun had gone off too precipitately. In his case the War Department had borne the cost of his training to no purpose. His relatives were responsible for the epitaph "Fallen for Führer and Fatherland." I learned of this incident only after my return to Berlin.

In the event of my being caught, my instructions were quite clear. First, keep silent; secondly, wait; thirdly, hope. The third point was in fact not an official instruction but the private codicil of my tutor, Jürgensen. Agents captured by their own people often had to wait weeks and months until the M.I. got them out again.

It happened only rarely that a man was entirely forgotten. But the lack of coordination between the M.I., part of the War Department, and the Reich Security Central Office, the Espionage Headquarters of the S.S., often led to devilish complications.

The train travelled slowly. There had been an air attack and the lines had only been provisionally patched up. Next to me sat an Army judge and two other officers. They were chatting together about this and that, nothing of any special importance.

At one station a military police patrol entered the compartment. A squat sergeant carefully scrutinized my service passport and looked me up and down suspiciously. The train travelled on.

"Haven't you ever been a soldier?" one of the officers asked me.

"No," I answered.

"But you're very young."

"Yes."

"Is there something wrong with you, then?"

"No."

Then they left me alone. They ate sandwiches and drank schnaps out of the bottle, including the judge.

The train arrived at The Hague one

minute late. On the station I once more underwent a thorough scrutiny. My papers survived the test. Civilians were not in favour here. I deposited my suitcase, which had my transmitting apparatus concealed in its false bottom, in the cloak-room. I took the view that the more nonchalantly I treated this piece of luggage, the safer I should be.

I went on foot to find some accommodation. This had to fulfil certain quite definite requirements. There had to be a minimum of iron in the building to avoid interference with my radio transmissions. It had not to be over-full but at the same time it should not be too sparsely occupied. Then in addition I needed a room the walls of which would deaden the sound of the Morse keys.

I found a pension which fulfilled these conditions. I fetched my suitcase and took it up to my room. The apparatus was all dismantled but I was able to get it ready for service within thirty minutes. I went down into the dining-room. Two German officers were drinking gin with three service girls. They took me at first for a Dutchman, and greeted me boisterously when I made myself known as a German. I learned a few inconsequential things from the officers which I could make use of if necessary.

There was, however, no necessity. The city was full of German soldiers and there was plenty of schnaps about. All soldiers carry their heart on their tongue if you treat them to a drink. In one of the bars I met a group of fellow-countrymen who were celebrating the acquittal of one of their comrades before a court-martial. He was a lance-corporal with a cheeky face.

They were all talking together until eventually the corporal succeeded in getting an ear for his story.

"This is how it was," he reported. "I was standing in front of the court-martial with my tail between my legs. I had been given away by a farmer because I had shot his cow. The thing in itself was nothing serious, but many more harmless cases have had a more serious outcome."

The others drank and laughed again together. I called for another round of drinks.

The corporal went on with his story.

"And why did you shoot the cow?" the Judge Advocate had asked him.

"I was on sentry duty."

"Well, and . . . ?"

"The cow attacked me. If a German soldier is attacked he must defend himself."

"And then of course he has the cow to eat?"

"Well, the soldier is responsible for seeing that no food is wasted."

They got more and more hilarious. I called for another round. They should now have been on their guard. Every soldier learns in his elementary instruction that civilians who treat him to drinks must be regarded with the greatest suspicion. But every soldier snaps his fingers at his instructions when he's got a free pass.

My companions belonged to a battery which was trying out some new mortars. This contrivance, which was later to be put extensively to use on the Russian front, was on the secret list. Needless to say I got to know everything there was to know about it.

I went back to my pension. I had a good look at the anti-aircraft positions and marked them on to a map of the town which I had bought. The number of troops, the names of the Commanders and similar things I had already known for some time. Every Dutchman knew them, of course. At midday I had my report ready. I coded it. I carried the code in my head. In a foreign country one should as far as possible transmit reports over short distances between the hours of three and five in the afternoon. These are the peak hours for radio communication and the solitary transmitter does not arouse so much attention as he might at other times. The agent must avoid stretching his transmitting time above four minutes. It normally takes about ten minutes to locate a secret transmitter. Four minutes doesn't give anyone much chance to take bearings. I made my report as short and precise as possible.

The transmitter stood on the table beside my bed. Above my bed hung an unprepossessing still life in oils. The sole chair had only three legs and the table wobbled. I looked at the clock. Ten minutes to go. I was feeling nervy. Just as one feels when one's sitting for the first time at the wheel of a newly acquired motorcar. Or introducing one's girlfriend to one's parents. Really I was enjoying the sensation. Fool that I was. . . .

I gave three, four signals to Berlin. The answer came at once. I got my report through in three minutes fifty-one seconds.

"Understood," answered the Morse voice from out of the ether. "We will be in touch again at five o'clock tomorrow morning."

I went out, my mission forgotten. It was finished. I did not drink much. I felt a vague tension inside. I went back into my room, put the earphones on and lay down on my bed. I could not sleep. From the dining-room came the sound of the voices of women Luftwaffe auxiliaries again. At four o'clock all was quiet. I had to wait another hour. I wondered whether the answer would come before the military police called on me. Yes. The answer ran:

"Well done. Return to Berlin at once."

I reported in Berlin to Jürgensen. He was positively radiating good-will.

"Excellent," he said. "We'll report to The Hague today. They *will* be pleased!"

There were endless conferences that day at the War Department. The officers were discussing one of the strangest cases to come out of the war. A German flight-sergeant — I will call him Fritz Söldner — had been shot down over London. He fell from the burning machine but succeeded at the last moment in opening his parachute. He landed on an apple-tree and was brought down by three oddly-armed members of the Home Guard. He had been injured in the course of his descent and was taken to hospital. Thus far the story was, by wartime standards anyhow, nothing unusual. However, the nurse who was deputed to look after the German flight-sergeant was placed there by the British Secret Service. Her name was Maud Fisher and she was a secret service agent. She knew her job. The German flight-sergeant fell in love with her. Head over heels. They went out together. Söldner was given far more freedom than was usual for a prisoner-of-war. He asked Maud to marry him. She did not actually refuse, but said she could not marry an enemy of her country. Söldner declared himself willing to go over to the other side and was put under training as an agent.

Söldner was sent to Berlin with instructions to get hold of the drawings for a particular apparatus from an electrical firm. The R.A.F. appeared over the Reich capital with two hundred aircraft. As the bombs fell indiscriminately, Fritz Söldner jumped out of a Lancaster. This time he made a smooth landing, burned his parachute equipment and presented himself with false papers to the electrical firm. He was given employment there.

A few days later, however, he fell under suspicion and was arrested. He broke down under interrogation and admitted everything. He appeared very distressed and said he could not imagine why he had let himself be talked into doing such a thing. He now wanted to place himself at the disposal of the German M.I. The whole day was spent discussing whether we should accept his offer. Opinions were divided. Meanwhile Fritz Söldner sat in handcuffs in an adjoining room and awaited his fate. A high-ranking officer of M.I., later involved in the events of July the 20th, and subsequently shot, was against sending Söldner back to England as an agent.

"It is quite ridiculous," he said. "At the moment no doubt he has the best of intentions, but as soon as he sees the nurse again, he will get soft and capitulate. We can't possibly make use of him."

Söldner was shot.

# CHAPTER 4

## SPAIN — AND MY FIRST MISSIONS

I was sitting in the train on my way to Spain. It was there I was to carry out my first real mission. An absurdly simple one.

My papers showed me as a Dutchman. They had been expertly forged in the S.S.'s own workshops in Oranienburg concentration camp.

Beside me on the seat lay a small brown-paper parcel. It weighed about two pounds and measured about sixteen inches by eight. It contained money. Real money. Swiss francs, 250,000 Swiss francs. The money had to be taken to Spain and was destined for some very important people, for the run-of-the-mill agents were paid with so-called Himmler bank notes, that is to say, counterfeit money.

On the international agents' market at that time Swiss francs were the accepted currency; they were easier to place than dollars. I had to deliver the money to a cover firm in Madrid — Item Number One.

I had entrained in Berlin. Needless to say, I had no one to see me off. Not only because it is not the usual practice on missions of this kind to be seen off at the station, but because there was simply no one who could have seen me off. The day of my departure had seen the end of an affair between Ingrid and me. It was a strange end, an end at which time had stood godfather.

I had got to know her at the theatre. She had been sitting next to me and had smiled at me. Tickets were scarce and one got them only if one had the right connections. I had them. Seemingly Ingrid had them too. Naturally I did not know then that her name was Ingrid. I only knew that her strange unselfconscious smile had captivated me.

Ingrid had no moods, no cares, no work. She wrote no letters to some absent soldier. She never mentioned the war. She always wore silk stockings. I never saw her with a shopping bag. She was a luxury article in a time of need.

When we had already known each other for three weeks, we knew no more about each other than that we were in love. I was getting the strangest ideas into my head. I wanted to give up my job with M.I., enlist in the Army and get married. Everything which had pressed me on towards my career as a spy, everything which had lured and intrigued me, paled by the side of Ingrid.

"What do you do actually?" she asked me one day.

"Armaments," I replied. "I don't know whether I ought to enjoy my work or not."

"There are worse things," she said. She looked at me and stroked my hand. Her hands were soft and delicate. It was not often during the war that one saw soft and delicate hands.

After that we often came to talk about my activities. Quite spontaneously. Naturally I kept quiet about what I was really doing. I had already got that far, but perhaps one day I may have told her one small thing too many.

I was ordered to report to Jürgensen. He was in a bad mood. There was a rumour circulating that he was going to be sent to the front. (He did, however, keep his post until the end of the war.)

"Don't spend so much of your time with women," he said. "Women are poison for agents. You should know that by now."

"I don't know what you mean," I replied.

"Then I'll jog your memory," he con-

73

tinued. "Where were you yesterday evening?"

"I had dinner at Horchers."

"With whom?"

I hesitated.

"Come on, man," he prodded me. "I haven't got all day for you. You were with a woman, weren't you?"

"Yes," I admitted.

"Right," he said. "And you told her that you were shortly going to Spain. Or am I mistaken?"

"No, you're right."

It was like a blow between the eyes. How could he have known? There had been no other diners in the room. No one could have overheard what I was saying. There could be no other explanation: he had got it from Ingrid. I confronted her with it, and she smiled, as always. There was no wavering of her self-assurance.

"You are a funny, sentimental old thing. Fancy getting so het up about a little thing like that."

"It's not a little thing," I replied.

"But this is war." Ingrid stood up and lit a cigarette. She put it into a long holder and walked up and down the room.

"We are all in its service, one way or another. Everyone in his place. You doing

74

your job and I doing mine. It's wartime, that's all. Or haven't you noticed it?"

"Yes," I replied. "So if I understand you correctly, your kisses and your love were all part of your war effort."

"That's putting it very crudely," said Ingrid. She was still smiling. Just as she always smiled, but it was the last time she was to smile at me. What I had taken for love had been nothing but M.I.'s final test of my reliability as a spy. The lesson was Silence, always and everywhere Silence. And secrecy.

I forced myself to think no more of Ingrid. That was finished. Now I had to fulfil my mission. We were all working for the war in our own way. All right then!

I was on the train for Spain and had to concentrate on the job in hand. According to the teaching of the Hamburg school for agents I had to break four barriers. First, our own police. Secondly, the German frontier control. Thirdly, the foreign frontier controls. And fourthly, the enemy secret service. At Hendaye I crossed the French frontier. At Irun I crossed the Spanish frontier. I spoke fluent Spanish.

So far so good.

"Have you anything to declare?" asked

the Spanish customs official. Barrier number three!

"No," I replied.

He pointed to the parcel containing the 250,000 Swiss francs.

"What have you there, Señor?"

"Prospectuses," I replied. "For my Spanish clients. Shall I open the parcel?"

He hesitated. Spaniards always have plenty of time.

I remained calm. Too calm perhaps. I watched him as he thought the matter over. If he should decide to have the parcel opened, I should be arrested. Nothing was more certain than that.

I had considered it advisable to carry the parcel quite openly in my hand. That might have been a good idea; or it might equally well have been a bad one. A hundred yards from where I stood the frontier agent of the German M.I. would be waiting. He would witness my arrest, and I should have tripped up on my first mission. Perhaps after long drawn out negotiations, the German Embassy would succeed in getting the money out again, but the career of Erich Gimpel, the German spy, would certainly have come to an end. I should have failed and that would mean that I would be transferred to the eastern front . . .

"That's all right, Señor," said the Customs official. *"Buen viaje!"*

I did not of course know our frontier agent personally and we had agreed upon a sign of recognition. Everything immediately fell into place and we travelled to Madrid together. There I had to telephone a certain number.

"We'll send a car at three o'clock," I was told.

An English motor-car with a liveried chauffeur arrived punctually to the second.

"Are you Señor Carlos?" he asked me.

"No," I answered, "I am Mario."

Now I had to ask him: "Are you Señor Juan?"

"No," he replied, "I am Filippo."

The right password had been given. I got into the car. I delivered the money. Naturally I did not get a receipt; it was a matter of trust. Hundreds of German agents later made off abroad with the foreign currency which had been entrusted to them.

I was taken to an elegant villa about six miles outside Madrid, the home of the German manager of a cover firm. Actually he was S.S. General Bernhard. Short, thick-set and corpulent, with a round head and rather sparse hair, he looked more like a retired bus conductor than the head of a branch of the Secret Service. He greeted me warmly. He was one of our best men, and for years directed the entire Spanish side of our work with great skill.

I was to see a good deal more of him. As part of the camouflage, General Bernhard had his whole family with him, including the children's nurse. He ran a large household and was on excellent terms with the Spanish Government. At that time Spain was swarming with secret agents and if you came across four foreigners playing cards you could wager that one was working for England, one for America, one for Soviet Russia and one for Germany.

"What can I do for you?" asked the general.

"Technical information," I replied.

"For example?"

"In Spanish Morocco British agents are operating secret transmitters. They are quite novel affairs. We should like to get hold of one intact."

"I'm sure that can be done," replied General Bernhard. "And what else do you want?"

"They've been installing magnetron and klystron tubes in electric armatures in British aircraft recently. So far we haven't

78

been able to get hold of one. They are coupled with explosive charges, and if you try to dismantle them they explode. You often get Allied aircraft making emergency landings here, don't you?"

"Yes," replied the general. "Yesterday a four-engined aircraft came down near Seville. I will arrange an opportunity for you to have a look at the engine." He smiled. "Well, if there is nothing else I can do for you. . . ."

I was dismissed. My next destination was Seville. There my luck was out. For the tubes I was after were not in the machine in question, and the armatures, which I had dismantled with the greatest caution, also did not explode. It was to be months before we eventually got hold of these tubes. They were important for radar development. We needed them above all to enable us to evolve suitable countermeasures.

I made several more journeys to Spain. It was my knowledge of the language that singled me out for these not unpopular missions. It was very easy for us in Spain, of course, as the sympathies, if nothing more, of the authorities there were on the side of the Germans.

It was in a bar in Barcelona that I first

heard of an incredible plan. Although it seemed like a figment of the imagination I pursued the matter and found that the incredible was true. I at once reported it to Berlin and received by return instructions to investigate further but not to become involved.

Gibraltar was to be blown up. Incredible, fantastic, but, true. And it almost came off!

Gibraltar. . . . For us the fortress was more than a nuisance. It commanded the entrance to the Mediterranean and our U-boats had to submerge as they passed this stronghold in order to avoid bombardment. In the narrows between the Spanish mainland and North Africa there was a dangerous underwater current. The German U-boat fleet had therefore to suffer repeated losses at this spot.

Then Eisenhower opened his headquarters in Gibraltar to direct the war in North Africa. The Spaniards looked with hungry eyes at the rock fortress. The fall of Gibraltar! This was the dream of Germans, Italians and Spaniards alike. A direct attack was hopeless and was not even attempted but a dare-devil plot was hatched out.

A man on the English Governor's staff was bribed. At incredible risk to his own skin, the man hid a time bomb beneath the coach-work of his Chief's Rolls-Royce and got it past the sentry undetected. From this moment the assailants had six hours.

They acted with lightning speed. I would never have thought it possible that the attempt could have succeeded even so far. I watched with my hands metaphorically in my trouser pockets, as I had been told to, but I felt uneasy. If it succeeded it would be just as well for me not to have taken part in it. If it went wrong, I would have it on my conscience that I had not restrained the men involved. But the conscience of a spy was controlled from Berlin.

Vast quantities of munitions and supplies of explosives were stored in the underground caves of Gibraltar. If there should be an explosion there the entire fortress would, according to the experts, be blown sky high.

The would-be assassins had now four hours. And they were lucky again. They broke through the second barrier. How they did it remains unknown to this day. Another hundred yards. Another hour. Above General Eisenhower was dealing with the day's affairs. Below the time bomb ticked steadily on.

Betrayed! It was all over! The bomb was

found and rendered harmless. General Eisenhower went on with his deliberations. One man was hanged. Three men were condemned to life imprisonment. Otherwise all was quiet at Gibraltar.

Four weeks later I approached my superiors with a Gibraltar plan of my own. My project was not quite so desperate but it had greater chances of success. The matter was taken up and I was set to work on it. They were beginning to take notice of me. Suddenly I had a name and was not only a number. I was no longer an apprentice. I was being taken seriously. At that period in Berlin they were prepared to take any risk. Nothing was too crazy for them. Nothing was too foolhardy or too chancy not to be given serious consideration.

We were going around, so to speak, with hand-grenades in our pockets. If there was only a one per cent chance of success, we went ahead, investing our lives, our blood and our money in these wild projects. The war was going badly, and it was up to us, a few hundred men in M.I. to stop the rot with any means at our command.

M.I. was also in a bad way. Gradually at first and then with one final stroke it was taken over by Amt VI — the Central Office of Reich Security, a secret department of the S.S., immediately under Hitler and furnished with unlimited powers. I received orders to report to Amt VI.

My leave-taking from M.I. was short and casual. I was asked one day to report at the Reich Security office in Tauentzienstrasse. During the same night bombs hailed down on West Berlin, and the building at the rear was destroyed. In this house a mouse-breeder had set up his menagerie; the animals made for freedom and rushed into the offices of Amt VI. On the following morning I had three dozen mice to greet me in my new official quarters.

I introduced myself to the Deputy Head of the Department, Dr. S., a man of medium build and nondescript appearance.

The offices of Amt VI were in a great barrack-like building on the Berkaer Strasse which had begun its career as a home for aged Jews. The front of the building faced some allotments; behind you could see straight inside a tenement building. In the yard was a bomb-proof bunker for the exclusive use of the officers of Amt VI.

"Please sit down," said Dr. S. "We already know you, or rather, we know your work. You were in Spain. . . . Ah well, we'll talk about that later."

He looked me over with fastidious distaste. I came from M.I. and for Amt VI that was no recommendation. This natural rivalry, which later developed also into a political rivalry between the two authorities — they both had exactly the same function — had even at this time assumed grotesque proportions. The agents were devoting more energy to watching, shadowing and bringing the other side into disrepute than to their own duties. The two departmental heads were Admiral Canaris (M.I.) and Brigadier Walter Schellenberg (Reich Security). After the attempted Putsch of July 20th, 1944, Canaris was arrested and later executed. The victor, Schellenberg, was imprisoned after the war in Landsberg, went later to Italy, embraced Catholicism and died a year ago in a monastery. I worked for both departments and knew their methods and their respective degrees of success. Canaris was a head without a fist and Schellenberg was a fist without a head.

"I think we'll send you straight off to Spain again," Dr. S. said. "We haven't many people with your experience. . . . You were a fair time there, weren't you? Have you any suggestions to make?"

I thought about my Gibraltar plan.

"Yes," I answered. "I can perhaps see a possibility that without too great an expenditure of money and blood, the harbour of Gibraltar could be blown up."

He stood up, offered me a cigarette, and paced up and down the room.

"You must explain that to me in greater detail, my friend," he said.

"Very well," I replied. "In the bay of Algeciras there are, as a general rule, forty cargo ships lying at anchor. The mainland side of the bay belongs to Spain, and from that side we could start our men."

"What men?" Dr. S. interrupted.

"I am thinking of frogmen like they're using in Italy at present. Half a dozen would be enough. I could smuggle them across the frontier disguised as entertainers. There's no difficulty about that at all. After all we can count on the Spaniards' co-operation in anything directed against Gibraltar."

"And how do you think your men can get to the ships unnoticed?" Dr. S. asked me.

"That's quite simple. We must start a mock U-boat attack at exactly the same time to divert the attention of the men in the harbour. Our frogmen would need to cover a stretch of only 200 yards in the water and they will manage that all right. After all, they'll be men with plenty of experience."

Dr. S. warmed to my plan, and later became positively fired with the idea. The whole of Amt VI was for it — except for one man and as he was so influential his full co-operation had to be enlisted before we could go ahead. Unfortunately he disapproved of the plan for some reason unknown to me. It was just his department that would have been responsible for carrying out my project. He opposed it and later persuaded Schellenberg to drop it. I am still absolutely convinced that the assault on the bay of Algeciras would have succeeded.

This was typical of the inter-departmental confusion that existed throughout the war. Operation Gibraltar did not take place, but I hadn't got time to feel sore about it, as other more daring, more fantastic projects claimed my attention. We worked day and night. We received four times the normal rations and as many cigarettes and as much schnaps as we could consume. Money was no object, but we didn't get anything for nothing.

I had quickly settled down in my new department, and the initial mistrust of me disappeared.

One day I was summoned to the presence of the head of Department VIF, Sturmbannführer L. While on my way to his office I was told that it was a very special and highly confidential affair. Everything of course was confidential. The death penalty for betrayal stood — even for betrayal through negligence.

"Are you pushed for time?" L. greeted me. "It's a long story I've got to discuss with you."

He gave instructions that no one was to be admitted to his office.

"You have sailed through the Panama Canal, haven't you?"

"Yes," I replied. "Half a dozen times."

"And you can still picture it to yourself?"

"Yes, of course. Every detail."

"Splendid!" replied L. "You must turn your knowledge to good account. You are my man. From now on you are in charge of Operation Pelican, which is something the world has never seen before, you can depend on that!"

"And what am I to do?"

"I will explain in detail. You can have everything you need, money, men, ships, aircraft. You will have every support. Operation Pelican has absolute priority. It must come before everything else. You are

87

responsible for it to me alone, and I request that from this moment you work on it exclusively. It must be put in hand at the earliest possible moment."

I still did not know what he wanted me to do.

"Now listen," he said. "The American and British fleet can, as you know, change its dispositions at a moment's notice. That is to say, if the Americans on the Japanese front need reinforcing, they can throw in all their weight in the Pacific, but if we start something here in Europe they can call off the ships from there and fling them in against us."

"That's quite logical," I replied. "And there's nothing much to be done about it."

"But something can be done about it," he said. "Why is it that they can so quickly change their theatres of war? Why? I will tell you. It is because of the Panama Canal. If it weren't for the Panama Canal they'd have to sail round Cape Horn and lose valuable time. As things are they can do in days what would otherwise take weeks. Therefore, if we can blow up the Panama Canal, the Americans will be put off their stroke for quite a time. You see what I am getting at?"

"And how do you propose to blow up

the Panama Canal?" I asked.

"That's your affair," he said. "You can have anything you need from us. Just see that you get on with it. It must succeed!"

# CHAPTER 5

## A PLAN TO BLOW UP THE PANAMA CANAL

I had long since accustomed myself not to have any personal opinions about the instructions I received from my new Department. An attack on the Panama Canal? Splendid! Why not land on Mars? Why not kidnap President Roosevelt from the White House? It was 1943, and the war, particularly the war on the silent front of the secret agents, was taking a desperate turn.

I fully realised for the first time that L. was really serious over his Panama Canal project when I learned that I was to be granted new powers extraordinary. Orders went out to the Navy and the Air Force that *everything* I needed should be placed at my disposal.

I tried to give an impression of confidence while I gambled on the conviction that Operation Pelican would end up as a piece of paper in a desk drawer just as so many other plans had ended.

I was reminded of the case of Dr. Dudt, an escapade of Amt VI which was running its course at about the same time as Skorzeny was getting Mussolini out of his mountain fastness. Dudt, an adventurer pure and simple, was a tall, thin Indian, who in some inexplicable way had succeeded in convincing one of the leading officials in Amt VI that he could produce the petrol which was so urgently necessary for the further prosecution of the war, by some new synthetic chemical process. The Indian was comfortably housed in the hotel Fürstenhof and received every day an official issue of two bottles of red wine and a bottle of cognac. He received, furthermore, also officially, two ampules of morphia every day, with which he injected himself.

The firm of Siemens was ordered to place a whole shed at his disposal, and the engineers and scientists attached to the firm watched the experiments of this gaunt Oriental Cagliostro, with scorn in their eyes and with clenched fists in their trouser pockets. They had instructions to grant his every whim, and his whims changed with every day.

His demands became more and more monstrous. *Pâté de foie gras,* oysters, caviar, champagne. He ate only white bread and left the crusts. Every morning he had to have some sort of milk dish which he usually threw on the floor of the Siemens canteen. The women workers there, overworked and under-nourished as they were at the time, were up in arms at this high-handedness, but were threatened with a charge of sabotage if they should make any difficulties for Dr. Dudt, of whose capabilities so much was expected. The Indian's sexual appetite was greater than one would have imagined from his gaunt and spectral figure, and Amt VI had repeatedly to take a hand to smooth out, finance or put an end to his various love affairs. Dr. Dudt's experiments lasted for four months and cost the country several million marks. They produced about ten cubic centimetres of petrol which the magician had siphoned from a laid-up motorbicycle. He ended up in Dachau. The man responsible in Amt VI was sent to the front and the Dudt case remained a top secret affair.

Was I, against my will and needless to say, without all the exceptional perquisites of the genius inventor, to become the Dr. Dudt of the Panama Canal?

I got a surprise.

I discovered that it was actually possible to put the Panama Canal out of action. It was even quite simple if everything went according to plan.

I travelled to Breslau and met the engineer, Hubrich, an old gentleman with a boyish face who, at the turn of the century, had sought and found the adventure of his life in Central America. Later he had become one of the leading engineers of the Panama Canal and still had all the plans in his possession. I cannot remember now who had hit upon the idea of approaching Herr Hubrich but I know that as I went on my way to meet him I was still opposed to the project which I was to direct.

We met in a restaurant, drank lager beer and ate a tasteless fricassée with potato salad which had been mixed with water.

"I want to consult you on a somewhat strange affair," I began. "Do you think there is any chance of our being able to blow up the Panama Canal?"

"Anything that man has built can be destroyed by man," replied Hubrich. It occurred to me he bore a striking resemblance to my first teacher.

"Yes, but there's one snag," I continued. "I haven't as much time to blow it up as you had to build it."

"What's in your mind?" he asked with interest.

"Assuming," I explained, "that we can succeed in some way, yet to be decided, in sending aircraft into the Panama zone and that they can launch an attack on the Gatun locks . . ."

"Why particularly on the locks?" he interrupted me. "Have you any idea what the Panama Canal looks like?"

"Yes," I replied.

The waiter approached our table and I ordered another portion of fricassée.

"You must have a lot of coupons," said Hubrich. "I'm in a bad way just now. My daughter's gone off with a fellow in the Luftwaffe, and I have to manage with the housekeeping as best I can."

He picked up a beer mat and took a pencil from his pocket.

"Now look," he said. He drew a line. "This, here, is the spillway by Gatun lake, the overflow over the dam, built of very solid material. However, in 1907 of course we weren't thinking of aerial bombardment. I don't know if you can imagine how much water there is in the Panama Canal and what it represents in pressure. With the water of one single lock, a town with a population of a million, like Boston, could be provided for one whole day."

"That is quite clear," I replied.

He was pleased that he had found someone with whom he could talk about the highlight of his life.

"I still have the actual drawings at home. At the time I worked out myself how strong the spillway had to be to withstand the pressure of water, and you can depend on it that my calculations were correct."

"That I can well believe," I replied.

"Of course I don't understand much about aerial bombardment," Hubrich went on. "I don't even know if they could hit a lock, but that is beside the point, for a lock could be repaired in two to three days and all your trouble would have been in vain."

I nodded.

"If, however, you were to blow up this dam, the following would happen: the dammed up water in the Gatun lake would break through the dam, sweep over the canal and flow into the sea. The Panama Canal has a steep gradient, in fact that was the difficulty in its construction. The water always wants to flow back into the sea. If the dam were destroyed there would be nothing to hold it back, and in my estimation it would be at least two years before the Panama Canal could be put into use again."

He drew a few more lines on the beer mat.

"Come home with me," he said, "and then we can take a look at the drawings. Tell me the explosive power of your bombs and I will tell you whether the spillway will blow up or not."

It had to blow up, our explosive experts would see to that. But first it had to be hit, and before it could be hit dive bombers, which, as is well known, have a very limited operational radius, would have to be sent by us to the Panama Canal. Now that I knew that it was technically possible to destroy the canal, I really got down to work. I was seized with Panama fever and so was Hubrich, the engineer. We sat in a Breslau tavern and made up our minds to take a decisive part in the conduct of the war.

I flew back to Berlin and reported at the Reich Air Ministry. I showed my special authority and was received coolly. I was referred to a Colonel, but as I did not want to tell him anything he in return did not want to give me anything. It was a very silent piece of negotiation. Finally I had to tell him what was afoot.

"I need two fast dive bombers," I said. "I want to use them to attack the Panama Canal."

"That's all very well," he replied. "You

can have the aircraft if you can tell me how you are going to get them across the Atlantic."

"That is my affair," I replied.

"Thank God for that," he grunted. "You can have the machines when you like, but it's a pity. It means two less for us. You will want volunteer pilots I suppose?"

"Yes," I replied.

I travelled to Kiel, to the Staff Headquarters of Grand-Admiral Dönitz. Our talk was almost a replica of that I had just had in Berlin.

"I want two U-boats," I said to a naval commander. "I shall probably need them for about ten weeks. Is it possible to get dismantled aircraft over the Atlantic in a U-boat?"

"Yes, it is," replied the officer. "But how are you going to reassemble them again? The whole idea is quite crazy."

"That's my affair," I said.

"Ah well, another two boats less for us," he replied. "Every day someone comes and wants something else."

I now had two Stukas and two U-boats. The two pilots and the U-boat crews were prepared to go through Panama-fire for me. I rented a long lakeside site on the Wannsee and made it a military area. Here we built an exact model of the Panama Canal. My two pilots meanwhile practised starting and landing on sandy soil. They were splendid fellows, and were already dancing South American boleros and roasting oxen on a spit in their imaginations. Ten to twenty times a day we destroyed the Gatun spillway.

Then came the most difficult part of the undertaking. My mechanics practised dismantling the Stukas and putting them together again, and finally managed to do their jig-saw puzzle in two days. In Kiel, meanwhile, the U-boat crews made a systematic and practical study of stowing the parts in the hull, and that too was accomplished. Then I ordered four Stuka bombs of specially concentrated explosive power and these were duly delivered.

My plan looked like this: I would penetrate into the Caribbean Sea with the two U-boats, at a certain point we would surface, get our aircraft parts ashore and assemble them in two days. The aircraft should start from the level shore. The pilots knew exactly the spot on which they were to drop their bombs. As the Stukas dropped their bombs from a very low altitude they could pin-point the spillway. The four bombs had to suffice.

We had to ensure that we got through with both U-boats to the intended landing place. For the landing itself we needed good luck and a thousand hands. If one of the U-boats should be sunk on the way, there was still a chance, given certain conditions, of putting Operation Pelican in hand with one machine. After the attack the two pilots were to fly to a neutral South American country and have themselves interned there. The U-boat men would have already started on their return voyage.

The Panama Canal is 50 miles long and has six double locks, each of which is 330 yards long and 36 yards wide. Without the Panama Canal the voyage from New York to San Francisco was longer by nearly eight thousand miles and the ships would need several weeks more to transfer, for instance, from the Asiatic theatres of war to the European.

Everything was in order. We were to start on an autumn day in 1943. We said our farewells, received schnaps and food coupons and money.

The two Stukas lay stowed away in the hull of the U-boats. The crews were on board. The time of departure had been fixed. We smoked and drank. We looked at the town with the eyes of those who would not see it again for a long time. There was a speech about the Fatherland, heroism, the Führer and Greater Germany. We listened and thought about the Panama Canal, about the spillway, about the section which we were to blow to smithereens.

"A telegram for you," I was told.

I went to the control room. It must be important if they wanted to get in touch with me at this hour. My mission was of course a secret one, to be divulged to no one. I decoded the message. I could not believe my eyes. I decoded it a second time. But there it was again.

"Operation Pelican called off. Report to Berlin at once."

I went back. I could not imagine what had happened. After all the money, work and energy that had been invested in this project. And what wonderful prospects of success it had had! All of us, the tough chaps of the U-boat crews, the dashing pilots, the devotedly keen mechanics — all of us had believed in 'Pelican.'

"Tiresome business, Gimpel," they greeted me. "It's a good thing that we could still get hold of you. Otherwise we'd have had to call you back over the high seas. We have it from a reliable source that the whole thing has been given away. There's no doubt about it. You wouldn't have got very far. You can congratulate yourself that we made our discovery in time."

"And who's behind this betrayal?" I asked.

Who? Who had given the whole thing away? The question hovers over the entire espionage history of the Second World War. Where were these traitors? Why had they become traitors? Had they done it for coffee? Or was it a matter of ideals? Was it love of adventure, or was it patriotism? Who knows? Who will ever know?

I know nothing of politics and I don't want to. I have never had anything to do with politics, and I never will. So perhaps I shall never understand why there was so much treachery in the war.

When only a few months later I sailed in a U-boat for forty-six days, as a soldier in the Second World War fighting on an invisible, silent and brutal front, this operation too was betrayed to America. I do not know who the informer was and I do not know if the traitor has any idea what it is like to be betrayed behind the lines, in the very heart of the enemy. I will tell him in a later chapter so that he may know.

Operation Pelican had, as I have said, been exploded. As was the custom in Amt VI, I was immediately put on to something else. Things were going badly for us in America. Our whole network of agents over there had been hastily contrived after the war had actually started. When we were at peace and preparations could have been made with comparative ease, the Foreign Ministry had declined to do so for political reasons. They feared to compromise themselves, a thing they were anxious to avoid at all costs. It was only shortly before the outbreak of war that they intensified espionage activities in the States, but even then they were working too much with amateurs, and not enough with experts. The overseas organisations of the N.S.D.A.P. were made responsible for the greater part of these activities with the poor results one might have expected. They put the members of harmless skittle clubs, folk-lore societies and rifle clubs of German origin under pressure, and tried to persuade them to work for their former Fatherland against their present home country. In many cases they succeeded in doing this, but the resulting information was on the whole worthless.

The Luftwaffe built up a relatively useful network of agents across North America, but it was discovered at one blow by the F.B.I. shortly before the outbreak of war and we suddenly found ourselves with no secret agents in the country of our principal enemies. We knew absolutely nothing about the Americans. We had no production figures. We knew nothing about their armaments, their standard of Army training, or their reserves; we did not even know the state of their morale. The dilettantism of the Foreign Ministry, blindly devoted to Hitler and headed by the ignorant Ribbentrop, hustled Germany into war with the richest country in the world. But we had no idea how rich America really was until afterwards.

Towards the end of 1944, the atomic bomb appeared like a ghost on the horizon. We had heard of America's 'Manhattan project.' Even before the war the German Professor Hahn had succeeded theoretically in splitting uranium, thereby releasing atomic power. Through his assistant, Lisa Meitner, who emigrated, the results of Hahn's research were taken abroad and reached America via Denmark. Professor Einstein realised immediately that Germany would in a short time be in a position to use atomic power for purposes of war, and that would mean victory for Germany. Einstein warned Roosevelt, and Roosevelt gave the word that the Manhattan project, that is to say American atomic research, should go forward with all speed. With unlimited resources of money, material and manpower, the atomic bomb was developed on an American scale and at an American tempo. That was the position when I was summoned to the Deputy Head of Amt VI, Dr. S.

"That is how things stand," said S. "We have tried everything possible. We have sent agents out there and they have either gone over to the other side or been caught. We can't work with foreigners any more or with stooges. We've got to put one of our own men on to it and that's where you come in, Gimpel."

"And what am I expected to do?" I asked.

"You are to go to America," he said. "How you are to get there I will now explain to you. We still have a few people to turn to, and through them you will come to the Manhattan project. You will get everything you need. You can take as many assistants with you as you like. As far as I am concerned you can have the whole of the Navy and what's left of the Air Force, but you must go, and go at once."

In Amt VI I had become used to anything and everything, but for a moment I wondered if I could be dreaming.

"And how am I to get over there?"

"I have already worked out a number of plans. . . . You can fly over with a specially equipped Focke-Wulf 200 and bail out."

"That's ridiculous," I replied.

"Yes, I don't particularly advocate it either," said S.

"And what other possibilities have you in mind?" I asked.

"By ship," he replied. "We can charter a freighter, give you the appropriate papers, and depend on your having your usual good luck. But in this case, of course, you will have to get in via South America."

"I don't much like the look of that either," I replied.

"You can please yourself how you get over there," he went on. "Perhaps in three days' time you will have thought of something, but remember, it's terribly urgent. I am sorry, I would have liked to spare you this task, but if anyone has a chance of getting through with it, it's you."

I went. The secretary in the ante-room asked me to have a word with Captain H.

He had thought up a plan of his own to get me to America.

He had come across a crook who passed himself off as a Hapsburg prince and a nephew of the ex-Empress Zita, who throughout the war had been staying in New York. The man had lost his papers and Captain H. now wanted to fit him out with some new ones. The crook should go through Switzerland to Spain, from there to South America and from there get into the U.S.A. The whole world knew that the Hapsburgs were sworn enemies of Hitler and this is what Captain H. wanted to exploit. I was to accompany the 'prince' as private secretary.

I have a sixth sense which tells me whether a thing has any chance of success or not. I had a look at the 'prince.' He was a tall lanky fellow with an impudent mouth and rabbity eyes. I have never had much to do with real princes, but this one looked just the stock picture-book aristocrat. Perhaps that was just as well for our purpose, perhaps not. I proposed to H. that we should first of all send the prince to Madrid on a trial mission. We gave him papers and money. He had nothing to do but cross the frontier, show his passport and convince the frontier officials of his identity.

He went off on the express train and immediately attracted attention. He was arrested as he was about to cross the frontier. H. was sent to the front.

So I had to get to America not with the help of the aristocracy but with U-boat 1230. It was all ready for service. Operation Elster had already begun.

# CHAPTER 6

## THE START OF A GRIM ADVENTURE

The Führer looked down at me with dull eyes from out of a square, dark brown wooden frame. The room had just been redecorated and smelt of paint. The electric fan revolved silently. Dr. S. was fiddling uneasily with his blotter; I was sitting facing him. It was ten o'clock in the morning. My time in Germany was up. I was about to leave on the American mission.

I looked past the Führer into the street where women, weary from the strain of air raids, weeping and waiting, were going about the day's affairs. All of them, the nameless, the anxious, the heavy-laden, the long-suffering, the greedy, all had their story. They would now be on their way to get their few ounces of cheese on Coupon VII/3, or their half-pound of apples on Special Points II/I. But it was not my job to worry about them. I was about to leave on the American mission.

A few weeks before I had still been in Spain. Sun, Mediterranean, peace, fiery-eyed women. The agent's war fought over a glass of whisky in the bar. Dancing. I had made acquaintances and friends there and they were all preparing to leave the sinking ship, organising their luggage for flight. They had forged papers with false names, they had dollars and Swiss francs, and no inhibitions about discussing their plans for the future. What was it all to me? I was about to leave on the American mission.

"Believe me," said Dr. S., "I should have liked to spare you this, but we have no one who speaks the language as well as you do and above all, no one else upon whom we can depend. . . . So you have made up your mind to get there by U-boat?"

"Yes," I replied.

He stood up and walked jerkily the length of the room. He was pale and stooped just a little. One could see that he had a great deal on his mind.

"I am not very much in favour of the project," he went on, "but after all it's your affair." He remained standing. "You know, of course, that six of your predecessors ended up on the electric chair."

"Yes, I know," I replied.

He shrugged his shoulders.

"Obviously," I went on, "it would be safer to stay at home."

109

He nodded and a smile passed over his face for a moment.

"Of course," he said. "Well, how do you propose to go to work?"

"I have one condition."

"Condition?"

"Yes. I need a proper American. The real stuff, not some seedy adventurer. You understand? He must know the latest dance steps and the latest popular songs. He must know what width one's trousers should be and how short one should have one's hair cut. He must know everything about baseball and have all the Hollywood gossip at his finger-tips. This man must stay with me at least until I become assimilated."

"Have you such a man in view?" asked S.

"That's the trouble," I replied. "I have absolutely no idea where to look for him."

"We'll find him," replied S.

The interview was at an end for that day.

The search for my assistant was as eventful as it was incidentally humorous. In the year 1944 I had to find an American who was prepared to work against his own country and who at the same time was courageous, sensible and trustworthy. For if he proved to be unreliable later he would automatically become my hangman. I enjoyed the privilege of being able to select my own executioner. The main thing was to act quickly.

We combed the prisoner-of-war camps. We looked over the American fliers who had been shot down. They were fine, high-spirited young fellows who accepted their miserable rations in good heart and regarded America as the centre of the world. The case of the German flier Söldner who had been persuaded by a British woman agent disguised as a Red Cross nurse to spy against Germany occurred to us. We were now trying a create a Söldner case ourselves. We introduced women agents to some prisoners whom we had carefully selected from a large number, but we had no luck. Our candidates' love of their country was stronger than their need of a woman: furthermore, we simply had not got enough women agents. Himmler liked to see the women in the kitchen, and, with his limited imagination, failed to grasp how important they were on the silent front. The Russians and the English have frequently based whole systems of espionage on women and with great success. If we wanted to avail ourselves of this weapon we had to do it behind Himmler's back, and always under the threat of being called to account by him.

I came across an anglicised Dutchman who had spent twelve years in America. I observed him for two whole days before I approached him. We drank together. After the second bottle he showed his unsuitability for my project. He wanted money. All my life I have despised people who spy for money, and that accounts for ninety-nine per cent of all secret agents. For one idealist, if one can call him that (today I would call him a fool), there are ninety-nine blackguards. The men with whom one has to work in the secret service are often the most despicable rabble that the world can throw to the surface. Prostitutes, procurers, cut-throats, traitors and criminals of all types and of all countries. Whomever they work for and whatever they work for, ninety-nine per cent of them are always the scum of humanity. I had time to reflect on the qualities of my so-called colleagues later when I was awaiting the hangman. Shortly before execution your last illusion also meets its death. . . .

Then they brought me a young, lanky American flight-lieutenant who with his 'Lightning' had voluntarily landed behind the German lines, and, to the astonishment of all the interrogation officers who had been in contact with him, had declared that he wished to place himself at Germany's disposal. We discovered that his Group-Commander had robbed him of his betrothed. He was embittered and it was for that reason that the young fellow wished now to fight on the side of the Germans. His story seemed so incredible that for some time we took him for an agent, but were finally convinced that due to some mental black-out he had simply run away. I took him to one side.

"Listen," I said, "you can get your revenge on the Americans. That's what you want, isn't it? We're planning a big affair."

"What is it?" he asked indifferently.

"You'll find that out later. . . . In any case we're going to America with excellently forged papers and a whole heap of money. You needn't worry; we've plenty of experience of these affairs."

"I know all about that," he said. "Why do your people end up on the electric chair when they've got so much experience . . . ? And why do you think I've run away from America?" he asked me.

"Because you hate the Yanks," I replied.

"Quite right, and for that reason I've no wish to go back to them! See?"

"You really want to fight on our side?" I asked.

"Yes," he replied, "but not as you think. Not with machine-guns, nor with forged papers. Just give me a microphone and I'll talk to my erstwhile comrades over the radio. They've had a bellyful already, anyhow. But that's all that I will do for this goddam war."

I took a good look at him. I could see that he was afraid. Fear was a thing which at that time I did not fully understand. I let him go but time was getting more and more pressing. . . . U-1230 was ready for me, and while it was having a final run over, I was measured for the uniform of a naval chief engineer. The uniform, of the best possible cloth, suited me well, and I would have liked to wear it for the rest of the war. But the time of departure was drawing ever nearer and I still had not found my companion.

Then an acquaintance at M.I. telephoned me.

"Go to the V.I.P.'s quarter in The Hague." He named a well-known part of the town which I already knew by hearsay. It was the part of the town reserved for the S.S. The S.S. officers who spent their leave here rode the horses from the Royal Stables and had the swimming baths warmed. If you were posted to The Hague and knew the right people you could live like a lord.

In the midst of this oasis of peace and pleasure sat Billy, the American, young, well-fed and contented. No one knew what to do with him, but at the same time his ticket had been paid for by the German consul in Lisbon.

When we met for the first time Billy had no idea who I was. He obviously took me for one of the S.S. officers who were staying there.

"You're an American?" I said.

"Yes," he replied, "but my mother's German. I don't want to be an American." He said this in English. He didn't know a word of German.

"And is that why you've come here?" I asked.

He nodded. "I hate America. I'll show that arrogant lot. I'll show them what they've brought me to."

"Well, I have nothing against it," I replied. We went out together. You could never leave Billy alone; he always got into difficulties. As he spoke only English he was frequently taken for a spy or at least for a shot-down American airman. On one occasion an over-zealous S.S. man pummelled into him. On another occasion three Red Cross nurses to whom he had spoken cornered him and had him marched away by the military police.

I looked him over. He was a soft, easily-influenced young chap, but perhaps something could be made of him. I have often had to rely upon my intuitive knowledge of people and I was certain that Billy's hatred for America was genuine. Whenever we spoke of the U.S.A. his face twitched, whether we were sober or not.

We often went drinking together. Billy, or to give him his full name, William Curtis Colepaugh, was one of the thirstiest and most accomplished drinkers I have ever met. I knew his life history from our files. It read like a novel written with a broomstick.

Billy came from Boston, the son of a German mother and an American father. When Billy was still at school the marriage broke up. Billy was on his mother's side and she took care that he received a good education. He was an apt pupil, distinguished himself in the Boy Scouts and was publicly honoured for rescuing two children from drowning at the risk of his own life. He left high school with the most glowing reports one year before the usual time, became a student at the Massachusetts Institute of Technology and later at the Admiral Farragut School in New York and the Grand Lakes Naval Centre. In 1939, after the outbreak of war, he made friends with the crew of the German cargo vessel *Pauline Frederik* which was unable to sail back. There was a good deal of camaraderie and a great deal of whisky. There were the quick German victories, there were the celebrations, there was confidence that Germany would win the war.

Billy was very much aware of his half-German descent. He was proud that the German sailors called him Wilhelm and clapped him on the shoulder. He was at the Captain's birthday party and met the German consul in Boston, Dr. Scholz, there. The consul realised at once that something could be made of Billy's devotion to Germany.

Billy became a spy without realising it. He completed his course at the Naval College with great success. He sailed as midshipman on convoy ships from America to England and reported his experiences immediately upon return to the zealous Dr. Scholz. Then came the blow. Billy was refused a commission because of his friendly attitude towards Germany.

War was declared between America and Germany and Dr. Scholz went home. Billy had to register at once for military service, the greatest possible humiliation for an up-and-coming naval officer. Billy fled from America, made his way to the Argentine and, referring to Dr. Scholz, presented himself at the German consulate there. They showed him the door but as a matter of prudence reported the matter to Germany.

In the Wilhelmstrasse Billy was adequately vouched for by Dr. Scholz and they cabled for him to come to Germany at once. But Billy had disappeared for the moment and they had to search for him. However, men like Billy can always be found in a sailors' tavern. He had forgotten his sticky reception at the German consulate and was prepared to go to Europe immediately. He got himself engaged as a steward, travelled to New York, passed all the control points, and eventually got on to the diplomatic ship *Gripsholm* as a potato-peeler. He landed in Lisbon and presented himself at the German Embassy there for military service. He was smuggled over the frontier.

But what was to be done with him now?

He received his basic training in a German S.S. company but he could speak no word of German and showed himself to be quite impossible as a soldier. That was how Billy came to The Hague. We had known for a long time that the F.B.I. were looking for him as a deserter. Billy's own story was investigated in detail and it was found to agree with the records. This was proof of his reliability. I was still uneasy on one or two points but time left me no choice.

"Things are getting serious, Billy," I told him. "You must come with me to Berlin."

"Afraid I can't," he replied. "I can't leave Trujs alone."

"And who is Trujs?" I asked him.

"My fiancée."

The girl did not fit into my programme at all. I observed her, she was a pale blonde, an easy-going girl who made eyes at all the men. We would have to get Billy away from her, but that would not be difficult.

"See to it," I told my confidential colleagues, "that the girl gets into different company, and that Billy gets into the right train." It worked. Trujs changed her affections to a young German officer and a week later Billy came to Berlin.

I returned from The Hague on the 20th

119

July, 1944. It was the day of the uprising against Hitler, but no one knew anything about that officially. I had to share my sleeper with an Army colonel. I introduced myself.

"Oh, a civilian," he grunted. "That means trouble at the frontier."

"Perhaps you'll be able to do something for me, Colonel?" I said.

"We'll see," he said without enthusiasm.

At the frontier I was allowed to pass without a word. The colonel was asked politely but firmly to go to the control office on the station.

"Oh, let the Colonel have his sleep," I said, and the patrol left him in peace too.

Yes, even on the 20th July, 1944, the papers I carried were a *passe-partout*.

My American mission, Operation Elster, was a high priority top secret affair, but all the same there was no one in Amt VI who did not know about it. Only a few people actually mentioned it to me, but everyone I met looked at me in a diffident or embarrassed sort of way. They couldn't understand why ever I had taken it on.

And why had I indeed? Obviously I had known for some time that the war was already lost, but I stubbornly refused to accept the fact. My father had distinguished himself in the First World War, my brother had fallen at Stalingrad, my friend had had both legs shot away and my cousin had been killed in an air raid. With every week that passed I lost another friend and I simply saw it as my duty to travel the path so many others had travelled whether they had wanted to or not.

I was warned, condoned with and laughed at but from the first moment my mind was made up. I would embark on U-1230. However, it was only at this juncture that I learned the exact details of my mission. My superiors wanted to know whether the Allies intended to drop atomic bombs on Berlin, Munich, Hamburg, Breslau and Cologne or whether they planned to go on using only the 'ordinary' high-explosive bombs. I was given instructions in the theory of atomic physics. A spectre was taking shape which was filling us with horror, and I was told that I — Agent 146, radio-engineer Erich Gimpel — was the only man who could meet the threat. I was a hero in anticipation and I quickly accustomed myself to the role.

One day a bulging dossier arrived on my desk. Notes, telegrams, newspaper cuttings, reports. It was the 'Pastorius' case, one of the most tragic failures of the

German M.I., one of the most dastardly pieces of trickery the war produced.

I read through the file, page for page. I was anxious to learn all I could from it. The words danced before my eyes. This one file was enough to rob a man of his reason.

The Pastorius plan had been devised by amateurs and carried out by amateurs. And it had cost the lives of six men. When the M.I. had reluctantly taken over the Pastorius plan, I was a trainee. I could still see them before me, the men who went voluntarily to America, among them young Herbert Haupt, his gold teeth glittering as he smiled, his eyes clouding over with sadness whenever he spoke of his parents; massive John Kerling, a real dare-devil; handsome Hermann Neubauer who knew his way around so well with women. I saw them before me as, laughing, they went aboard the two U-boats which were to take them to America, laden with money, explosives, and the good advice of people who did not know what they were talking about.

A certain Herr Kabbe had devised the plan and become its absentee manager. For he did not accompany the men; he preferred to warm his feet by the fire while they were ploughing across the Atlantic. Their mission was to sabotage the production of aluminum in the U.S.A. Supported by American helpers whose addresses they had with them they were to blow up the factories. They travelled in two U-boats, four men in each. One group landed on Long Island, near New York, the other group somewhere in Florida. The explosive material bore a German trademark; dollar bills which they had sewn into their belts were partly invalid and considerably short of the proper amounts, these candidates for death having actually been robbed even before they left Germany. All of this was not pure chance, nor was it sheer negligence. It was treason.

The two U-boats crossed the Atlantic. The first group to land were surprised by a coastguard as they were burying their explosives, but they did not fully realise what was going on and went home and went to bed. The F.B.I. slept too. Dasch, the leader of the group that landed near New York, betrayed his comrades and became their murderer. He reported the operation to the F.B.I. New York branch. They did not believe him. They did not even trouble to pass his report on to Washington. Dasch went to Washington and was laughed at there. It was not until he put 80,000 dollars down on the table that they began to take him seriously.

The fate of the men who had come to America to fight for Germany was now sealed. The fate of Herbert Neubauer, Heinrich Heinck, Richard Quirin, Werner Thiel, Herbert Haupt, and Edward John Kerling.

They were put under constant watch. Their photographs were in every police station file. They visited relations, friends and helpers in the States. This, of course, they had been strictly forbidden to do but they were only beginners and one could hardly expect them to do otherwise. And so, unknowing, they dragged their mothers, their fathers, their brothers and their sisters down into the abyss with them. The F.B.I. kept a record of every visit they made. Anyone who had spoken with them and did not later give evidence against them was for it. That is universal practice.

The men of Operation Pastorius were suddenly arrested.

The hearing was in New York. There were eight death sentences, and a pardon for Dasch, the traitor, and a pardon for Bürger who was the only man who could prove that he had not come to America voluntarily but had been coerced. Roosevelt immediately confirmed the death sentences. Six men awaited their end.

I read on. I forced myself to it. Now it came, the horrible, incredible end. I looked at the photographs and read the reports of the last hours of my predecessors. It had all been recorded with American precision — how the end had come, how the men had died, how the executioners drew rubber masks over the distorted faces so that only the eyes and noses protruded, how they were fastened to the chair and how once more the death sentence was read over to them.

You sit in the chair and cannot move. Then the button is pressed. The current is turned on, but every body reacts differently. There is no norm. It depends on the heart, the weight, the individual sensitivity to electricity. With one it may happen quickly, another may take longer. In some cases three shocks are necessary.

I tried to imagine how my predecessors had prepared themselves for death: Kerling would have been defiant and stubborn, Haupt would have broken down completely, Quirin would have been in despair, Thiel would have been quite detached. No pardon, no mercy, no words of comfort.

On my desk lay a photograph of the car in which their bodies had been taken away after execution. The bodies of the men who had gone to America before me. Men whom I was to follow, who had died, betrayed, betrayed by their comrade, John Dasch.

But he was by no means the only traitor. There were others in Berlin, in a section of M.I. which spied upon the other section. The Americans claimed that they knew about Operation Pastorius even before the U-boats left Germany, that they had got the information from a high German authority and had paid for it with coffee which was sent into Germany via Switzerland.

I wanted to thrust my thoughts away from me. The traitors had not yet been caught. Would I be betrayed too? Would there be the fragrance of coffee somewhere in Germany while the hangman was putting the rope around my neck?

I had two days in which to complete my preparations. My department insisted on taking out a Life Insurance Policy for me.

"We'll look after that," said Dr. S. "Naturally the affair will be camouflaged. We will go on paying the premium for you. If anything happens to you your dependants will get 100,000 marks. You have only to say to whom the money should be paid."

"To my father," I replied.

We spent the last evening in Berlin in the Fürstenhof hotel. There were three of us. My girlfriend, Margarete, Billy and I. We sat in the lounge and drank wine. Billy was drunk. Now and again he would stand up and say something in English.

"Keep your mouth shut," we told him each time.

As he caused so much trouble we had forbidden him to open his mouth in public.

In his suitcase lay the uniform of a German naval lieutenant. For the forty-six days of the U-boat voyage, Billy, who could speak not a word of German, was to be promoted naval lieutenant.

"I shall never see you again," said Margarete.

"Nonsense," I replied.

"The whole thing is hopeless. Everyone says so."

"They would do better to keep quiet," I replied.

Margarete indicated Billy.

"I don't trust him for an instant," she said. "You wait, he'll give you away."

"I don't think so," I replied.

"What's she saying?" asked Billy.

"You keep your mouth shut," I replied.

"Just look at his ape-like arms," continued Margarete, "and his eyes. He can never look you straight in the face. You've certainly got a nice one there. The pride of Amt VI. You've got some surprises in store!"

We went on drinking. We got merry. We got sad. We stayed another hour in the Fürstenhof. Just as we were getting up to go a Nazi district leader in uniform entered the crowded lounge. He was drunk.

"Listen, folks," he said, "the whole of London is on fire! The new secret weapon is in operation. London is in flames! The world has never seen anything like it before."

He turned round in every direction.

"Heil Hitler!" he shouted.

"Shut up," said Billy in German. They were the only German words that he had learned from us.

The resplendent official was hanging on to the back of a chair.

"All together now, three *Sieg Heils* for our Führer!"

No one made a sound. He thrust out his hand and pointed from table to table.

"After the war," he said, "we'll hang the whole lot of you, and I'll bury you all."

"That's a nice send-off for you," said Margarete to me.

We still had four hours to go. In four hours' time we had to say farewell to our personal happiness. We were conscious of every minute and kept looking at our watches. Margarete was looking especially charming in a tight-fitting coat and skirt. Her face was white and the paleness suited her. We did not want to talk about Elster but somehow we always strayed back to the same subject. You always do think about the very thing that you most want to put out of your mind.

Margarete wanted to come to the U-boat with me, but that was not allowed. Not only because the mission was a top priority secret affair, but because U-boat men are superstitious and say "a long hair in the screw will make the boat sink." Also no flowers were allowed on board. "Flowers turn a boat into a coffin."

Billy and I travelled to Kiel in civilian dress. My companion was beginning to show signs of nervousness. Up to this moment he had borne himself splendidly. He was delighted with his role as supporting hero and felt specially intrepid after a few drinks. He was given the agent's number 146/2, an appendage, so to speak, of Gimpel. My department trusted him completely; to them he seemed made-to-measure for our requirements.

Our equipment was loaded on to the ship: two kit-bags with extra strong padlocks. They contained 60,000 dollars, diamonds to the value of 100,000 dollars, automatic pistols, radio parts, photographic apparatus and invisible ink. I had systematically practised stowing my long legs in the U-boat. I was by no means the right proportions for a U-boat sailor and until I got used to it I ached in every limb. My arrival in Kiel was a minor sensation for the U-boat men. They took me for a real chief engineer.

The U-boat which was to land me in Frenchman Bay was commanded by First-Lieutenant Hilbig. We got on famously from the first moment. He had instructions to avoid any encounters on route. Only he knew about Operation Elster.

We got a great send-off as was usual with U-boats leaving port.

I narrowly escaped making an awful gaffe when three U-boat commanders presented themselves to me, and besieged me with technical questions.

"What's the position with radar, sir?" they asked. "Are there still no counter-measures? You know of course how things are with our defence apparatus."

"Yes," I replied, "I know how things are."

I extricated myself as well as I could. I told them that it was precisely for that reason that I was embarking on this voyage — to gather experience connected with radar research.

"Hilbig's in luck's way," said one of the U-boat commanders. "He would have to be the one to get the C.E. on board, while we're still doing the hell-or-heaven stretch."

The crew of U-1230 had mustered, officers to the right, other ranks to the left, Colepaugh and I among the officers. Lieutenant Hilbig presented the crew to the Commander of the base.

"Get moving, men," said the Commander. "I know your voyage is no pleasure trip. It isn't the first time you've done it. I wish you a safe return, from the bottom of my heart. I wish you good luck and success. Just remember that everything you do is for the Fatherland, for Greater Germany."

The mothers, the wives and the children

of the crew were standing in the background. They all looked as if they had been weeping. They were two to three hundred yards away from us and perhaps some stray words of the speech were reaching them on the wind. The Commander came up to us and shook hands. When he looked at me he faltered for a moment and then quickly took his leave.

The crew were allowed another ten minutes to go to their loved-ones. As I watched the scenes of parting I felt relieved I was alone.

The last preparations for sailing had been made. I ran over my luggage just once more. Billy stood by my side, silent, bewildered, anxious. I gave him a clap on the back.

"Now we're off, Billy," I said. "Are you scared?"

"Not specially," he replied.

"Now we shall see," I said.

We went on board. An engineer guided me through the boat, explaining the technicalities, but I was not listening, my thoughts were working independently, swinging between Margarete and my American mission.

Billy did not move from my side.

"Here are the diesel engines. We call

them Hein and Fietje."

I nodded. I was longing for a cigarette.

"I'm sorry, that's not allowed," said the engineer. "You may smoke only in the tower because of the danger of explosion. You'll soon get used to it."

A few minutes later we sailed off into our grim adventure.

# CHAPTER 7

## TO AMERICA BY SUBMARINE

Needless to say, I had crossed the Atlantic more comfortably than was the case in U-1230. We had a good send-off from the R.A.F. Hundreds of British aircraft appeared over Kiel and when we left, the town was in flames. We were sitting in the officers' mess eating beans and bacon and listening to the explosions, when between the second and third waves of attack the order came to leave port.

There were three vessels sailing in line ahead, with U-1230 under Lieutenant Hilbig in the lead. In the interests of more concentrated firing power we had to proceed in close formation as far as Horten, the Norwegian war harbour in Oslo fjord. The men were wearing overalls, their faces were still clean-shaven and they went about their tasks with quiet confidence. As far as they were concerned my name was Günther and I was a chief engineer. They viewed me with a certain reticent curiosity. I was a 'silverling,' so-called because of the silver cord on my service cap. The regular naval officers wore gold.

U-1230 was of the 9-C type. It was 80 yards long, had a displacement of 950 tons and commanded two twin batteries and one anti-aircraft gun. The gun platform was known as the 'winter garden.' The gun crews remained at action stations as far as Horten. The water was too shallow for us to submerge. Our best psychological defence was hope, hope that we should not be attacked from the air. Our most formidable menace lurked on our very doorstep, and the channel in which we sailed was strewn with the wreckage of sunken German cargo ships. We threw the 'Klapper,' a sound-producing device, overboard and dragged it after us on a cable as some defence against submerged mines which were exploded or touched off by the noise of the propeller. By this time the British had made the Baltic Sea their *'mare nostro.'*

The men, with their strong, rough hands and ashen faces, had the imperturbability which comes from constant contact with danger. They knew exactly what they needed; they needed good luck, only good luck. And they knew what was their due: once a month a bar of chocolate; once or twice, or if they were lucky, perhaps even five times a day, a solitary smoke in the tower; three weeks' leave after every sortie; special rations on board if after submerging the tins had not burst with the pressure. (If they did burst, the crew had to be put on half rations.) All of them, the commander, the first officer-of-the-watch, the junior officers and the men, all had a mother, a sweetheart, a wife, a child, a brother, but the war didn't care about them. . . .

We reached Horten without mishap and devoted the following week to submerging trials. If in 1944 a German submarine wanted to cross the Atlantic it had to do so stealthily, and, what is more, it had to submerge very deeply, for radar could guide the depth-charges with deadly precision. Here we could dive more deeply than was possible in harbour. A piece of rope was stretched tautly from one side of the vessel to the other and when Lieutenant Hilbig called into the loudspeaker after a submerging trial, "Trial ended — surface," the rope was hanging quite slack, such was the terrific pressure against the sides of the U-boat.

The U-boat had two w.c.'s, but the one forward in the bows was put to a use far removed from that for which it was intended; it had to act as a store-house for our special supplies. Shaving or washing on board was impossible. The sailor had to do his best with eau-de-cologne, which was all part of the naval issue. A man could withdraw only with the verbal consent of the officer-of-the-watch. If when the boat was submerged a member of the crew went from aft to forward or the other way round, he had to report at the control room so that the equilibrium of the boat could be restored by balancing the water tanks.

There were no cabins. The men's hammocks were slung between torpedoes, pieces of machinery and in a variety of odd places brought into service with great resourcefulness. Salamis, hams and other smoked meats hung between armatures, pressure indicators, tubes and levers. The companionway looked like a farm kitchen. Our supplies — the boat had been provisioned for a six-months' voyage — swayed with the pitching of the boat.

We had 240 tons of oil and fourteen torpedoes on board. The torpedoes could not be used on the voyage out. In common with all other sea-going vessels we had, once a day, to our chagrin, to report our position to Germany over short-wave transmitter. The Allies awaited this information jubilantly every morning and held their locating apparatus ready. Dozens of German U-boats fell prey to the enemy because of this bureaucratically-ordained self-betrayal.

The presence of two unusual guests on board caused a bit of a stir among the crew on the first few days. Even if I, the 'silverling,' could in an emergency produce something resembling that which was expected of a chief engineer, it was beyond any dispute that Billy Colepaugh was the strangest German naval lieutenant who had ever put to sea. We had camouflaged him as a war reporter, and as a sort of badge of office we had hung a magnificent camera round his neck. However, he put his hand to his camera at such totally unsuitable moments that his photographic skill was very soon seriously doubted by all the sixty-two members of the crew. The men could see that Billy was no German and no real naval officer. Whenever they spoke to him he just grinned and said yes.

I told the crew that Billy came from one of the former German colonies and that that was why he could not speak German.

They listened to my story and continued to bait him.

One day, a stoker placed himself in front of Billy in one of the passage-ways.

"May I pass please, sir?" he said.

Billy shook his head.

"You do not understand?" continued the stoker.

Billy grinned.

"You're no lieutenant," said the man, "you big camel."

"O.K.," said Billy.

Scenes like this, whenever the men could relax, were a daily occurrence and speculation as to our real identity became a favourite topic of conversation among our ship-mates.

We sailed out from Horten and on to Christiansund, the next and last German U-boat base. An anti-aircraft cruiser gave us escort cover. Lieutenant Hilbig was besieged with questions about us.

"Are you out to win the Knight's Cross with a special mission?" the first mate asked him. Then, when Hilbig remained silent: "I hope you haven't got a sore throat, sir?" Hilbig laughed. He was tall, slim and fair and had flown sorties to England at the beginning of the war as a naval pilot until the lack of fuel brought about his transfer to the Navy. He was the archetype of active service naval officer. Although he never raised his voice or threw his weight about, although he never had much to say, he commanded absolute obedience. He had a minute cabin to himself, and this was the nerve centre of U-1230.

During the whole of the voyage, I saw Hilbig thrown off balance only once. We were just half-way across the Atlantic when he received news by radio that he had a baby daughter. Five minutes later depth-charges were crashing about our ears.

We completed the voyage to Christiansund without mishap. The crew were preparing for their last shore leave. We met other U-boats in harbour, flying pennants on their aerials to show the tonnage they had sunk. The base was in a state of great excitement. That same morning distress signals had been received from a U-boat which technical difficulties had forced to surface while an enemy air attack was on. Three or four German ships had gone to its aid but all they had found was an enormous patch of oil which flowed slowly away to the north. Crosses were placed against sixty-two names. . . .

I went on shore in the afternoon, my last opportunity to see one of the servicemen's film shows. It was a love story full of heroics and men in immaculate uniforms. After the performance, the order was flashed on the screen in huge letters: "Attention! Please remain in your seats! Officers leave the hall first."

I went to a quay-side tavern and drank Holzschnaps. I had been warned about it but I had to get used to running greater risks than drinking Holzschnaps. This was the second time I had been in Norway. I had undertaken a mission there about eighteen months previously, at the end of 1942, which had nearly cost me my life.

I had been sent out to Norway then because our radio observers had located some secret transmitters there which we had so far not been able to put out of action. We had however, been able to decipher one or two messages at least partly, and it was from these that M.I. had first heard of Operation Schwalbe and discovered that the enemy planned to attack the 'Norsk-Hydro' near Vemork. The great Norsk-Hydro plant was the only factory in the world producing 'heavy water' (deuterium-oxide) in any considerable quantities. 'Heavy water' was needed to split the atom (in the case of the Hiroshima bomb the Americans were forced to use graphite as a substitute for 'heavy water').

I was told of a Norwegian contact in Oslo and I looked him up. We knew that the man was playing a double game, and I passed myself off as a British agent who had landed by parachute. I held a wad of money under his nose and asked him to bring me into contact as quickly as possible with two other agents whom I had lost sight of in the course of landing.

He gave me the address of an inn. I had it watched and within fourteen days we knew the names and addresses of all the people who regularly consorted there. We learned in fact that a few days previously an Englishman had had a talk there with two Norwegians. The Englishman was working under the cover name of John. I had to find this John whatever happened.

I had the two Norwegians taken into custody by the Norwegian authorities. On the third day of their arrest they were told that they had made derogatory remarks about Quisling, the Norwegian pocket Führer. At that time you could have held any Norwegian on this charge. After another four days, I let the men, who had never set eyes on me, go free again.

If they had known their job they would now have voluntarily isolated themselves.

But they were no experts and it was upon this that I had set all my hopes. Their every step was watched. Two days later we trailed them into a street in a western suburb of Oslo in which — as the bearings had shown — a secret transmitter was being operated. We were certain that the transmitter was in the street but we had not been able to discover in which house. We refrained from searching the whole street to avoid attracting attention.

The two Norwegians disappeared into number eleven. I stood on the opposite side of the street. I had two other men on the job that evening. They were standing in the porch of number nine. The street was dimly lit by one solitary lamp. My two companions and I knew what John looked like. He was tall, very thin, very loose-limbed and had sparse hair. There were perhaps 50,000 Norwegians who answered to this description but we were determined that evening to arrest every man who was tall and loose-limbed and had sparse hair.

11.37 p.m. The police report prepared later recorded the minute exactly. The door opened. A man came out without an overcoat. He might be John. He must be John. He stopped, lit a cigarette and looked to the left and to the right. That might have been pure chance but it was not.

I could wait. I restrained myself from grabbing the man immediately but my two companions were too hasty. They went up to him, and one of them got his torch out of his pocket and shone it on him as he continued to stand there motionless. I was perhaps twenty yards away from him. My colleagues had approached him to within a distance of about six yards.

"Hands up!" one of them called and levelled his gun at the man.

Slowly, limply, looking rather bewildered, the man who was to be arrested raised his hands.

"Idiots!" I grunted to myself.

Then it happened. Suddenly and unexpectedly.

There was a shot, three, four, five shots. The man was still standing there with his hands up, but my two companions lay on the ground.

John had shot from the hip. By means of a trigger mechanism that could be operated even with raised hands. There was some sort of connection between the hand and the trigger. On this evening, we of M.I. lost two men and gained a new shooting device.

John made off like lightning with me in pursuit. I fired as I ran, shooting past him of course. But he disappeared, as if the earth had swallowed him.

I caught the two Norwegians, who were likewise trying to get away, for the second time. After lengthy interrogation they admitted that they had been working for the British. Parachute agents had been in contact with them and they knew that a British landing was planned in the neighbourhood of the Norsk-Hydro. I reported the matter to Berlin and was recalled.

A little later the German Military Commander in Norway, General von Falkenhorst, went personally to Vemork to inspect the defence installations there and have them reinforced, but in spite of that the British soon showed them to be destructible.

The British knew all about Vemork because the founder of the works, the Norwegian physicist Dr. Thronstad, having fled to England via Sweden when the Germans invaded Norway, had warned the British authorities that Germany should not be allowed to come into possession of the means of producing atomic bombs. When Germany ordered that the production of 'heavy water' should be stepped up from

1,500 kilogrammes to 5,000 kilogrammes a year, the Allies realised that their enemies were on the point of producing the atomic bomb, and they acted like lightning. The first thing they did was to drop four parachute agents who made contact with the workers with a view to discovering what were the possibilities of destroying the works. The factory was seven storeys high and built of steel and concrete. An attack from the air would be useless unless the bombs could be aimed with minute accuracy.

Then came two Halifax bombers with two freight gliders in tow. They came to grief on a mountain and there were a few dozen dead. But of what account were they when the atomic bomb was at issue?

On Christmas Day 1942 six more agents landed in Norway. The day was chosen because the British, not without justification, hoped that the Germans would be sitting round the Christmas tree drinking punch. The saboteurs made their way into the completely desolate and uninhabited region of Vemork in a snowstorm. They were driven off their course and became separated, and it was weeks before they came together again. Two months after landing they had at last penetrated through to the

Norsk-Hydro. On the 27th February, 1943, they overpowered the augmented watch, got inside the works, blew up the central plant and put the whole installation out of action for nearly twelve months. When the works were ready to go into production once more a few hundred American aircraft arrived whose exceptionally heavy bombs proved stronger than steel and concrete.

It was intended that the supplies of 'heavy water' which remained should be moved to Germany, but in February 1944, the train ferry in which they were being transported blew up. The British Secret Service — as ever the best in the world — had attached a time-bomb to the train. With this setback Germany fell finally into the rear with the production of the atomic bomb.

And now, a few months after the destruction of the Norsk-Hydro, I was sitting in a quay-side tavern in Christiansund drinking Holzschnaps. It tasted awful. In 1944 everything tasted awful. A few more hours and I would be on board U-1230 again, bound for America, to discover how far the Americans had got with the atomic bomb, and to ascertain by what means their production of it could be stopped. The Allies had all this behind them.

On the following morning U-1230 left port. We sailed mostly at a depth of 260 feet. Ninety revolutions a minute produced a speed of two knots. We were able to manage about fifty miles a day.

It was uncanny. The Atlantic was ruled above and below water by the Allies, and there we were, attempting to cross it in a tiny boat at snail's pace.

U-boat crews have a code of their own, and Billy and I had to fit in with it. During the war no boat sailed on the 13th or on a Friday. We had to get used to the toilets — one had to climb through a hole sideways and only reached one's objective after performing a variety of contortions. Those who managed it for the first time received a mock diploma in accordance with time-honoured custom.

The first bombs began to explode round the boat on our fourth day out. Warning of air attack! Alarm, submerge! The conning tower hatch was closed down immediately. Daylight disappeared, the boat went down, the air became foul. The interminable gramophone records, to be heard in every part of the U-boat from morn till night, fell silent. The captain gave his orders. Billy stood by me and held me tightly by the hand.

"What shall we do," he asked, "if a bomb hits us?"

"We will drown," I replied, "and then it will all be over."

He forgot to smile that time.

We listened to the bombs. We could feel the shock of the explosions. The detonations sounded unusually long drawn out and strangely distant, as if shots were being fired in a tunnel. Then the lights came on. The faces of the men relaxed.

"All over," said a mate who was near me. "You just have to make sure you disappear in time. But depth charges are far worse."

We remained below water. Once the enemy has located a U-boat he spares neither time nor persistence in its pursuit. We doubled back on our tracks. We changed our course. Lili Marlene could be heard once more but we knew that she might be reduced to silence by an explosion at any moment.

"Do you know yet where we're going to land?" asked Billy.

"No," I replied.

"What fools we were to let ourselves in for this," he went on. "It's quite crazy."

"You should have thought of that before. You said you hated America."

"That's quite true, I do," he replied.

"But I value my life."

"And don't you think I do?"

I looked at him. Fear is quite a natural thing, I told myself. I recalled Margarete's words. I saw her before me, a small person with intensely blue, lively eyes and soft, well-cared for hands. I heard her say: "I don't trust him for a moment . . . you'll see, he'll betray you. Look at his ape-like arms. Look at his eyes. He can never look anyone straight in the face. You *have* picked out a fine one for yourself. The pride of Amt VI. You've got some surprises in store."

It was too late to worry whether I could trust him or not. I was dependent on him for better or worse. He carried his heart on his tongue. Well, what of it? He was young and had not had much experience of this war. And where is the heart that can go on beating calmly when bombs are exploding all round?

We crawled on across the Atlantic at two knots. Throughout the day no word could be spoken aloud because of the enemy sound detectors. Even under water we could only whisper. Every day when darkness fell we rose to periscope depth, 42 feet. If the sea was calm the Schnorchel was raised. This supplied engines and crew

150

with oxygen. If because of nearness to the enemy it could not be used, the engines were worked by electricity. The oxygen in the boat sufficed for human lungs for a further thirty-six hours. Then it was exhausted.

The constant state of tension seemed to devour the time. We were altogether forty-six days en route, watching and being watched. We got used to the close quarters, the foul air, the depth charges, the whispering, the great odds stacked against us, the feeling of being alone and defenceless. The men spoke little of home but it was doubtless very much in their thoughts. At this period no U-boat would have dared to penetrate so far into the Atlantic without special orders. We wondered whether we would ever return. Who had the greater chance of survival, the crew of U-1230 who had to cross the ocean again or I who had to make my way to the atomic plant?

It was just bad luck for anyone who fell ill, for there was no doctor on board. Any man who still possessed an appendix would do better to stay at home. If a man died he was wrapped in a hammock, and had the German flag wound about his body. There was an adequate supply of flags on board.

Death stalked us between the Faroes and Iceland. We successfully evaded the bombs, but we should all have died from suffocation if Engineer Böttger had not taken instant action on his own initiative. The Schnorchel used to protrude above the water as little as possible and every time the waves washed over it the pressure fell within the vessel. Ears felt as if they would burst, the heart beats quickened, breathing became more difficult and the head began to swim. The food tins burst or became misshapen.

On this particular unlucky day we had to use the Schnorchel in a heavy sea-way. A huge wave washed over our ventilator thus preventing the exhaust gases from escaping. They therefore streamed back into the vessel and went straight to our heads. We began to lose consciousness. The diesel engines, which had been going at full speed, suddenly cut out, a thing which at that moment no one could understand. That is, no one but Engineer Böttger who was standing by the diesel. He immediately grasped what was happening, pulled out the clutch of the diesel engines, disconnected the shaft from the motor and changed over to the electric power. He was just in time. Eight men, Böttger among them, collapsed.

The boat, which with the failure of the diesel engines had suddenly started to sink, slowly rose again.

"Surface!" ordered Lieutenant Hilbig.

Drawn up by compressed air, U-1230 shot out of the water like a fish. The tower hatch was opened and the fresh night air streamed in. It was just in time. A split second's hesitation and the exhaust gases would have killed us. The eight unconscious members of the crew were hauled on ropes through the tower on to the deck. It was fortunate that at the time no enemy warship was in the offing.

Nearer and nearer to America. Nearer my fate. I went over my luggage. Was it nervousness or was it my sixth sense? I opened the packet of dollars I had been given only to find that they had been packed in bundles and that the wrappers round the bundles bore the words *"Deutsche Reichsbank."* With infinite trouble I had been equipped with American shoes, American shirts and other articles of clothing, American revolvers, but they had forgotten to remove the wrappers which would have been a complete give-away.

We were still separated from America by four days, keeping in constant radio communication with our German headquarters and steering a direct course for the agreed landing-point, Frenchman Bay in the State of Maine, when the signals rating rushed out of his cabin and thrust a wireless message at Lieutenant Hilbig. In a few minutes Hilbig had decoded it. I stood beside him. He looked at me, flabbergasted.

"The swine!" he said.

He read out the message in utter disgust and handed me the note.

"What do you make of that?"

I read:

"We have reason to believe that the enemy may be apprised of our undertaking. Act according to your own discretion."

I sat down.

"What are you going to do?" asked Hilbig.

"Have a cigarette," I replied.

He nodded.

"I'll come into the tower with you," he said. When we were up above he continued: "It's enough to make a man weep. Do you want to land now or not?"

"Of course I'll land," I replied. "But not in Frenchman Bay."

"Right."

"One more thing," I continued. "Colepaugh must be told nothing of this message."

We went back into the officers' mess and studied the charts in an attempt to find another landing place, but we were in for a painful surprise. Wherever we looked the water was too shallow to bring a U-boat into shore. In these circumstances there were only two possibilities, either to turn back or land in Frenchman Bay.

"It's not going to be any picnic," said the commander. "If the Americans have got their wits about them, they'll know well enough that we can only land in this bay. They only need to set up sounding apparatus and they'll have us. That being so, I must make a few preparations and get the boat ready for scuttling. We might fall into enemy hands and in that case I'm responsible for seeing the boat's scuttled."

"Yes," I replied. I knew that according to the code of U-boat commanders there was no greater disgrace than to allow one's vessel to fall into the hands of the enemy intact.

But we were in any case unable to steer a direct course for Frenchman Bay. There was yet another hitch in the form of a short circuit in the transformers which put our depth-sounding apparatus out of action. Without this apparatus it was hopeless trying to operate in a relatively shallow bay. The ship's engineer informed the commander that with the means at his disposal he was not in a position to repair the apparatus. I recalled that I had once been a radio engineer.

"There's just a chance," I told the commander. "The transformers must be completely dismantled and re-wound."

After three days of unremitting work the electrician managed to do this, and I myself fitted it back into the instrument. And it worked.

When we had neared the coast, I took bearings from a Boston radio station and confirmed our new position. We were in Fundy Bay.

"If your bearings are correct," said Hilbig, "we shall be seeing the lights of Mount Desert rock in two hours' time." My bearings were correct.

The crew were told that Billy and I were going to land. Nothing more. They could think the rest out for themselves. No more details had so far been given to the crew as there was always the danger that they might be taken prisoner.

The bay was guarded by a destroyer. We dived below it and remained on the sea bed. Throughout the day ships moved over us. We could hear the sound of engine and screws with our ears alone. We waited for the night and high tide. We rose to periscope depth and let ourselves be carried into Frenchman Bay between two islands. If the American coast defences had not been asleep we should have been discovered long since. The coastguards had to answer for all this later before the court-martial. The Americans made no use of their sound detectors or their radar apparatus. They already had victory in their pockets while we were trembling for our very lives. Current had to be saved and we could have no more cooked food. The cook prepared his cold dishes while the boat, fore and aft, was being made ready for scuttling. The captain allowed me two gallons of water to wash in, from his own special supplies. The first officer-of-the-watch cut my beard with an electric hair cutter, and after three attempts I managed a proper shave with a razor.

It seemed incredible. We could hardly believe that we had remained all this time undiscovered: and still no depth charges, no U-boat chasers, no attacks from the air. We ate sandwiches and waited for night to fall. The men who passed by me pressed my hand. I had assisted as officer-of-the-watch and had got to know them all. The cook was a real character, known throughout the Navy. He was sea-sick on every voyage and on every return to port he volunteered for the next voyage out. The men murmured their good wishes. They wanted to question us, to warn us, to sympathise with us, to admire us.

I pondered for a long time whether I should go ashore in uniform or civilian clothes. If I went ashore in uniform and was captured I should have to be treated as a prisoner-of-war. If I wore civilian clothes I was a spy and would be hanged. But in any case I would have to remove the uniform some time for I could hardly be seen circulating in America in the uniform of a German naval engineer. Burying the uniform seemed to me more risky than landing in civilian clothes. Billy too had to take off his uniform. He was green with fear and shaking at the knees.

"Everything will soon be all right," I told him. "Once we've landed we'll be all right. It's more dangerous here in the bay than on shore."

The time passed with immeasurable slowness. The seconds, the minutes, the hours stretched themselves like so much elastic, and the whole boat seemed to crackle with the tension.

"In two hours' time we will surface," said Hilbig. "We want to find out how near we can approach the coast. I will let the boat run backwards. We will remain on the surface while you row to land. I think you'll need fire cover."

"I'd rather you made off," I replied.

"No," he said, "I have orders to see that you are put safely on shore, and standing by is all part of my duty."

My baggage was ready, but I still did not know if I would be able to go ashore that day. I might have to wait several days yet. Perhaps I should have to ask the sixty-two men of the U-boat crew to wait another thirty-six or forty-eight hours in the threat of depth charges. We knew what the system of coast defence was but we did not know exactly how it functioned on this section of the coast, how the shore was watched and how many observers would be on duty. Another hour, a half-hour, a quarter of an hour. I stood beside the commander. He looked at his wrist-watch. We turned on the sound detectors. Nothing could be heard.

"Rise to periscope depth," ordered the commander.

Almost without a sound the boat moved upwards. The periscope came out of the water and through it we watched the coast. It was positively alive with activity. We were still too early.

# CHAPTER 8

## THE LANDING IN AMERICA

Our pulses raced as we stood there in the tower, smoking, comparing the time by our watches. Before us in the periscope the coastline of the country into which I was to slip unnoticed seemed near enough to touch. How different it seemed from when I had studied it on a map in Berlin. A tongue of land hemmed around by reed beds, then hedge-growth and behind that a wood, dissected by a road upon which car headlights could be seen moving. The moon had wrapped the reeds, hedges and woodland in a milky veil. Wisps of mist wafted out to us from inland. That anyhow was one good augury for Operation Elster. There were three things we needed — time, mist, and luck.

A fresh breeze bore the mist away again, and suddenly everything lay clear and naked before us. With the fantastic magnification of our periscope we could see every bush and tree in detail. We were perhaps still about 350 yards from land.

"I'll try to get in a bit nearer," said

Hilbig. "I'll turn the boat round once more and approach in reverse, but I shall have to take care the screw doesn't get caught."

The boat turned, smoothly and quietly, its engines at half throttle. Engines have no eyes, no heart, no feelings. The navigator had to call out the soundings without pause: 70 feet, 65 feet, 60 feet, 70 feet. Hilbig's lips were tightly compressed. He said not a word; he gave no orders; he had no need to; his men read his orders from his face.

We approached land by another sixty to seventy yards. Only our conning tower was showing out of the water. To the left was a house. No light was showing from it. We looked it over through the glasses. There was no sign of movement. Then another lorry came down the road, and was overtaken by a private car. One could see all this quite plain. Two dogs were sporting together and their howling sounded like the crying of a little child.

"Now," I whispered.

The commander nodded.

"One moment," he replied. "First we will train our artillery and machine guns on to the shore. If you are surprised jump into the water and swim back to us. I'll give them something to think about on shore meanwhile."

The inflatable rubber dinghy was fetched, its bottom still limp. It could not be pumped up until after it was taken on deck as it would not pass through the narrow tower hatch inflated.

"We'll wait twenty minutes after you've landed," said the commander. "If nothing happens then, we'll start on our way back. We can arrange our next meeting place tomorrow or in a few days' time. You can always reach us with your transmitter."

"If I once get over the landing I'll get through," I replied.

As we pulled the rubber dinghy through the hatch a beam of light came towards us, ever nearer. At night one always has the feeling that one is standing directly in the beam of a headlamp even if it is a mile away.

The rubber dinghy was thrown back and we waited motionless. It was a private car. We held it in our telescope. It was now on the spot at which the road ran closest to the coast. Soon the light would move away again. Another second, another two seconds. We already knew how the road curved from having watched the lorries go by.

But the light did not move away, it came

nearer and nearer. It was quite uncanny. A car was drawing aside from the road. Why? How was it possible? We looked at each other. We followed the car with our glasses. It must now be 100, 150, 200 yards to the side of the road.

And then the mist came again, and once more we were blind for a while. Had the car something to do with the coastguards, or was it a navy shore patrol car? We knew exactly how the American coast defences were organised. Destroyers sailed up and down on the three mile limit, naval aircraft kept the coast under constant observation, while the shore was covered by the shore patrols of the coastguards according to a carefully worked out plan. The coast roads were covered by Army jeeps. The American coast defences formed a net five to six layers thick.

"Just look at that!" said the commander.

The mist had parted once again and the moon was now more clearly visible. I pressed the glass to my eye and saw the car. Was it a dream? A figment of the imagination? A man was sitting at the wheel with a woman beside him. He had put his arm round her and their faces were pressed close together. What was this? A tryst in a motor-car? That was something that could be seen on any road in the States. The Americans stay put in their cars whether they are going to attend divine service or see a Wild West film, so why should they get out of their cars to kiss and make love? And for that matter how often had I driven along such a stretch of coast-road myself with a girl beside me? I had done it in Lima with Evelyn Texter, and wherever you go there is always an Evelyn Texter. There is always the need for her too when you have had too much to drink and not enough love. And there are plenty of Lovers' Lanes in America. You can suddenly turn off the main road, drive over a stretch of waste ground or over a field to a lane and here you can be alone. Alone to whisper, to kiss and swear eternal love.

But you usually turn off the inside lights of the car, a thing which our pair of lovers had evidently forgotten to do. We observed them through the telescope. Could we be mistaken? Were they what they appeared to be?

I stared at the car, but the longer I looked at it the more blurred the picture became. We stood there observing the couple for twenty minutes and were just thinking that we should have to postpone our landing operation when the car started up again and drove back into the night.

At just about the same moment snow began to fall in thick, wet flakes.

"Now!" I said to Billy.

The dinghy was brought up again, the compressed air tube attached to it, and in a few seconds it was inflated. Two hefty sailors stood ready. To deaden the sound of their paddles they had wrapped them round with rags. The commander shook hands.

"Good luck," he said. "You'll need it. I'll come back at once if you call me."

I nodded. My movements had become purely mechanical. I pulled Billy after me. He was stiff with fear, and was staring at the coast with terrified eyes.

"We'll soon be on shore," I said.

The dinghy was lowered carefully on to the water and we got in.

The snow was driving out from land and we could not see a thing. The water was slightly choppy. We sat in the dinghy, the two sailors paddling strongly and rhythmically. . . . Five yards away from U-1230, then ten yards, then fifteen, then twenty.

It would take us two minutes to reach the shore. Maybe three, maybe four. We sat there like two drones. In moments of danger one often tries desperately to think of something pleasant. We were now halfway there. We had 120–130 yards still to go.

Once more the headlamps of a lorry appeared on the horizon and we could hear the motor.

It's in third gear, I thought. No danger. It's going on. If the driver had been going to stop he would have changed down by now.

Another eighty yards. I had two revolvers in my pocket, both with the safety catches off. What would I have done if I had been on shore and had seen an enemy submarine? What indeed! If I had been alone, I would probably have done absolutely nothing. Or I might have gone to get help. Or I might have kept observation. There is no knowing if the night has eyes.

Another fifty yards.

"Remember the Dasch case," Colonel M. had said. "Don't be a fool. Have you still got the facts of his landing well in mind?"

"Yes," I had replied.

"Dasch was surprised by a coastguard, a dull-witted old man. And he stood there palavering with him instead of shooting

167

him. Don't you make the same stupid mistake. Shoot, man! Remember your life is at stake!"

He had paused for a while and lit a cigarette. "And your mission too," he had added.

What should I do if the person who discovered me happened to be a woman, or a child or an old man? I had had to do many things that I had hated and despised, but I was certain that I could never bring myself to fire on women and children. I had agreed with Hilbig that I would try to take a prisoner and get him on board the U-boat. Throughout the voyage my mind had been filled with this idea. I had imagined how astonished everyone in Kiel would be when U-1230 arrived back with a prisoner on board, a prisoner straight from the American mainland.

With a slight creak the dinghy made contact with the bank. We were there. The two sailors remained seated. They looked as if they were about to say something.

I motioned them to be silent and gave them my hand.

I put one revolver in my left pocket. The other I held in my hand. We had packed the contents of the kit-bag into two suitcases. I gave Billy a gentle kick. He did not want to leave the dinghy.

We went on shore, each of us carrying a suitcase and a revolver. The ground was soft and mossy and squelched with every step, but after ten to fifteen yards it felt firmer. The snow was still falling and the branches of the trees brushed into our faces. We could not help making some noise.

The dinghy now moved off again. The two sailors had waited a few minutes although their orders were to row back to the U-boat at once. We could still see U-1230 with our naked eyes. Hilbig was waiting, his artillery trained upon the road.

We were now through the undergrowth and had reached the woods.

"The worst is over," I said. "Billy, if someone speaks to us, you answer."

I felt suddenly as if I could not trust my English. It was stage-fright. I tried to think of various English words but my mind was a blank.

I had a minute luminous compass attached to my watch and had worked out even before I left Germany what direction I would have to take when I was once in the woods. The nearest sizeable place was Ellsworth, a small town two to three miles away, and this we wanted to avoid, for strangers always attract attention in a small town.

It was hard going in the woods; we tripped over tree-roots, fell down and picked ourselves up again. And oh, those damned suitcases! There was no point in going on like it. We would have to get on to the road, whatever the consequences.

So we marched along the roadside, I on the left, Billy on the right. The first car approached and the light of the headlamps raked us from head to foot. The car came nearer, the light got brighter. We felt naked, caught, trapped. Billy made as if he wanted to take a dive back into the woods, but I held him back.

"Stay where you are, you idiot," I hissed at him. "If you go rushing off now you'll make yourself look much more suspicious than if you just carry on walking."

It seemed an eternity as we waited for the thing to overtake us.

It drove right past us; it was a lorry. On the hoarding at the roadside we read: "Melas Potato Chips. The best in Boston." And on the other side: "Drive carefully. Death is so permanent."

"There you are," I said to Billy. "It's quite simple, and it's far better on the road than in the woods."

He nodded. He suddenly seemed to be in possession of himself again. Yes, I thought, it's a good thing I brought him with me.

How close we were to arrest at this hour on the Ellsworth to Boston road we learned only later. The whole of America had, of course, been warned by the Department of Psychological Warfare of the danger of spies and saboteurs, and the country had at first fallen a willing prey to Fifth Column psychosis. You can convince the Americans of anything if only you spend enough money on propaganda. But only for a limited time. The rabid enthusiasm with which they had first embraced the idea was not maintained, and when, after six months, then a year and then two years nothing much happened, no one took spy warnings seriously any more. No one, that is, but the children.

Half an hour after our landing a Boy Scout had cycled past us. He had been taking part in an evening sing-song. He was fifteen years old, had close-cropped fair hair, blue eyes, a vivid imagination and a propensity for logical deduction. I got to know him in court much later, and there I learned his story.

He still believed in spies. We were car-

171

rying suitcases and no one in America carries a suitcase, at any rate not on a remote country road. We had no hats, and everyone in America, at any rate when he is out walking, wears a hat. We were wearing trench coats, while an American, at any rate in a heavy snow-storm, would have been wearing a thick winter overcoat.

To the fifteen-year-old boy we immediately became objects of suspicion, but he was not content with that. The American Boy Scouts cherish a unique romanticism which is something between practical neighbourly love and a game of Red Indians. The boy searched for foot-prints and found them in the soft snow. He took his torch and examined them. He applied himself diligently to his task and followed them right back to the shore. He was therefore convinced that we must have come from a ship, and he knew that there were two of us.

That same evening the Boy Scout reported his findings to the nearest police station. A fat sergeant roared with laughter and advised him to go home and get some sleep so as to be fresh for his lessons in the morning. But the boy would not give up so easily. He got in touch with the local branch of the F.B.I. At first they tried to throw him out, but when they saw that he was not to be diverted from his purpose they listened rather unwillingly to his story. He described his observations, presented his conclusions and reported the direction we had taken.

"You're a very good lad," he was told. "Carry on like this and you'll make a fine soldier one day. The only trouble is, the war will be over by that time. Oh no, there haven't been any spies here for a long time. It's only the Boy Scouts who still find spies. At the rate of fifty a day. . . ."

We knew nothing of all this, of course, as we trudged along the road, tired, bad-tempered and already a little apathetic when we were not actually in the beam of a headlamp. Our hair was plastered down on to our perspiring brows, our feet ached, our arms were numb from carrying the heavy cases. I no longer had any illusions about our appearance. At best we looked like a pair of criminals. Even the most dim-witted policeman could not fail to notice us and the least he would want to do would be to examine our cases. And then that would be that. Or else I would shoot him as Colonel M. had instructed. Then perhaps I should be hanged four weeks sooner. . . . Once more a car approached us. The glare hurt our eyes. The fellow at the wheel did not dip his lights, but slowed down. As he changed gear there was a slight scraping sound. Something obviously was not quite in order. I thrust my hand into my pocket and put my finger on the trigger.

The car approached us slowly and stopped. The driver wound the window down.

"Hallo, boys!" he called over the road. Billy made as if to run away but I grabbed hold of him.

"Come on," I told him, "let's go over."

The man in the car was alone. We breathed again. He was perhaps fifty, had a chubby face and spoke with a north-eastern accent.

"What *do* you two look like?" he greeted us. "Where do you want to go?"

I had primed Billy as to what he should say. Now this was his moment. An opportunity like this would never occur again. He threw me a helpless look but I glared at him so fiercely that he finally realised that it was now up to him.

"We've had a bit of bad luck," he said. "A goddam awful business. My friend," he said, indicating me, "is that mad he can't even bring himself to say anything. I drove

174

his car into a ditch: you can just imagine what I feel like."

"Have you got any money?"

"Sure."

"And where do you want to get to?"

"We've got to get to Bangor."

"You're in luck's way," said chubby-face. "This happens to be a taxi. It's out of service just now, but even so, it doesn't mind earning a dollar or two."

We got in. Billy sat in front on the right next to the driver. I sat behind, my hand still in my pocket, my finger still on the trigger of the Colt. Just as in some ridiculous crime novel. So far I had never killed a man. How would it be, I thought, if I were forced to do so now? Supposing, for instance, I had to kill the man who was sitting two yards away from me, talking to Billy? Talking about his eight-year-old daughter who wanted a pedal-car for Christmas. It had to be a red pedal-car, but it wasn't going to be a new one. He was getting a second-hand one. Even in America there were people who had to look at every dollar before they spent it.

"What are you going to do about your car?" asked the driver.

"Oh, we're not worrying our heads about that," said Billy, laughing. "It's only an old bone-shaker. We'll have it hauled out of the ditch tomorrow. We may even let it stay there."

The driver laughed.

"I wondered first of all if I would even stop. You didn't look any great shakes, the pair of you. . . . But then I thought, well, you might have had some sort of accident. Whoever would be walking about in weather like this, carrying a suitcase, if he wasn't obliged to?"

"How far is it now?" asked Billy.

"Oh, another ten minutes or so. Would you like me to drive a bit faster?"

"No," answered Billy, "it's all right. There's not all that hurry."

I did not say a word. I sat slumped down on the back seat with the suitcases beside me. I hoped everything would be all right. But in any case my mind was made up. I knew that I should not shrink from the worst if anything should go wrong; if the man were to get difficult, or if he drove us out of our way. It was the night of the 29th–30th November. We had come on shore at two minutes past eleven. We had taken eight minutes to reach the road. We had walked for twelve minutes along the road before the taxi driver met us. We had now been six minutes in the taxi. It must now be about half-past eleven, if my calculations were correct.

I looked at my watch, an American one of course, procured in Germany with great difficulty; I was seven and a half minutes out. I listened to the conversation in front and wondered whether we would still be able to catch the train coming in from Canada in Bangor. We might just manage it. I sat there repeating to myself:

"My name is Edward Green. I am thirty-three years old. Honourably discharged from the American Navy on grounds of ill health. With the rank of Captain. I was born in Bridgeport, Connecticut. . . . My name is Edward Green. I am thirty-three years old. Thirty-three years and two months. I have been discharged from the American Navy on grounds of ill health. Honourably discharged . . ."

"There are the lights of Bangor already," said the taxi driver. "Where shall I put you down?"

"At the station," answered Billy.

That was of course thoughtless, but not without justification, for the silliest thing of all would have been to spend any longer in the neighbourhood of our landing-place. Billy paid six dollars. I still said not a word. I had both the cases. I tried to walk to the waiting-room in a matter-of-fact sort of way. Billy was already standing at the ticket office. He took two tickets to Portland. The train was due in four minutes. We had made it. That was something which we could not have expected before-hand.

We sat in a typical American day-coach in which everyone could see everyone else and hear everyone else's conversation. The arrangement of the compartment was similar to that of a German local train. In one corner sat five noisy G.I.'s. They had a bottle of whisky half-full and were telling some wild stories about a certain Elizabeth. Next to them sat a priest, his lips constantly moving as if in prayer. Two country women were discussing poultry farming. The train travelled smoothly and rapidly through the night.

Billy and I said not a word to each other. Our two cases were stowed away on the luggage rack, and I tried to keep my eyes away from them as much as possible.

Another twenty minutes, another sixteen minutes, then ten and then four. Then came the lights of Portland. We would still have to pass the barrier. Then we would be another step forward.

The G.I.'s were making an awful row on

the platform. An officer looked at them disapprovingly, and they moved on a few steps, grumbling about the "damned officers." Then they threw the empty whisky bottle down on to the lines. Everyone who was about at the time, and it was one hour after midnight, was diverted by the G.I.'s. Everyone was laughing, or grumbling, about the soldiers and did not notice that we weren't wearing proper winter overcoats and were walking bareheaded through the driving snow.

Excitement makes you hungry. We handed our cases in at the luggage office and the whole future of Operation Elster hung upon a yellow ticket, with which plus twenty cents I could re-claim my transmitter, invisible ink, diamonds, dollars and firearms.

We left the station and went along one or two main streets. They were more lively than German streets normally were in 1944. Santa Claus was already to be seen in the shop windows, wearing a white cotton-wool beard and a red coat as ever and always. He had long since fled from Germany.

Neon lighting was the order of the night. There was no blackout. Everything in the shop windows was still illuminated, gold watches, fountain pens, wallets, food, wines and spirits. At the worst money was tight.

It had stopped snowing. We went back to the station. We still had an hour and a half and then we would go on to Boston. If our landing had indeed been observed, no one would imagine that we could be in Boston on the following morning. There was only one snag about Boston. It was the birthplace of Billy Colepaugh. We could not avoid Boston but it was quite clear to me that I should not be able to let my companion out of my sight there for one instant. He had relatives and friends in the big city, and he was getting more and more jumpy the nearer we approached it.

We found a buffet on the station. A man in a white apron asked us what he could get for us.

"Ham and eggs," I replied. They were the first words of English I had spoken since we had landed.

"What bread would you like?" asked the man.

This was my first blunder. What bread? Were there various kinds of bread then? I faltered. The man repeated his question:

"What bread would you like with your ham and eggs?"

"Oh, anything," I replied.

He looked at me astonished.

"Well, would you like toast?"

"Yes," I replied, "toast will be fine."

I ate as quickly as I could and disappeared. The fact that in America people ate five different kinds of bread had caught me out.

There could be no doubt that the man had been surprised.

We took our seats in the Portland to Boston train. My blunder at the buffet had made me unsure of myself again. I had prepared myself so carefully in Germany, but I had not known about the five different kinds of bread.

I ran through my knowledge of America once again, asking myself how long was the Mississippi, how high was the Empire State Building, what were the names of the last ten American Presidents, who was leading in baseball?

I can't remember how long the journey was but anyhow the day was dawning as we stepped out of the train.

We now had to find a hotel and chose one near the station, the Essex. In America there is no compulsion to register at hotels and as a matter of fact no one carries any identity papers. You give your name, stay there, pay your bill and go. The man in the reception desk wrote our names in a black book without even looking at us and I felt pretty sure he could not have described us afterwards.

We took a double bedroom and slept until midday. It would have been better to have stayed in different hotels, but I had to take care that Billy didn't do anything foolish in Boston.

We ate in a cheap popular restaurant, and after that went to a department store near the station. I lost no time in buying myself two hats and we also got thick winter overcoats. I wore my trench coat only once more and that was in New York. I had gone into a shop to buy myself a tie and the salesman pointed to my coat:

"That coat wasn't bought in the States," he said.

"What do you mean?" I countered.

"I could see it at once from the cloth and the cut."

"You're right," I declared. "As a matter of fact I got it in Spain."

That day I finally parted from the trench coat.

We went back to the Essex and lay down on our beds with our hats and coats on to banish the too-new look of our American clothes. I had once read that Anthony Eden, at that time British Foreign Secretary, always adopted this method of removing the vulgarity of pristine newness from his suits. The tip now stood me in good stead.

We intended next day to travel on to New York. But we felt safer in Boston at night than on a railway train. At ten o'clock in the evening we were still in our room, which was not one of the best, with the wallpaper grinning at us. I did not want to go out, but I knew it was wrong to isolate myself. I had to get used to speaking to people. I must conquer my inhibitions. My English had a slight accent, not a German accent but rather a Scandinavian one, but how many Americans are there who speak English entirely without accent?

I would have to go where I would be least expected, if I was expected at all. I decided on the night club known as The Carousel.

True to its name, this was a sort of roundabout. The bar with bar stools and the guests seated upon them turned on its own axis, and only the waiters in the middle remained stationary. There was real Scotch whisky to be had. Doubtless it had crossed the Atlantic more safely than I had in U-1230. A five-piece orchestra was playing hot or sweet, according to taste, and without extra charge.

As we drank, I felt the tension ease, but every time the door opened and someone else came in I felt it there again. Could we be sure that we wouldn't meet any of Billy's friends? It was true that Colepaugh had not been in Boston for five years, but is not the life of a secret agent a constant battle with fatal chance?

A platinum blonde singer was performing in a ghastly mauve evening dress. She smoked as she sang, through an enormous cigarette holder. Billy made straight for her without the slightest hesitation, and she came back and sat between us at the bar.

"You don't belong here?" she asked.

"No," replied Billy.

"And who's this?" she said, pointing at me.

"A friend."

"You've got some very silent friends."

She turned to me.

"What's your name?"

"Edward."

"I've heard nicer names, but I like you. Shall we dance?"

"But nobody's dancing here," I said.

"Ah, dancing's in the next room," she replied.

The music was relayed by loud-speaker. Elly pressed herself close to me. She understood every word I said. She asked no more questions about where I came from and she did not ask where I was going to.

We drank champagne. We clinked glasses. It sounded gay and happy.

The champagne was paid for by Reich Security, but nevertheless it tasted good. I looked at my watch. I still had a few hours in hand. My train went at two minutes past nine in the morning, the train that was to take me to New York, the city where I was to carry out my first instruction.

But the bottle of Pomeroy was still half full. . . .

# CHAPTER 9

## TRICKED BY BILLY IN NEW YORK

New York received us with all the casualness of a great metropolis. It was swarming with soldiers due to go overseas within the next few days and meeting their dear ones for the last time before sailing. For this reason finding a hotel room was a major problem. Billy and I arrived at Grand Central Station. We left our luggage in the cloakroom and went to try our luck. After two hours' search we found a modest double bedroom in the Kenmore Hall Hotel on 33rd Street in Manhattan. I strolled past the skyscrapers with studied nonchalance although I had never seen them from close to before and was terribly impressed with them. I dare not stand gaping at them and give myself away as a stranger.

We had now been in America for three days, and I was beginning to feel more secure. I was speaking fluently now and letting the devil take care of my accent. Billy was enjoying the whisky, the generous supply of pocket money (5,000 dollars, in fact, which I had given him soon after landing), and the willing attentions of the sort of girls whom one can buy anywhere in the world for round about two and a half dollars.

My immediate task lay in reading dozens of newspapers, visiting the cinema four times a day, making friends with chambermaids, taxi drivers and waiters, in the interests of achieving complete acclimatisation. As far as America was concerned at this period, the war was taking place mainly in the newspaper headlines and the New Yorker was ignoring it in a way which made the hopelessness of my mission only too obvious. But it was not for me to have private doubts; I had to carry out my instructions.

Now, on my third day in the States, I was able to approach a policeman without a thumping heart, I could look a military patrolman smilingly in the face, I could deal with officials and was no longer embarrassed when I was asked what sort of bread I wanted with my hamburgers.

"It's killing," said Billy, "to discover that the F.B.I. are so sound asleep. They should have caught us long ago."

"Yes," I replied, "they should have!"

"Nothing can happen to us now. We're

well in. The worst part was the landing."

"It certainly was — apart from our mission," I replied.

But he didn't want to hear anything about that. He strutted about town distributing tips, the size of which made my blood run cold. But I needed him desperately and I wanted to keep him in a good mood. New York was offering him more than bomb-damaged Berlin had been able to offer him a few weeks earlier.

I got busy assembling my transmitter. There were two possible methods for sending my news back to Germany. I had a note, written of course in invisible ink, of some cover addresses in Spain and Portugal. But to have written there would have been so obvious that the dumbest official in the Censorship Department would have become suspicious. It would have been better to use the names and addresses of certain American prisoners in Germany. We had made a close study of their family connections and respective habits and I could have sent a fabricated letter which would have given the impression of being utterly genuine, but between the lines, invisible to the censor, would have been the real text. The International Red Cross could have been made the unsuspecting go-between for my reports and the letters, which would have been directed to certain real names and addresses, would have been opened by M.I. and de-coded. But even this course did not commend itself, for it would have been weeks before my reports reached the right quarter, that is to say, Amt VI.

I assembled my transmitter. The good old short-wave, I decided, was as ever the spy's best friend. There were in America, even during the war, many amateur transmitters. Conditions were by no means as strict as they were in Germany. If my set were to be seen — which of course I would try to prevent with every means in my power — I could still be taken for an amateur. The important thing was that all parts of the apparatus should be of American origin. Short-wave amateurs were not in the habit of working with German transmitters. . . .

I bought the various parts for my set from several different New York radio shops. I wanted to have as little to do with radio dealers as possible, and therefore took a very close look at their window displays before I went in so that I should not invite special attention by asking for something they had not got in stock.

I was standing in front of a shop window in 33rd Street wondering whether I could get a 6-L-6 tube there. For the last hundred yards a massive city cop had been walking behind me. He had been strolling along close to the pavement edge, wearing a sky-blue uniform with an outsize badge on his cap. Like all New York policemen he carried a light baton, and this he was swinging round and round from his finger by a cord.

He was walking quite slowly and keeping close to me. Gradually a feeling of suspicion, excitement, horror, crept up my spine. I looked straight in front of me at the shop window. He was perhaps now one yard away from me. I wondered if one of the radio dealers into whose shops I had been had become suspicious and sent the man after me. He had a good-humoured, rather bloated face and did not look in the least like a crafty captor of secret agents. But it had happened often enough in the past, that through some odd chance the most dim-witted policeman had caught the most accomplished spy.

He came to a halt beside me. At his right side he carried an enormous Colt revolver, the weight of which dragged his belt down. He pushed his cap slightly to the back of his head, pointed with his stick to a radio receiver, and said:

"That's a nice job, isn't it?"

"Yes," I replied, "very nice."

"I wonder if it's any good?" he continued.

"You can never tell just from looking at the outside," I replied.

He pulled his cap forward again and placed it once more at the regulation angle.

"Perhaps I'll treat myself to it for Christmas," he said, and wandered slowly off. "I'll have to see what the wife says about it."

My nerves were jangling, but I waited until he was out of sight and then I took a taxi. There were still one or two surprises in store for me that day. I changed from 12th Avenue into 50th Street. At Pier No. 88 lay that luxurious ocean-going giant, the *Normandie*, half submerged. In 1942 the ship had been set on fire by German saboteurs.

We drove on. It's no fun driving through New York. You have to stop every hundred yards or so. I had had enough and had just made up my mind to ask the taxi driver to stop, when it happened.

At a road junction, at the top of 28th

Street, I think, the lights changed to green. The driver, a short, stout man of about fifty, put his foot down and drove off with a jerk. At the same moment a woman pedestrian who had not paid attention to the traffic lights, ran straight into the car. The driver jammed on his brakes and did a quick turn to the left. But he hit the woman with his right mud-guard. He put his foot down on the foot-brake; there was a screech and the car came to a halt horizontally across the road. The woman had been thrown against the pavement with the force of the impact and lay there unconscious. It all looked terrible.

The driver was nearly green with excitement. He turned round to me and said in a shaking voice:

"You saw it, sir, didn't you? It wasn't my fault, was it? The woman stepped straight in front of the car. I did everything I possibly could to avoid hitting her."

"Yes," I replied.

A crowd began to form. The driver pulled up by the pavement on the right. More and more people came rushing up to the scene of the accident. A young man took his jacket off and laid it under the woman's head. Two policemen arrived on the scene. The street was sealed off. The crowd was getting bigger every second.

"Clear off!" I said to myself. The slightest hesitation on my part and the police would register me as a witness. They would check up on my papers and all my personal details. They would notice my foreign accent, and would ask questions, dangerous questions. I went the first few yards slowly and when I had got free of the crowd of onlookers I ran as fast as I could. A woman was the first to notice me; she took me for the driver, and assumed that I wanted to run away.

"There he is," she called shrilly. "Catch him!"

Police whistles sounded behind me; passers-by called out; a man barred my path and I elbowed him out of the way.

I was now four to five hundred yards from the scene of the accident. I turned into a side street, ran to the left, then to the right, then once more to the left. I took a taxi and drove for two minutes. I got out, rode for three stations on the underground, got on a bus, took a taxi, got out of the taxi, went into a department store, bought some lemons, a wrist-watch and a new hat and ate some steak.

No one was following me. Once more I had got away. . . .

Cautiously I returned to my hotel. Billy was not there. There was a note on my bed:

"Just gone to have a drink. Hope you don't mind. Back in two hours."

I lay on my bed. I had already put my radio parts together. I sat up and decoded the address of a New York business man who was to put me in touch with people in the atom industry. I learned the address by heart and burned the note. I paced up and down the room. I ordered a whisky, but it did nothing to still my disquiet.

Obliquely opposite my hotel was a cinema. I went in. It was frightful. For an hour and a half I sat through a film which purported to show how German soldiers were mishandling Russian civilians. A Russian woman who had given shelter to a partisan lay on a dung heap and gave birth to a child. Meanwhile German soldiers stood around making jokes. Then came the heroine. A blonde Russian put her arm round her lover, who was a Captain in the German Army, and indicated who should be shot. This piece of trash could hardly have been surpassed for lack of taste and for the hatred it tried to inspire. It was the American counterpart of Veit Harlan's *Jew Suss*. I went back to the hotel, drank a few more double whiskies and went to bed.

Suddenly I was awake. I looked at the clock. It was three o'clock. The other bed was still empty. Billy was missing. I was immediately wide awake. I sat up and dressed without turning on the light.

Had he been arrested? Would he have betrayed me intentionally, or unintentionally? What methods did the F.B.I. have of getting a man to talk?

I left the hotel. No one noticed me, at least I hoped not. I walked over to the other side of the street. There was a house which was not locked up. I stepped inside and observed from the passage-way what was happening in front of my hotel, wondering what the F.B.I. would do if . . .

Perhaps they would send Billy back to me alone. Perhaps detectives would come and search the hotel. Perhaps they had men posted on the other side to keep an eye on me from close quarters. I smoked one cigarette after another, holding the lighted end to my palm to conceal the glow.

My cases were in the hotel room. I had with me only a small wallet containing some money and a revolver. My observation post was by no means ideal. At any minute someone might come out of the house or enter the house, and a strange man, who at three in the morning stands in the unlit passage-way of a house, is already half arrested.

Half-past three. Four o'clock. The night seemed to stretch itself endlessly. There was no sign of Billy. In my imagination I could already see him being put under pressure by the police. I could see his face quite close to me, white with sweat, uneasy, tormented. Then I visualised him sitting in a bar with a blonde woman on his lap and stuffing five-dollar bills down her dress. What was true and what was false in these workings of my imagination? Five o'clock. A mist descended over New York. I wondered whether I should leave my hiding place and walk up and down the street. But I told myself that that would certainly be a mistake. The whole street, not only the occupants of the houses, would notice me then. The seconds passed slowly by; sixty seconds one minute, sixty minutes one hour. You can't have any conception of how long an hour can be if you have never stood motionless and fearful on one spot, waiting, waiting, smoking, staring into the night until your eyes burned, until you've seen movements that were not there and experienced things which existed only in the imagination.

Half-past five. The mist was lifting slowly. Traffic on the road was becoming more dense. Soon the early risers would be getting up. I had now been in America for four days. I stood there waiting, hoping, trembling with my eyes fixed on the entrance of the Kenmore Hall Hotel. I realised that I could remain in my observation post for only a few minutes more. The patches of mist had disappeared, and it was growing lighter with every minute. I would have to leave this entrance and I had to make up my mind either to leave my suitcases where they were or wait in the hotel room for Billy and thereby risk arrest. I looked at my watch. "I'll stay another three minutes," I said to myself. Then two minutes were left. Then only one minute remained.

Traffic was increasing; workers on early shift were passing along the street. I gave myself another two minutes, and then another four. I was just about to leave the house when I heard Billy. I heard him before I saw him. He was not alone and he was not sober. He was laughing uproariously as he staggered slowly nearer. I could see him now. Whisky was written all over his bleary face. He was propping himself up against a woman who was also drunk. The two of them had their arms around each other supporting each other and were laughing and giggling.

Was it a trap?

I remained in the background. In the shadow of a house. Billy and his companion came nearer. If they were putting on an act for my benefit on instructions from the F.B.I. they were brilliant performers. But no, it was genuine. It must be genuine.

They stood in the hotel doorway, he clutching on to her. She had trailing peroxide-blonde hair which fell in untidy locks over her shoulders, a face that had once been pretty and a figure that was still good to look at.

"Come along up with me," said Billy.

"You alone?"

"No," he replied, "a friend's with me."

She muttered something to herself. Then I thought I heard her say: "Why don't you move out?"

"That's just what I will do," replied Billy. "Just wait and see."

"And then come on to me," she said. "Why don't you come with me straight away?"

He was standing twenty yards away from

me hanging on to the wall. I wanted to step forward and jerk him back to his senses, but I did not want his girlfriend to see me.

"No," answered Billy. "Not until to-morrow . . . but tomorrow I'll come, baby. You can depend on that."

She went on her way alone, staggering along the street. I shadowed her. I wanted to see if she still staggered when she was out of sight of Kenmore Hall. I followed her for ten minutes and no longer had any doubt that she was really drunk.

Billy had already undressed when I got back. There was no point in trying to talk to him there and then. I would wait a few hours. In fact, I could now take a few hours' sleep myself.

I woke up at nine o'clock, pulled Billy out of bed, dragged him to the wash-basin and held his head under the cold water tap.

"Leave me alone!" he cried.

"The devil I won't," I replied. "I've just about had enough of your nonsense. You stay with me now and stop drinking."

"I'll damn well do what I like," he answered.

He sat crouched in front of me looking as if he'd have liked to hit me.

"Six weeks on that damned U-boat," he went on, "then that hell of a landing with the rope nearly round your neck . . . and then when we get here you start lecturing me like a bloody schoolmaster."

His jacket was thrown over a chair. I took the wallet out. He still had 3,500 dollars. In three days Billy had spent 1,500 dollars. Anyone who goes around town spending money like that attracts attention and for us to attract attention to ourselves was as good as the end.

What was I to do? I needed him, but I could not chain him to myself with handcuffs. Later, some weeks after this episode, an official of the F.B.I. was to say to me:

"You made only one mistake . . . you should have given Billy a shot between the eyes as soon as you landed. . . ."

Billy and I sat at breakfast. I had scrambled eggs and ham. He had soda water and headache powder. He looked pale.

"I don't want to make trouble for you," he said, "but you don't understand. After what we've been through a chap must have a bit of pleasure."

"I've nothing against that," I replied, "but you can't go around giving twenty dollar tips for a couple of steaks and a bottle of wine."

"And why not?" he asked. "Do you know New York, or do I? Either I'm the pilot on this trip or not. In New York it's the small tips that send the eyebrows up, not the big ones."

I let him go on talking and he soon stopped on his own accord.

Everything was now ready. The transmitter was working and Billy was half-way towards becoming a reasonable human being. For the moment we had only temporary accommodation. For the following day we had new quarters in view, an apartment, not a hotel. At last I could conduct myself with some degree of confidence. I had deciphered the New York addresses. The first was the address of a Mr. Brown of 41st Street. It was a business house. Mr. Brown had apparently made himself useful to Germany a few years previously on matters of espionage. I decided to call on him in the afternoon.

Billy wanted to stay in bed and I had nothing against it. I could not do with him around when I went to make my call.

I took a taxi and went the last six hundred yards on foot. Mr. Brown ran a stockbroker's office on the eighth floor. I went up in the lift. The business occupied only two offices, a reception room and the boss's room. A red-haired secretary received me.

"What can I do for you?" she asked.

"I want to see Mr. Brown."

"And what is your name?"

"Kenneth W. Smith."

"And what do you want to see him about?"

"I want to see him on business."

"He's not in," she replied, "but you can have a word with his wife if it's important."

"It's not as important as that," I replied. "When is he expected back?"

"Tomorrow."

She lit herself a cigarette and opened the window.

"You can stay in the cinema until then if you like, or don't you need any tips on how to kill time in New York?"

"No, thank you, I don't," I replied. "I know my way around."

She looked charming and I should have liked to have invited her to have a meal with me, but it was not a good thing to have a girlfriend who was the secretary of a 'business friend.'

In Amt VI they swore by this Mr. Brown, but they had sworn by a good many people in Amt VI to no good purpose.

I bought myself a few papers and went

slowly back to my hotel. I covered the first stretch on foot. The fresh air did me good. Once I had been able to get in touch with Mr. Brown on the following day everything would be in order. I would now go and have something to eat with Billy, then we would go to a cinema and then perhaps I'd go to a night club for two or three hours.

I covered the last stretch to the hotel in a taxi. I walked slowly across the foyer. The doorman looked up.

"Have you forgotten something?" he asked.

"What do you mean?"

"Well, you've already moved out, haven't you?"

"I don't understand," I replied.

"But the bill has been paid. Your friend saw to everything. He said you'd already gone away. That was why I was surprised when I saw you walk in again."

I tried to conceal my consternation as well as I could. Billy had disappeared. Billy had flown.

"Is something wrong?" asked the porter.

"No," I replied. "Everything's fine."

I walked on a few yards and then turned round once more.

"What did he do with the luggage?" I asked.

"He took it with him."

"Both suitcases?"

"Yes. Both of them. I was going to call a taxi but he said it wasn't necessary; he hadn't far to go. He seemed to be in a great hurry."

I gave the man a few cents and went out into the street. The situation I now found myself in was indescribable. The transmitter, the revolvers, the diamonds, the dollars. All gone. All gone with William Colepaugh.

There I stood with my mission hardly begun and with about three hundred dollars in my pocket. Everything swam before my eyes. With three hundred dollars I had somehow to find Billy somewhere in America. If I did not find him within the next few hours it would be all up with me.

# CHAPTER 10

## I WORK OUT MY OWN SALVATION

The trail of a man who walks through New York in broad daylight carrying two large suitcases is not all that difficult to follow. The doorman at the Kenmore Hall Hotel on 33rd Street knew the direction Billy had taken. A newspaper man had seen him, and a shoe-shine boy had seen him too. I followed the trail. I had to take care not to make myself conspicuous by asking questions that were too pointed.

Billy had evidently been thinking only of the money and the diamonds. The cases had extra strong locks, and the keys were in my trousers pocket. It would be impossible for Billy to break the cases open without the help of an expert. He would first have to take his booty to some safe place and think up a story with which he could later approach a locksmith.

Another point to be borne in mind was that Billy was wanted all over America as a deserter and in that way he was in a more difficult position than I was. I had already been taken into American custody in 1942 and had been the subject of an exchange repatriation. But I knew for certain that on that occasion the F.B.I. had neither photographed me nor taken my finger-prints. I had in fact been only an internee, and internees were not worried overmuch, at least not in the opening stages of the war.

"What would you do," I kept asking myself, "if you were in Billy's place?" Leave New York! That was quite clear. As quickly as possible, and preferably by train. That way would arouse the least attention. In one of the long-distance expresses. Change trains once or twice on the way. And where should I get in? At the nearest station of course!

Which station was the nearest? I went into a snack bar and consulted a street map of New York.

"Are you looking for something special?" asked the bartender.

"No," I replied. "I'm just wandering around New York. I only wanted to see where I was."

"Is this your first visit here?"

"No, I've been once before," I replied. "But I didn't have time then to take a good look at the town."

I drank some coffee and ate doughnuts,

swallowing down the haste, the anxiety, the horror, forcing myself to keep calm. I knew that I should have to go after Billy with my head rather than my legs. He had acted upon impulse; that much was quite clear to me. Billy was the sort of man to do a thing first and think about it afterwards.

I had a sudden flash of inspiration. Of course, Billy would have gone to Grand Central Station. If he had not found a train at once he would wait somewhere near by. For two or three hours perhaps. He would not stand on the platform with the suitcases. He would hand them in at the left luggage office as we had done when we first arrived in New York.

I went to Grand Central Station. There was not a sign of Billy. I confirmed from the time-table that no long-distance train had left the station in the period immediately preceding. I wandered through the restaurants and bars, walked over the platforms and into the lavatories. No sign of him. There was just one chance that remained. The left luggage counter.

"Check your baggage." The words stood on all four sides of the left luggage office, which was placed right in the middle of the station so that one could walk right round it. It was half-past five in the afternoon.

The place was swarming with tired rush-hour crowds. Queues were forming at the quick service buffets. News-boys were striding up and down the main concourse shouting the headlines.

"Body in the Hudson identified . . ."

"Unhappy love affair drove her to the river!"

"If Bill had kissed her yesterday, she would still be alive today!"

I let myself be carried by the crowd as near to the left luggage counter as possible. I was obsessed with one fixed idea. "Your cases are here," I told myself. Hundreds of cases were standing close together and piled on top of each other. The two top-most rows of shelves were still empty. If luggage was left for a considerable time it was always put up high. Only when those racks which were easily accessible from all sides were full, would the officials use the full depth of the shelves, and stack the cases one behind another. I could only see the luggage from the outside, but if Billy, when he handed the luggage in, had said he would be back for it in an hour or two, it would just be left on the ground.

Twenty times, thirty times I walked round the left luggage place. Driven and impelled by one thought: It is here; it must be here; here is your last chance, your only chance. I bought a newspaper, went back into the crowd and stood there reading. Again and again I forced myself to look at the cases. I changed sides; I heard comments on the war situation, listened to background details about the love drama in the Hudson river, learned the advantages of a new nail varnish and the disadvantages of a second-hand car.

I went round to the second side. That was where lost luggage was claimed. Still less hope of success. And perhaps I had only half an hour, ten minutes or perhaps only five minutes to do what I had to do.

I posted myself on the opposite side of the luggage place, pushed this way and that in the stream of humanity, looking at the cases, walking and walked upon. Two policemen were pushing their way through the crowd with a determined air. Were they after me already? No, they passed me by.

And just at that moment I saw them. I saw my cases! Three or four yards from the ramp, standing there solidly and indifferently, side by side. Two harmless pieces of luggage in company with a hat-box, an umbrella and a hold-all. There was no doubt about it; they were my cases. There was the property of Amt VI, stolen by my colleague. There was Germany's last desperate attempt at espionage during the Second World War. Favoured by luck, whipped on by desperate hope, I had found my cases again in the biggest city in the world!

It was a quarter to six. I stood there and pondered. Any moment Billy might arrive. He would sneak up to the counter and of course he would see me. That could not be avoided. But what would he do then? Would he come up to me or would he run away?

I knew him and I believed that he was now more frightened of me than he was of the F.B.I. But would he go to the American authorities and try to save his own head by forfeiting mine? That he would not do. He knew precisely what Americans did with traitors, even if they had done them a service. They would accept his information, interrogate him, hold him under arrest and put him before a court-martial, just as they would do with me. In that way they would be consistent. We should both get the death sentence. In the case of the traitor Dasch, at least on the occasion of Operation Pastorius, it had been like that. It might be that after the trial Billy's sentence would be commuted to life imprisonment, and I alone would be put to death, as in the case of Dasch. . . .

Ten to six. Six persons, four men and two women were standing at the counter. The handing out of the luggage was going quickly and smoothly as I watched. The officials looked at the numbers only superficially, the people pointed to their cases, and had them handed out to them a few seconds later. I got nearer to the ramp. Six yards separated me from my cases. I could not simply take them. There were too many people around for that, but I must have them. There were three clerks at the counter. I wondered when they would be relieved. I had been hanging about the place for so long that I felt they might have noticed me. If I had aroused suspicion then it would be hopeless to try to get my property back in the conventional way.

When, a few days previously, Billy and I had handed in our luggage at Grand Central Station and the whole future of Operation Elster had hung upon a number on a ten-cent ticket, I had asked Billy in fun:

"What should we do if we lost the ticket?"

"Oh, it wouldn't matter that much. If you can show that you've got the keys they'll always give you the cases. They're not so punctilious in America, and it's not often anything is stolen. No one's going to get himself sent to prison for the sake of a suitcase. If a man is a criminal he'll concentrate on something more profitable."

Was he right? Should I try it? I had to try it. But not until the present three clerks had been relieved.

I must move away from the ramp and wait in the background. I must keep my eye on the entrances. I must look out for Billy and at the same time watch the left luggage counter.

Two minutes to six. When would they be relieved? Could I enquire about this? No. No one takes any interest in the working hours of luggage clerks. I bought myself a paper. The corpse in the Hudson River had had further repercussions. "Was it murder?" ran a sub-heading. Americans had had enough of the war. What a refreshing change it was to have a murder, so long as you'd had nothing to do with it yourself.

Three men in uniform caps went up to the counter. Was this the relief? It was! The men exchanged a few words, nothing of any importance, I could see. Oh God, how long were they going to hang about? Why didn't the other guys go home? It was time. They ought to be glad to get off.

Their wives would be waiting with a meal for them and the children would be looking forward to seeing their fathers. Dammit all, men, get moving!

They went off in leisurely fashion, obviously in no hurry. What could they know of me, my fears, my hopeless situation, my mission? They walked past me. One of them looked me in the face, but I didn't think he was at all suspicious. There were two people at the counter. Now there was only one. I went up to the ramp. Would my English be all right? Of course it would! Enough of all these anxieties! I hurried the last steps and was quite out of breath; at least I pretended I was. One of the three clerks came over to me at once and said: "You're in a hurry, aren't you?" and laughed good-naturedly.

"I've got to catch a train," I replied.

"Your ticket, please?"

I searched my pockets. My left overcoat pocket, the right one, my ticket pocket, my trousers pocket. I got more and more flustered and more and more desperate.

"Take your time, sir," said the clerk. "You'd better lose your train than lose your luggage."

"But I can't lose the train!" I blurted out.

"Where are your cases?" asked the man.

"There they are."

"Well now, just look for your ticket quietly," he recommended.

The game began again. Was my act convincing? One or two people were looking at me. Supposing Billy were to come now, or a policeman were to tap me on the shoulder, or a detective of the F.B.I.?

I looked at the man at the counter. I remember thinking to myself that he was about fifty, five feet six tall, and would weigh about twelve and a half stones. He was at least ten pounds overweight, was married and wore a wedding ring. He might already have been a grandfather. In three years he would be bald. He already had no hair at all in front, and was very sparse at the temples. Just above the left corner of his mouth he had a wart. I'd get rid of it if it were mine, I thought. I'd either lance it or use nitrate of silver.

"It's ridiculous," I said. "I've lost the ticket. What am I going to do now?"

"You can go into the office," he said. "You may be lucky, but there are bound to be some complications. I think you'd do best to go home and look for the ticket. You'll have lost the train by now in any case."

"Where's the office?"

"Here. Behind the glass partition."

It was odd how all the luggage clerks looked the same. The man in the office had his cap on. Perhaps that was one of the rules. He was sitting down with his legs stretched out, talking to two women. One of the two women was very young and pretty, but I had no time for pretty young women.

"In 'Latest News'," said the elder of the two, "it says quite clearly that he murdered her."

"Nonsense," said the clerk. "That's only what the reporters write. In the morning they'll say that the police made a mistake. They always do it like that."

"He's a handsome fellow, the murderer," continued the woman. "Did you see his photograph?"

"He wouldn't be to my taste," said the young one. "His cheek bones stick out too much and his nose is too squat. He looks to me like a prize fighter."

"Lily's got extravagant tastes," said the older woman. "Anyhow it doesn't really matter. He's not in the running now."

"Can I help you?" At last the clerk took notice of me, looking towards me without any particular interest.

215

I told him my story about the lost luggage ticket. The two women listened. They made no attempt to leave the room. The younger one had bright blue eyes and a high vaulted brow, but I still had no eyes for feminine beauty. She stared at me openly, at the same time managing to look as if she were gazing past me.

"I can't let you have your cases," replied the clerk. "We have to abide by the rules."

"But there must be some solution," I replied. "It must sometimes happen that someone loses his ticket. What do you do then?"

"You take a form," he replied, "and describe the contents. Then you wait three months. If no one else has been to claim the luggage in the meantime the cases are then opened. If the contents tally with your description they are then returned to you."

I took the keys from my pocket.

"Here are the keys," I said. "Look at the lock. It's a very heavy one. I can tell you exactly what's in these cases, but I can't wait three months. I've got to get to Chicago today."

The clerk nodded.

"What I should like to know," said the older woman, "is how he did it. He can't have strangled her in the water. But if she

216

was already dead when he threw her in the water, the police would have found the marks of strangulation on her throat yesterday."

"You ought to have joined the police force," said the young woman.

"Well, let's take a short cut," said the head clerk of the left luggage office.

"What a good thing we're not in Germany now," I thought.

"What's in the cases?"

"Shirts, socks, two suits, a suit of pyjamas."

"You must give more precise details than that," said the clerk. "That description would fit any suitcase."

"Two white, one green, one pink shirt. And a camera, a very valuable one, a Leica."

There were so many Leicas in America that the German make would not seem particularly strange.

"One moment," said the clerk. "Show me the cases."

I held them in my hand! But only for a few seconds. I carried them into the office. The clerk opened them. The left lock jammed. I helped him. The case had a false bottom. In the false bottom were radio parts, two revolvers, a bag of diamonds, a wallet with about 55,000 dollars. . . . If the man were to take a good look he would find everything. A telephone was at his elbow. He could call the station police. A flick of the finger would be enough and I would be arrested.

The clerk took the Leica in his hand.

"That's a fine camera," he said. "Set you back a bit, didn't it?"

"Yes," I replied, "at least 450 dollars. It's a German make."

"Damn the Germans," he said, laughing.

He put the Leica back in the case, locked it up again, opened the second one and examined it equally superficially.

"Well, you can have your cases," he said, "but you must first let me have your signature."

The man seated himself at the typewriter and typed an inventory with two fingers. He took a terribly long time over it. Or perhaps he only appeared to. Time always seems interminable when you are standing on hot coals. . . .

At last he had finished. I offered him a dollar tip but he thanked me and declined it.

"Give it to the guys outside," he said. "They need it more than I do."

Now away! I heaved a sigh of relief, but I

had to be careful not to move too hastily. I must go in the direction of the platform as the clerks at the left luggage counter would certainly be looking after me. And then I must double back. A train was just coming in and I was able to mingle with the people who were leaving it. I had done it again! There was still no sign of Billy. I looked at the clock, it was 6.31. I had to cover another fifty yards to reach the main exit. Now twenty, now ten. I was carried out of the station with the crowd.

"Taxi?" a driver asked me.

"Yes," I replied. I hesitated for a second and looked round once more.

It had been a million to one chance!

What luck I had had again!

But oh, my nerves!

"Hello, Erich!" a voice called behind me.

I swung round. Oh, the devil take it, my name was Edward! But who could be completely master of himself in such a situation!

"Erich, Erich, it can't be true!" the voice continued. Falling over me, embracing me and kissing me with all the demonstrativeness of the South American was Paolo Santi, an old friend from Peru. . . .

The people around me were standing still, either amused or annoyed by this touching scene. I took Paolo on to one side.

"Have you got half an hour to spare?" he asked me.

"Yes, have you?"

"Oh, I'll let my train go hang," he replied. "I'll take the next one. I'm on holiday so I needn't worry."

He smiled at me.

"You've got thinner," he said.

"Yes," I replied.

We took a taxi and went to a restaurant. I handed in my cases at the cloakroom. Santi had sent his luggage on ahead.

"Now tell me," he said, "how on earth d'you happen to be in New York?"

I rapidly improvised a story. Actually I had no idea what Paolo Santi could be doing. In Lima we had gone to dances together, played poker and pursued the girls. Then I had been arrested. . . .

"You know, don't you?" I said, "that I was deported from Peru? All because of this damned silly war. Now I've come to North America. They locked me up for a time, then they offered me my release if I would stay in the States and work. I didn't have much choice, and I'm quite sure Germany will lose the war perfectly well without my assistance; so I'm staying on here. Up to now I've been doing my own job in Boston."

"And what's happening now?"

"A silly business. My boss has a very young and pretty wife. You can guess the rest. At the moment I'm out of a job. I've only just arrived here. Tomorrow I'm going to start looking for something."

He roared with laughter at my story.

"Still the same old Erich," he said, and gave me a hefty thump on the back.

"What are you up to?" I asked him. "Married yet?"

"I've been married twice," he replied. "And the day after tomorrow I'm getting married for the third time. I've found the right one at last. D'you know, only the third American ever clicks. And so far I've only married Yankees."

Now it was my turn to roar with laughter.

"Have you settled down in the States for good then?"

"Yes," he said. "I have to pay my alimony in dollars."

"And you're living in New York?"

"Yes, I've been living here all the time," he replied. "I've got a nice bachelor apartment. It was very pleasant in between the two marriages. Now it looks as if I've got to give it up again."

I was on this in a flash.

"So your apartment is vacant now?"

He grasped the situation immediately.

"Of course," he said. "Fancy my not thinking of that before!" He thrust his hand in his pocket, dragged out a bunch of keys, and put them on the table.

"Here you are," he said. "Help yourself. It's on 44th Street. Number twenty, eleventh floor. The small key is for the lift. As far as the others are concerned you'll have to try them all until you find the right one."

I could hardly believe my eyes and ears. Paolo was beaming at me as if he would have liked to drown me in his smiles.

"Happy now?"

"Yes," I replied. "But you must let me pay you something for it."

"Nonsense. When I get back it will cost you a bottle of whisky, which we'll polish off together."

We took our leave and I let him go back to Grand Central Station alone. He looked put out for a moment. With South Americans you can do anything, but you must never be discourteous. I told him that I had a bad headache and was able to reconcile him to my apparent discourtesy.

I collected my cases and took a taxi. I changed taxis twice. The neon light advertisements were shining brightly, and there was a Santa Claus in every shop window. I felt so grateful for my good fortune that I wanted to raise my hat to him. I covered the last three hundred yards on foot. I found the lift key at once. I met no one — a further stroke of luck on this exciting day. Eleventh floor. The third key I tried fitted. I turned on the light.

It was a wonderful apartment with bedroom, living-room, study, kitchen and bathroom. It had every comfort, which was unusual during the war even by New York standards. And there I was, quite alone with three rooms and a kitchen and bathroom. I wished Paolo every success in his third marriage.

At the same moment as I was moving into Paolo's apartment, a thin, dark-haired young man arrived at the left luggage counter on Grand Central Station with a perfectly valid ticket and requested his two cases. He appeared timid and excited but not so timid and excited that it would have struck the luggage clerks if they had not later been interrogated by the F.B.I.

"My cases," he said.

"One moment, sir."

The luggage clerk searched, shook his head and went on looking. He went to his colleagues, showed them the ticket, and the three of them started to look. They looked, of course, in vain.

What happened now was recorded in the report prepared by the F.B.I. a few days later.

"We're very sorry, sir," said one of the men. "We can't find your luggage. Would you please come to the Chief Clerk. We must take full details."

"I handed the cases in just three hours ago," said the young man, Billy Colepaugh. "They must be here."

Passengers who wanted to get their cases out were piling up behind him, already getting impatient. Billy stood on the ramp not knowing what to do next. Completely thrown off balance, he let himself be taken to the Chief Clerk. He had still not tumbled to the fact that I had outwitted him.

"Your cases were collected twenty minutes ago," said the clerk, "by a Mr. Green, Mr. Edward Green. The man told us he had lost his ticket. He was in possession of the keys and gave us an exact description of what was in the cases. I'm very sorry, sir. Perhaps in this case we were not quite careful enough, but I must say we did act correctly. How was it that the man had your keys?"

Horrified, struck dumb and at his wits' end, Billy stood there, incapable of moving, incapable of speaking.

"I'll call the police," said the Chief Clerk.

"Please don't," said Billy. "I don't want to make a charge. The matter will clear itself up."

"Well, I must say it's a strange business. But just as you please."

"It's some piece of tomfoolery," replied Billy.

He went back into the town, into the metropolis of New York, alone, abandoned, without money, without friends, without colleagues, without a single human being with whom he could speak.

When he had stolen the cases from me my fate was sealed, and now that I had got them back he was hoisted by his own petard. For six hours he wandered through the city, mad with anxiety, rigid with fear, trembling with horror and looking for some person to whom he could tell his story. A man whom he knew, a friend. . . .

Meanwhile I was lying on the broad sofa in my new apartment, in a pleasantly central-heated atmosphere, well-fed, contented and happy, reading in peace the Hudson River murder story. The radio was providing some sentimental dance music — I think it was Glenn Miller. The lights were giving a pleasant indirect glow which did my eyes and my nerves good. I had drawn the curtains. I was alone and I was glad to be alone.

I pictured Billy's story to myself in every detail. I felt sorry about him. He could not go to the police. But how long would he be able to hold out before they caught him? He probably had 3,000 dollars with him still. If he had been a careful sort of chap he might have gone underground with that, but I knew he was not. Until they caught him I could work in peace, but once he was caught everything was finished. I had no doubts on that score whatsoever. He would hold out for two or three days, perhaps. That was if he did not act in anger at my turning the tables on him over the suitcases, and put the police on my trail at once. . . .

In that moment Edward Green died. I stood up, took my papers from my wallet, went into the kitchen and burned them. I still had plenty of other names and professions.

The next day I would go to Mr. Brown,

the contact man of the German M.I. The next day or the day after that I would perhaps already be in contact with the atomic people. If only Billy had not been caught by that time. I wondered if I should look for Billy? If I found him I would have to shoot him, I thought to myself. There would be no depending upon him and he had sentenced me to death first. If I caught him I could show him no mercy. And any court-martial in the world would up-hold my judgement. . . .

I thrust the idea from my mind. I had been reading too many crime novels. I selected a book from the book-case and then put it down again. I found a bottle of whisky and poured myself a drink.

I lay down luxuriantly on the couch once more, content that my working day was over. The music had come to an end and it was now news time. There were reports from the various theatres of war. Things were going badly in Germany, but there was no doubt that the reports were highly coloured. I simply would not believe that the war was already lost although the whole world, including me, knew it was really. At last the news was over.

"One hour in Paris," said the voice from the ether. A light orchestra was playing. I enjoyed the music as I was enjoying the warmth, the feeling of well-being, the apartment and the whisky.

Suddenly my feeling of well-being deserted me. Was it nerves? Were my senses deceiving me? No. There were sounds, footsteps, footsteps approaching the door. A key in the lock! I jumped up. I snatched the revolver from its holster and released the catch. With one bound I put myself in such a position that I would see whoever entered the apartment before he saw me. What if there were more than one?

The steps came nearer. The second joint of my index finger curled round the trigger. The door opened. I stood there as if frozen to the spot. It was a woman, young and fair. She stood there, frightened at first, then she laughed.

She was tall and was wearing a voluminous coat, which was held in at the waist with a belt. American women often have uncannily strong nerves. She did not call for help. She did not run away. She just stood there and smiled at me.

"Playing Indians?" she said.

I was on the threshold of the most ridiculous experience of my life.

# CHAPTER 11

## BILLY BETRAYS ME TO THE F.B.I.

I took in every detail of her face, the high vaulted brow, the slender nose, the delicate, made-up lips, the unaffected, almost invisible smile, the long hair lying casually just as it fell. I stared at her, pondering at the same time how the outsize revolver I was holding could be made inconspicuously to disappear.

"How did you get here?" I asked.

"I could ask you the same thing," she countered.

She closed the door and came a few steps nearer. She walked on her high heels with such assurance and such gracefulness that she might have come into the world wearing them.

"I am a friend of Paolo's," I explained.

"And I am a friend of his too," she said.

I had at length succeeded in shoving the revolver back into my pocket where it was making an ugly bulge. On the radio a jazz drummer was demonstrating his skill in a passage which lasted a full minute. I felt as if my head was being used as the drum.

"Paolo has gone away," I continued, "and has placed his apartment at my disposal for a few days."

"That's not bad," said the girl. "He must have several keys. He gave me one too. I've got the decorators in my own flat; the place reeks of paint and that's one thing I can't stand."

I decided to introduce myself. "My name is Edward Green."

"I'm Joan Kenneth," she said.

"In the circumstances I'll move out, of course," I said. "You must have priority."

"Well, well, so there are still a few gentlemen left in the world. But actually there's no need for you to go; after all there are several rooms, aren't there?"

I nodded and stood there feeling rather embarrassed. Evidently she liked my reserve. She had no idea, of course, that I was less concerned with her reputation than with my mission.

"Well, isn't there anything to drink here?" she asked.

"The whisky's over there. If you'd have arrived half an hour later you'd have had to drink milk."

"Oh, I always appear at the right moment."

She took off her coat, went into the bathroom for a minute or two and then reappeared.

"I'll take the bedroom," she said. "You can stay in the living-room. Turn the wireless on a bit louder. It's Tommy Dorsey, isn't it? Do you like him?"

"Sure, I do."

"We'll make ourselves comfortable. Or do you still want to move out?"

"Not necessarily."

"There you are, you see," she said. "And now come with me into the kitchen and give me a hand. Or aren't you hungry?"

"I'm not hungry but I've got an appetite," I replied.

We made hamburgers and they tasted heavenly. We found two bottles of beer and drank up the rest of the whisky. We listened to Tommy Dorsey, Glenn Miller and Louis Armstrong. Now and again the band stopped playing and a voice from the ether told us how many tons of explosive had been unloaded over the various cities of Germany.

"The war will soon be over," said Joan, "thank God."

"Yes," I replied.

"Have you been in the services?"

"Yes, I was a naval officer."

"My brother was, too. He was killed . . . at Pearl Harbour, right at the beginning."

"To hell with the Japanese," I said.

We lit a cigarette.

"It's nice here," said Joan. "I hate sitting around in restaurants in the evening but I also hate being alone."

"I'm just the same myself."

"You're not an American, are you?"

I felt my heart turn over. Suddenly all the warmth and comfort of the evening was dispelled. The alarm had sounded. Was she an agent of the F.B.I.? Was she but a charming trap? Was she a precursor of the hangman?

"Why do you say that?" I asked.

"You speak like a European, like a Scandinavian."

"My parents were Norwegians," I answered.

"Why are you so tense about it?" she asked. "I wouldn't mind a scrap if my parents had been Norwegian. Oh, Europe! Paris, Vienna, Budapest, Rome. . . . Oh, damn this war!"

She picked up her handbag, turned to me and said:

"Good night. I hope I won't disturb you getting up early. I have a little dress shop and I have to be first in."

"Good night," I said.

I listened to the radio for another hour. Joan had been to the bathroom and had then gone back into the bedroom. If the F.B.I. were already on my trail why should they post a woman agent here to watch me all night? Why didn't they come at once and arrest me? Clap-trap, I told myself. But then it occurred to me how very little notice Joan had taken of my revolver and how few questions she had asked me.

I thought and thought whether I should stay or go. There was a good deal of support for either course of action. If I were to go, Joan, even if she were quite harmless, would become suspicious. If I remained and Joan were not harmless I should be right in the soup. But in that case the house would certainly be surrounded and I should not have been able to leave it anyhow.

I went to bed with the last drop of whisky. I woke up five or six times. By four or five o'clock in the morning I had reached the point where I was indifferent to everything, and in that state of mind I settled down to five hours sleep.

When I awoke Joan had already gone. So as not to waken me she had had her breakfast in the kitchen; her cup was still on the table, a tiny trace of lipstick on the rim. I washed the cup, took a shower, ate two hamburgers left over from the night before and went on my way to Mr. Brown on 41st Street, 8th floor, to talk with him on a matter of atomic espionage. . . .

I turned the corner three times and made sure I was not being followed, thinking meanwhile how lovely it would be to sit by the Christmas tree with Joan instead of chasing off after the Manhattan project, to celebrate the festival of love and peace instead of working in the service of war.

Here it was. 41st Street. I took the lift up to the 8th floor. The red-haired secretary considered for a moment whether she would attend to her finger-nails or take notice of me. She finally decided for me.

"You're in luck today," she said. "Mr. Brown is in. Actually you meant to come yesterday, didn't you?"

"I intended to," I replied, "but it's never too late to see you, or is it?"

"Oh, oh," she countered. "There's a boxing match on this evening. If you'd care to get some tickets, I'll come with you."

"I'd rather go to a theatre," I replied.

"We'll talk it over when you come out," she said.

She put her nail varnish down, went into Mr. Brown's room and reappeared in a minute or two.

Brown was a small man with a somewhat agitated manner. He got up from his chair and greeted me with outstretched arms.

"What can I do for you?" he asked.

"First make the walls and doors sound-proof," I said.

He seemed taken aback for a few seconds.

"I don't do any secret business here," he said.

"You might," I said, "just a bit."

He sat down and offered me a cigar, which I refused.

"From 1938 to 1942 you worked for the German Secret Service," I began. "For your services you received in all 64,293 dollars and 40 cents. You were supposed to have paid your sub-agents with the money. You were the only man who escaped the wave of arrests that went on at that time. I am here now to see that you give value for money."

He looked as if his limbs had turned to water. His eyes opened wide like the eyes of a rabbit about to be devoured by a snake.

"Who are you?" he asked.

"As far as you are concerned my name is Kenneth W. Smith," I replied. I paused for a while and looked out of the window wondering whether the red-haired secretary could hear our conversation, then I continued:

"I am from Germany, from Berlin. If you will give me your assistance nothing will happen to you . . . you did some very good work on the previous occasion."

"You must be crazy," he said. "Things were different then. Now Germany has lost the war." He stood up and paced the room, throwing his arms about and muttering inarticulately. He paused by the telephone.

"What if I called up the F.B.I.?" he asked.

"They'd hang you," I replied, "and me as well, of course. They don't pull their punches. Anyone who has once worked against America can expect no mercy, and you don't need me to tell you that."

He nodded.

"I have a family," he said. "I have built up some sort of life for myself. The war is lost for Germany, but by God I'd have liked to see her win it. I hate America! For ten, fifteen years I washed dishes and was pushed around by every street-corner cop. Had to put up with every Tom, Dick and

Harry calling me a dirty bastard."

"But now you have a flourishing business," I replied, "and a pretty secretary. And you got it all with the money that came from Berlin."

I went to the window, looked down into the street and turned round to face Brown again.

"I'm giving you a fair deal," I said. "I will trouble you only once more if you will tell me what I want to know. Introduce me to the people I want to get in touch with and you will be free. As far as we are concerned you will be dead, regardless of what may happen afterwards."

I felt sorry for the man. My visit must have been a terrible shock for him, but I dared not take pity on him. Who felt any pity for me? Once you've walked on the devil's highway you have to go on walking there whether you want to or not.

"What do you want to know?" asked Brown.

"All there is to know about the Manhattan project," I replied.

This obviously wasn't the first he'd heard of it. He grasped the situation immediately.

"Tomorrow," he said. "And then it's the end."

"Then it's the end," I assured him. I was on the point of leaving when he said:

"Have you any money?"

"Yes, I've got a whole heap of money."

"Will you take a bit of good advice?"

"Yes, I can always do with that."

"Listen then," he said. "Take yourself off to South America as fast as your legs will carry you. You're running into disaster with your eyes open. Still to be working for Germany. . . . It's sheer madness."

"That's just what we are, fools, you and I," I replied. "And for the moment you must accept the situation."

The red-head had disappeared, which suited me down to the ground. I absented myself with the utmost caution. I was not afraid of Mr. Brown. It was quite obvious that he was afraid of me. He had got old and obese and secret agents who are old and obese are not much use for the dirty work. But at least they know the rules of the game. He would keep his mouth shut. He would buy his freedom by passing on fresh information to me.

Needless to say, the American War Department had done everything humanly possible to keep the atom project secret, but that was impossible. It was, strange to say, childishly simple to get into contact with the Hiroshima bomb. I knew that to produce this weapon of destruction they needed uranium, and uranium was to be found in northern Canada. Getting it was a laborious business involving many hundreds and thousands of specialists, and a thing like that could never be kept secret. To an experienced agent like Mr. Brown — I never got to know his real name — there would be no difficulty in getting at any rate some general information.

For the moment I had nothing more to do than wait. There was still no sign of Billy. Strangely enough the air was still clear. I re-doubled my vigilance and the more trouble-free my environment appeared to be, the more assiduously I studied it.

There was no F.B.I. agent on my tail but Santa Claus seemed to be following my every movement. There he was, on loudspeakers, on the radio, in neon lights and in every kind of advertisement. To the Americans, the coming of Father Christmas meant peace, but in Germany at the same time the festival of the Prince of Peace was being celebrated without joy; that year the German Christmas tree was bare.

I thought of Margarete and drowned my

melancholy in whisky, feeling like an octo-
genarian meditating in his bath-chair on
what he would do if he could live his life
over again. . . .

The next few days passed without special incident. Joan, my co-tenant in Santi's
apartment, supplied me with other pre-
occupations. I had already become expert
in drying dishes. What a sensation it would
be: "Germany's last secret agent wears
apron in kitchen, helping enemy girl to
polish off Allied food supplies." That
would be the sort of thing the newspapers
would run if I were caught. Fortunately I
did not realise how near to arrest I was. I
did not learn until later what had happened in the interim, how my fate was
catching up on me, and how the American
M.I. was coming upon the scent. The sequence of events was retailed to me later
by the F.B.I. officials in generous detail.

After his abortive attempt to recover my
cases at Grand Central Station, Billy had
gone on drinking for two days without
pause. And when the drink went to Billy's
head he was soft, soft as a jelly.

Some years before he had had a friend in
New York and this friend might well have
been fighting at Okinawa or Aachen. The
chance of his being in New York was a very

240

slim one indeed but in fact that was just where he was. He had been twice wounded, had become a much-decorated war hero and was now occupying an important position in the American armament industry.

Billy found him. He thought up a story and his friend, Tom S. Warrens, believed him. At any rate he believed him at first. Although the two friends were so different there was one thing they had in common and that was their liking for whisky. Billy still had some money and so they went from bar to bar. They put their arms around the girls' naked shoulders and stuffed money into their garters. They treated the assembled company and sang and danced. They went on like this for days on end. Tom failed to report at his place of work and reported sick. And he was sick, from too much alcohol.

Billy got a thick head. One day at four in the morning he got an attack of the miseries. I was familiar with this mood of his; I had witnessed it once or twice when I had been with him. The friend wallowed in misery with him, at any rate at first, but he was a little more sober than Billy, just a trifle, a fatal trifle.

Billy rambled on incoherently with the

crazy logic of the inebriated. He babbled, he stammered, he talked of U-1230. Tom had just laughed at him. He laughed at him for one long day and one short night, but Billy went on and on with the same story. He was now sobering up as his money was running short. His friend went on listening and the apparently inconsequential chatter began to take reasonable shape.

What was to be done? Tom S. Warrens was, like every other American, a patriot; he had been twice wounded in the war and had been discharged from the Army with honour; but he was also a loyal friend. To report the matter to the F.B.I. would be a breach of faith with Billy. And who would contact the secret service on the strength of the ramblings of a drunken man? Yet it all seemed to hang together. Supposing Billy really was working against his own country? Tom sought the counsel of other friends and their advice was clear and unequivocal: "Go to the F.B.I."

The friends recalled the Dasch case, when fathers and mothers were sentenced to death because they had held their sons in their arms and had not at once gone to the police to order the hangman for their own sons. There were no extenuating circumstances, not in wartime. As it happened, the sentences were not carried out, but twenty years' imprisonment was bad enough.

So the F.B.I. was informed and its officers took Billy in charge without any special enthusiasm. They waited until he was sober. He was then interrogated and at once broke down; his sole concern was to save his own neck, but it was already in the noose and the rope was already being drawn tight.

"I want to inform you," said Billy, "that a German agent is at large. He is called Edward Green. He's very dangerous. He is the most dangerous man of the German Reich Security. I crossed the Atlantic with him."

"You say you are an American," an official interrupted him, "and yet you admit that you smuggled a German spy into your own country?"

"I only did it as a means of getting back to America myself, so as I could place myself at the disposal of the Army authorities and hand the German spy over to you. I'm an American and want to remain an American."

The F.B.I. men still could not make up their minds whether they were dealing with a madman or a spy. Spies who spoke as freely as Billy were rare, and hardly worth taking seriously.

Billy's files were produced; they established that he was a deserter and that his sympathies for National Socialism had excluded him from taking a commission in the Navy.

Alarm! Special alarm! The most urgent alarm the F.B.I. had known in New York in the whole course of the war.

"Speak, you swine, or I'll push your face in." Billy was not being handled with delicacy. No, no country of the world deals gently with its own traitors. I, on the other hand, was to be cross-examined with singular fairness, but more of that later. Billy sat there, a small, cowardly figure, trembling with fear.

"What does he look like? Come on, talk! Tell us again! First you said he was not very tall, then you said he *was* very tall. Which is it? Come on, speak up, you swine!"

Billy was too frightened to utter a word. He asked for a cigarette which was given him with bad grace, and then he started babbling. He gave a full description of me. The officials were frightening him to try him out and see if he was lying. But why should he lie? He saw a tiny ray of hope; he hoped that if I were caught he might secure a pardon on the strength of the information he had given against me. The hope was a slim one, but when all reasonable hope has gone you can always dream up something.

"Come on! Don't be so dumb!" said a small, stout F.B.I. man. "Open your mouth, Billy. So he's about five feet ten, is he, your friend? Come along then, just keep on talking. What does he like to eat? What does he drink? Is he left-handed? Has he got a good digestion? Is he colour-blind? Does he go to church? Does he go to night-clubs? Has he got corns on his feet?"

"I don't know any of those things," said Billy.

"Well, what do you know?"

"Well, he's not left-handed," replied Billy. "I know that. His digestion's all right. Grilled steak is his favourite dish and he drinks whisky. He drinks plenty but he can stand it."

"Come on!"

"He's got an English accent."

"We know that already. We're trying to find out something we don't know."

The lamp was shining straight into

Billy's face and his interrogators were standing in the dark. They were relieved every twenty minutes. It went on like this for hours and was to continue like it for days. There was no pity, no sympathy for Billy or me. The chase was on, but so far the press knew nothing of it. . . .

"Desperate German Christmas offensive in the Ardennes." Such was the headline of the moment. New York, sure of victory, almost tired of victory already, trembled for a space, the space of a few days, haunted once more by fear of the Nazis, fear that the war could still drag on, fear that the invasion had been in vain.

And the Department for Psychological Warfare worked on. If a German spy should chance to fall into enemy hands at this time of all times, then he'd be specially unlucky.

"I've told you everything," Billy repeated again and again. "There's nothing more I know."

"Haven't you ever noticed anything about him, some little mannerism that's a bit unusual?"

"No."

"Think again, or we'll help you do your thinking."

"I don't know anything more."

The interrogating officer went close up to Billy and stared him straight in the eyes. His face had become gaunt and the eyes were lying deep in their sockets. The light was blinding and Billy wanted to close his eyes but he could not. Again and again the F.B.I. men forced him to look at them, to look into the light, to answer their questions. Always the same questions, put sometimes gently, sometimes quietly, sometimes angrily, sometimes indifferently.

"There's one thing that occurs to me," said Billy. He seemed now almost relieved. He thought perhaps there'd be an end to the questioning if he said something.

"One thing occurs to me," he began. "I have noticed an odd habit. When he pays for something and gets change, he always puts it into his left breast pocket."

One of the officers nodded to his colleagues, and a new identification sign for the German spy was broadcast to all police stations. Attention! Attention!

The search was on for Edward Green alias Erich Gimpel, the German spy. Top secret! The American civil population must not be made to feel uneasy. Every F.B.I. man available must be thrown into the task of finding Erich Gimpel.

They laid their traps to catch me and laid them on an American scale without regard for money, time or men.

But I still knew nothing of all this.

I had arranged to meet Mr. Brown in a snack bar on 31st Street. He arrived punctually, and alone. He had every reason to play straight.

"My car is outside," he said.

We got into an old Packard and drove this way and that through New York.

"I've a whole heap of information," he said. "Can I depend on it that this is our last interview?"

"If I find the information satisfactory, yes."

The traffic lights turned to green. Brown put his foot on the accelerator.

"The atomic bomb will be ready for use within a few months."

"How many months?"

"Five or six at the most."

"How do you know?"

"I'll tell you afterwards. My information is a hundred per cent reliable."

"And how are the bombs dropped?"

"They're still experimenting on that. The bomb is terribly heavy. It has to be flown in a special machine. The trials are being made in California. An air force captain has been practising starting and landing with excessive loading there for weeks."

I made a note of name and place. It would be easy to check up on this information.

"They reckon," said Brown, "that they can bring the war to an end with one or two bombs. The effect of the bomb is terrific."

"And how many bombs have they?"

"Only two or three," replied Brown. "But that will be plenty."

"And where are the works?"

"That I cannot say exactly, but mark this name: Mr. Griffiths. He's a physicist. He lives in a hotel on 24th Street. You may care to get in touch with him. But if you do, it'll mean the end for you. You realise that, don't you?"

"That's not your affair," I replied.

He gave me a mass of technical details. I repeated them over to myself until I could carry them in my memory. I wondered how much truth there was in what Brown had told me. I didn't know yet what his information was worth. . . .

"And the bombs will be used?"

"You can depend on that," answered

Brown. "America regards the atomic bomb as the only thing to bring the war to an end. There's only one thing that would prevent them using it and that would be if Germany or Japan had the atomic bomb too. You see what I mean?"

"Yes," I replied.

"And now will you take a piece of advice from me?"

"Why not?"

"Make yourself scarce," he said.

He stopped. I got out of the car. Our leave-taking was short and cool.

"Think of my family," he said.

"Give my love to the red-head," I replied.

I wanted to pass my report on to Germany that same day. I walked on for a few blocks. Fortunately I did not know how many of the passers-by were keeping an eye on me. Billy's description fitted me, of course, but there were thousands of men in New York whom it would have fitted equally well. Actually I did not think that Billy had already been caught, but I had no illusions about the fact that the days of his freedom and by the same token the days of my freedom too, were numbered.

Now for Griffiths! Whether I could approach this man without drawing attention to myself was another question. If there was a Mr. Griffiths and if he was living in the hotel which had been named to me, then it would prove that Brown had not invented his information. In any case my next task was to establish the reliability of Brown's information.

I found the hotel; it was a second-class establishment, neither good nor bad, and with the usual, obtrusive cleanliness. I passed into the small foyer. The porter was not there, but a black book lay upon his desk, the hotel register.

I stood there for a few moments drumming my fingers on the desk. Two women were sitting on a sofa in the corner and like all Americans at the time were discussing the Ardennes offensive. A man was sitting in an armchair. I could not see his face, which was hidden behind a newspaper.

Was he really reading? In a flash I was on my guard. I knew that trick. I had learned it myself. I noticed at once how the newspaper was lowered a trifle, how the eyes moved to the edge apparently nonchalantly, how the newspaper was raised again and how the manoeuvre was repeated two or three times.

The man who held the newspaper in his

hand had had the same training as I had had. That's the F.B.I., I told myself.

I turned my back on him. I opened the register and immediately hit upon the name Griffiths, but I turned on further, ran my finger down the page, stopped at a name and made a note of it. I could not see my shadower but I could feel him behind me. I felt instinctively that he was waiting for me, that he had recognised me, and that he was now about to act. In the next second perhaps. I straightened myself. The porter came back.

"What can I do for you?" he asked.

"A relative of mine was coming here," I replied. "Mr. James H. Miller."

"He's not here," said the porter. "I'm sorry, sir."

I stood about hesitantly for a few seconds more. My shadower was once more camouflaging himself behind the newspaper. His hands were quite still. The paper with the giant headlines was not shaking. What would he do? How had the F.B.I. been instructed?

While I was playing the part of a disappointed caller who couldn't make up his mind, I was doing some rapid thinking. The F.B.I. have a strict rule that no arrest may be made unless two men are present.

My man was alone. Perhaps his colleague had gone to the lavatory. Or perhaps he would have to get reinforcements before he could act. Perhaps the second man had just gone to get some cigarettes.

"Is there a toilet around here?" I asked the porter.

"Back there, to the left," replied the man.

I gave him twenty cents and went slowly off. I did not quicken my steps; even when I was out of sight I could still be heard.

I stopped. From where I was standing I could still see the porter's desk. If my nerves were not playing tricks with me the man with the newspaper would now get up, go to the desk and try to find out what name I had made a note of.

Right! There he stood, bending over the book.

I walked past the lavatory and past the kitchen. A staircase led upwards, but if I went upstairs I should land myself in the cart. If I went back I should be arrested. I might shoot, but I wouldn't get very far in a busy street. There wouldn't be much sense in that.

Quickly, quickly! I told myself, realising at the same time that I must flee with my head rather than with my legs.

I saw the words "Tradesmen's Exit" on a door. Oh god, if only it's not locked! There was my chance, one last small chance. I put my hand upon the latch. . . .

# CHAPTER 12

## LOVE — AND THEN ARREST

All was quiet behind me. The F.B.I. man was still standing at the reception desk and the two ladies were still discussing the Ardennes offensive. The sound of their voices carried to where I was moving and I could make out a word here and there. The porter left his desk again and went upstairs. Somewhere a radio was on quietly. The sun suddenly burst out and shone clear and strong through the window. A white-capped chef was making his way along the narrow corridor and I had to step aside to allow him to pass.

"Thank you, sir," he said and raised his hand to his cap.

The door responded to my touch. The tradesmen's entrance was open. This was pure chance, due perhaps to the negligence of some member of the staff. I tried to shake off my nervousness.

"Keep calm," I admonished myself.

Slowly, with the utmost caution, I opened the door, afraid that the hinges might squeak. But they had evidently been recently oiled.

The F.B.I. man could not see me from where he was standing, but he must have been expecting me to reappear at any moment. He would be getting suspicious. I wondered why he had not acted already. Why hadn't he simply put his hand to his revolver and said: "Edward Green! You are under arrest. I warn you that from this moment anything you say may be used in evidence against you."

I was standing in the yard. It was in the form of a small quadrangle with a drive-in for the delivery vans. This stood open. To the left against the wall of the hotel two men were working on a lorry. One was lying underneath it and the other was standing in the cab. They took no notice of me.

I walked slowly, very slowly. I had closed the door behind me. Surely the F.B.I. man must have noticed something by now; I was still twenty yards from the drive-in. A private car was standing in my path, a sky-blue Chevrolet of the latest type. The owner must have known all the right people. During the war there were plenty of jeeps being made but not many Chevrolets.

The two mechanics were shouting to each other but I could not understand what they were saying. I went up to the Chevrolet. Another five yards. Now I was level with it, and I saw something which made me catch my breath. The ignition key was in its place. I pulled myself together, glanced round at the two mechanics and looked back at the door I had come through. I sized up the way out. Everything was quiet. Everything was the same. Everything seemed to be going along as usual.

Now for it. The door was ajar. I seated myself at the steering wheel and pressed the starter. The engine started up straight away. Now down on the accelerator, slowly release the clutch. Turn left. Look in the mirror. A little more acceleration. Change to second gear. Now one more look in the mirror. Turn to the right. Accelerate again, third gear. . . .

Now away! I took the first two curves so sharply that the back wheels scraped along the curb stones. Right, left, straight ahead. The red light. Amber. The green light. Accelerate. Turn to the left. Straight ahead. Across the main road. Now slowly. Drive slowly. Take care not to arouse attention.

I looked at my wrist-watch. I'll use the

car for five minutes, I thought. The two mechanics must have noticed the theft at once. They would report the number to the traffic police, and the police had wireless cars. Everything would move forward at a great pace. If you want to steal a car it's just as well not to do it in America.

I crossed Times Square, did a few more zigzags, making sure that in my excitement I was not driving round in circles.

I found a parking place. Turn right, and now out!

For the first twenty yards, I walked quite slowly, then I crossed over to the other side of the street, took a left turn, increased my pace, then jumped into a taxi.

"Quickly now," I said to the driver, naming a railway station. "If you can make it in ten minutes, I'll just catch my train."

"Depends on the traffic," replied the driver shaking his head. "People are always in a hurry and yet I often have to stand around for hours waiting for a fare."

I replied in the same strain, meanwhile taking an occasional look behind me. The taxi was not being followed. How many F.B.I. men might there be after me now? The officer in the hotel would have given his first alarm. They would have found the car by now but I was still a couple of jumps ahead. I leapt out of the taxi, paid off the driver and gave him a dollar tip. I ran into the station, up to the platform, bought myself a newspaper, changed on to another platform and came out again.

The taxi driver had obviously driven on at once.

I continued on foot. How lovely New York was at this hour. The people seemed so gay, the Christmas bells were ringing joyously and the sound of fun and laughter could be heard everywhere. The passers-by were carrying bulky parcels, last minute purchases, and excited children were running along at their heels.

"Merry Christmas," resounded from every loud-speaker. "Merry Christmas, Merry Christmas, Merry Christmas."

"Flowers," I said to myself. "A handkerchief, a few pleasant little trifles." I got everything I wanted, took a taxi, changed taxis, went a stretch on foot and eventually arrived at the door of the apartment house. I pressed the lift button and was carried up to the 11th floor.

I could not find my key and rang the bell. For a few seconds my nerves nearly failed me again. Suppose they were waiting for me here? Suppose the F.B.I. were behind that door? Suppose they were armed?

Yes, someone was waiting for me. Joan. . . .
She smiled at me.

"Darling, you look exhausted," she said.

"Yes," I replied. "New York's a strenuous place."

"You've come at just the right moment," she went on. "I've put up the Christmas tree and the turkey's in the oven. Now you can make yourself useful."

We hung the bright baubles on the tree together.

"We'll decorate it the European way," she said. "I'll like it better like that. I intend that my first Christmas after the war shall be spent in Europe."

"Plans . . . dreams . . . they're the best things there are," I said.

"But I believe in them." She turned to me and smiled. "You are an old pessimist," she said. "After all, you've still got the best years of your life in front of you, haven't you?"

"Yes," I said.

We had finished decorating the Christmas tree. The wireless was on and the music sounded sweet, soothing, alluring. It was as if the spirit of the festival of peace was flowing from the instrument and drawing us ever more into its embrace. We sat together quietly; there was no need to talk.

The meaning of Christmas and how it should be celebrated is something you'll never find in a text book for secret agents. The previous year I had been in Spain for Christmas. There were plenty of good things to eat. When the faithful were setting out for Midnight Mass we were lying about on the floor. When they were getting ready to go to Matins we were trying to clear our thick heads with more alcohol. Two years previously I had spent Christmas in Holland. On the day before Christmas Eve two German agents had been shot. Two days later an English agent lay in his grave.

Christmas! What was Christmas? Flickering candlelight, the mild, lovable fragrance of scorched pine branches, the excited, exuberant joy of children.

As I sat there at Joan's side beneath the Christmas tree I felt something creep up my spine and catch me by the throat. Something said to me: "It's Christmas for everyone else, but not for you!"

Swiftly, clearly, my memory swung back over the years, over the decades. I saw my father, my mother, my teacher before me. Once before when I was only eight or nine I had experienced this same heaviness of spirit. My friend's father, a bank cashier, had shot himself on Christmas Eve. 12,000 marks were missing. That year the spirit of Christmas passed me by, excluded me as it was excluding me now.

I swallowed two glasses of whisky. Smiling, Joan removed the bottle from my reach.

"Not before you've eaten," she said.

We went into the kitchen to see how things were getting along. Everything was in order. We left the turkey to look after itself while we looked after ourselves.

And then came the radio news. They couldn't leave us in peace even on Christmas Eve. The Ardennes offensive had been crushed. Decisively. I wondered whether it was propaganda, and whether the Department for Psychological Warfare had cut the offensive short more quickly than General Eisenhower.

I was the war's last fool, holding out on an outpost that was already lost.

"This would be a good time for a transmission," I thought. Actually all the separate components for my set had been ready for some time and were in a suitcase which was lying underneath a couch in this very room, the room which housed our Christmas tree. No one would be paying any special attention to radio communications on Christmas Eve, but my reports were not ready. The information I had had from Brown had first of all to be checked and then followed up. There were still some difficult days and weeks in front of me. . . . I only hoped that Billy had not yet been caught. I wondered where he might be at that moment.

"You look like a general after a lost battle," said Joan.

"Have you ever seen a general?" I asked.

"Only on the screen," she replied, laughing. "But on the screen they're always victorious."

"That's why they are always much nicer in the cinema than in real life," I replied.

We took the turkey out of the oven, carved it and served it. It was beautifully tender and crisp. We sat facing each other, smiling, eating with enjoyment, toasting each other, going over to the radio now and again to see what programmes we could get. We drank Rhine wine. You could still get it in New York.

"It goes well with the food," I said.

"Yes," said Joan. "Today every American soldier gets a turkey from the Army."

"Yes," I replied, "and there are still 300,000 turkeys to spare. That's the number of men the war has cost us so far."

"300,000 Americans," she went on. "And how many English, French, German and Italian?"

"Let's talk about something else."

Joan stood up, walked over to the light switches, turned the ceiling light off and the wall light on.

"There are two G.I.'s I knew who will never eat turkey again," she said. "One was my brother."

I nodded. Suddenly all the magic of the evening was gone.

"Don't you want to know who the other one was?" she said.

"I can imagine."

"It was Bob," she continued. "He was tall and slim like you, and he had your fair hair. I was going to marry him. I had known him for three years. He was a lieutenant. This time last year Bob and I were celebrating together. Do you see now why I didn't want to go back to my own flat? I didn't want to be alone there."

I said nothing, but got to my feet and paced up and down in the room.

"I'm a fool," she said. "Now I've gone and spoiled everything. But on an evening like this you just can't help thinking. . . . He was killed in March. In the Pacific. Landing on one of those damned coral islands that aren't worth a cent. And after that they gave him a medal."

"They always give them a medal afterwards," I replied. "Oh, there's no sense in going over it all."

She smiled at me. Her eyes were shining. She went up to the Christmas tree and lit the first candle. Then she turned towards me and said:

"You must light the second candle."

"If you light them all," I said, "they'll burn all the more brightly."

"You're a flatterer," she said, "but it does me good. Do you know, I thought this evening was going to be awful, and look how differently it's turned out. I rather reproach myself that I can forget so quickly, that I can suddenly feel so gay at being with you. I feel I shouldn't be enjoying myself like this."

I put my arm round her. Then I went and fetched my little parcel.

"I've probably chosen all wrong," I said.

"I put your flowers in a vase ages ago."

"I'm sure you won't like the handbag; I've no experience with these things."

"It's lovely," she replied. "And if you were more experienced in these things I shouldn't like you nearly so much. But what nonsense. Of course you are experienced, but it doesn't matter."

She took a tiny box from her handbag.

"There," she said, "this is for you."

It was a pair of gold cuff links. I still wear them.

The flickering candle-light caressed her face, illumining eyes, nose, brow. I could not take my eyes off her. I went on staring at her, and she liked it. She was not embarrassed, she was not coquettish. She was just herself. Just Joan.

We sat together on the couch. The music had come on again, and the magic had returned. It was as if there had never been a war, as if there would be no more fighting, as if never again would a mother tremble for her son and a wife tremble for her husband. It was quite simply as if even the most evil, the most unenlightened, the most dangerous of politicians had suddenly heard and understood the message of Bethlehem. For us there was no battlefield. There was only that sitting-room on the 11th floor. I was not a German and she was not an American, and we loved each other and we did not need the banalities of speech to tell each other so.

We knew it.

I do not know how long we sat there, silent, relaxed, happy. The candles burned down to tiny stumps, and we had to snuff them out. Their flickering light no longer played over Joan's face but the fragrance and the magic of Joan were there in the dark.

"It's strange," she said. "Actually we know nothing about each other. It's even more strange that we've never asked each other who we are, what we do and where we come from. But I feel that's how it should be."

She frowned fleetingly.

"I feel as if I've always known you."

"I feel just that way myself," I replied.

We kissed, and I forgot all the things that I should have remembered. The time, the place, my mission and the fact that I was a hunted man. Agent 146 of the German M.I., the human machine, the man who went through with every mission that was entrusted to him without question — that man died for a few hours. I sensed, I felt, I realised that I was a human being with his hopes and longings like every other, a human being with a heart which had certain rights that no power nor state on earth could deny it. I realised all this that Christmas Eve in New York. In New York, the biggest city in the world, where the F.B.I. were after me like a pack of bloodhounds. I realised it all as I lay in Joan's arms.

"Will you stay with me always?" asked Joan.

"I don't know," I replied.

"Will you just forget me?"

"No," I said, "that I can promise you; I shall never forget you."

"It's strange," she continued. "I always seem to know just what you are going to say."

It was midnight now. The bells were ringing on the radio and the carol-singers were proclaiming Christmas Day.

We drew closer together. I was happy that things had turned out like this, that I was holding Joan in my arms instead of hunting British agents in Holland or lying with a heap of drunken men in Spain. The night enfolded us in its embrace. A clock was ticking. The sound was painful to me. If only there were no clocks. . . . The feeling of happiness to which I had surrendered became ever more poignant.

Joan had fallen asleep. She was smiling. She lay quite still, her face turned towards me. I had opened the window, and the cool night air was wafting into the room. I covered her with a rug so that she would not feel the cold.

And then once more the secret agent in me gained the upper hand. Uncompromisingly he reported for duty. For an hour, two hours I struggled desperately against the dictates of my conscience.

Life has not dealt gently with me. I have witnessed the death of friends. I have felt the clammy hands of the hangman measuring my neck. I have known the silent despair of a prison cell, the inevitability of the passage of time measuring out life slowly, day by day, hour by hour. In all these situations my role was a passive one, the inevitable result of circumstances beyond my control.

Now, however, I had to anticipate the grim drama. I had to leave Joan, sleeping, smiling Joan who would be looking forward to a joyous awakening at my side. I had to cast behind me all the joy of this evening, all the spirit of Christmas, all recognition of our mutual love. I had to pick up my bag and baggage and step out into the chill of the metropolis, into the heart of the enemy. I was an enemy of the people who were now celebrating Christmas; I was a spy, a spy for a country which had already lost the war.

I would have to waken Joan and explain everything. I was sure she would never denounce me. But therein lay her own undoing. She would be charged with having harboured a German spy. The law of warfare knows no love, no pity. She would be executed. Militant, uncompromising patriotism, that monster produced by war, would make no concessions.

No, I could not do it. No, not as long as a glimmering of understanding was left to me. Not so long as I had any sense of responsibility. No, not so long as I loved her.

She turned in her sleep and what light there was enabled me to study her face in every detail. I imprinted her features upon my memory. I would never see her again, and I would never be able to explain to her why I had slipped away. It was my lot to wound her. Perhaps she would never understand. She might weep, she might be embittered, she might curse the fate that had brought us together. She might hate the happiness that had united us for a few hours.

No, I could never do that! I crept quietly up to her. I would have to wake her. I would have to stay, I would have to risk everything to guard our happiness. The war was already as good as over. I would tell her what my part in it had been. She would understand and would say no more about it. I had money, I could speak Spanish, I knew my way around South America. I knew where I could go and not arouse attention. I knew the places where no one would think of looking for me. She would come with me. There would be two or three days' uncertainty before our getaway was finally accomplished, before we would be safe. We would travel separately. For Joan anyhow there would be no risk, and I knew how to go about it, how to cross frontiers and keep my nerves under control. For once in my life my training would be of some real service to me.

She knew nothing of the inner battle I had to fight, the despair I had to endure. She did not know that her problematical future was already my past.

I got up and packed my belongings. I pulled my case out from under the couch on which she was sleeping. A light sleeper would have been disturbed. I hoped she would wake. I hoped that the terrible, fateful decision would not be left to me alone.

But Joan went on sleeping. Scraps of white mist floated in through the open window. I closed it and again it was not possible to avoid making a slight noise. I carried my bag to the corridor. "At least

271

you can leave a note for her," one half of me said. But the agent remained obdurate. I made my way to the door. I turned once more and looked behind me. . . .

I ignored the most elementary requirements of caution. It was all a matter of indifference to me now and I acted entirely without thought or consideration.

I summoned a taxi and drove straight to an hotel. As far as I was concerned the whole of the F.B.I. could be waiting for me at the reception desk. For all I cared they could have caught me there and then. All I wanted was to be free of the whole business.

I left my bag at the reception desk. They needed only to open it and they would have all the proof they wanted against me. Then I bought myself a bottle of whisky and took it to bed with me. On the following day I did the same thing. That was how I somehow managed to live through Christmas Day. That day and during the days which followed, I forgot everything I had learned at the school for secret agents. Perhaps I could never have done what I eventually did if I had conducted myself like an expert.

The information from Brown gave me a

pointer and I carried on without thought or care for the consequences. Not once did I look round to see if I was being followed. It was as if life had put blinkers on me. I visited libraries and reading rooms, I spoke with engineers and workmen, and I posed my questions without any inhibitions.

Needless to say, the Manhattan project was absolutely confidential, but no country could keep an atomic bomb entirely secret. The route of the uranium ore that came from northern Canada — some of it also came from the Belgian Congo — could be precisely traced.

For the cooling of an atomic pile it is necessary to have vast quantities of water. I observed that a section of the Columbia River had been diverted. It also did not escape my notice that in Oak Ridge in the State of Tennessee a six-storey works building had sprung up within the space of a few months.

I also investigated the matter of test flights. Two distinguished air force officers, specialists in B29, the greatest American long-distance bomber of its time, had been drafted from the Pacific zone. They were now engaged in the seemingly pointless occupation of flying an exceptionally heavy mock bomb backwards and forwards in

Arizona. The pilots themselves had no idea of the significance of what they were doing when I reported everything to Germany.

I gritted my teeth and again became more cautious. My report must get through. Perhaps a terrible disaster could be prevented if the German government could be warned in time, and if they took my warning seriously. If. . . .

I assembled my transmitter. I had some difficulty in getting it to go at first, but I finally succeeded. At five in the afternoon, American time, all was ready. I formulated my message. It was too long. I shortened it and found I was able to save about fifty words. I coded the text, learned it by heart, then wrote it down once again and found I could cut another sentence. I would need eight to ten minutes. I seated myself at the keyboard, wondering if I would be located in New York, wondering if they still imagined that a German spy could possibly be transmitting a message from their very midst.

I tapped the keys. After a short time I received a reply. I was now quite calm. I was, so to speak, once more in my own element. My transmission took no longer than I had calculated. Reception had been clear; I received confirmation from the ether.

The first part of my mission had been completed. What would they think of my report in Berlin? I wondered whether they would simply throw it into the waste-paper basket as they had done with other important messages which they had not dared to place before Hitler. Or would they simply not believe what I had said? Would they think that I had fallen prey to pacifist feelings? Or would they think I had reported what I had reported just to make myself look important? Anything was possible. I realised all of this. When the war was over I was to know a good deal more besides. . . .

The second part of my mission was — sabotage. I was to marshal together a group of men who would carry out explosive attacks on the main works buildings of the American atomic industry. Men and money for this purpose were ready and waiting for me in South America. The only question was, to what extent were they dependable? It was quite within the bounds of possibility that both were counterfeit.

"What is the point of it all?" I asked myself again and again during this period. Was it all worth while? Was it still my duty to go on? Why didn't I just throw the whole thing up? Why didn't I just go under cover for a while? My colleagues and indeed my superiors were not to prove to be such sticklers for duty.

The arrangement was that I should get in touch with contact men in Peru by inserting an advertisement in a South American newspaper. Through the medium of a few innocuous words which I have since forgotten, I was to inform them that they were to come to New York as quickly as possible.

The advertisement appeared. The next step was for the contact men to confirm through an advertisement in the same newspaper that everything was proceeding according to plan. I had therefore to buy this particular paper every day. It was obtainable only at the larger newspaper stands in New York, and unknown to me that was where my fate lurked in wait for me. . . .

The last day of 1944 began for me like any other day. My room was over-heated, the wallpaper was grim. I shaved and had some coffee in a snack bar. I was in a bad mood, but I had been in a bad mood ever since I had left Joan. All the time I longed to go back to her. I wondered what she was doing, and what she was thinking of me. I wondered if she had somehow got over the ghastly surprise of the morning when she awoke to find I had disappeared.

I knew the little dress shop in New York that she ran. I had walked past it a few times. I wanted to see her once again. I hadn't even a photograph of her; it would indeed have been wrong of me to have had a photograph of her. I saw her face, her eyes, always before me. It was enough to drive me crazy. Meanwhile I was acting as errand boy for an idiotic war. . . .

I lunched at one o'clock on a double portion of steak and the usual *pommes frites*. I was suddenly terribly hungry. Then I bought myself a few newspapers. Passing over the war reports, I read a speech of Roosevelt's. I couldn't stand the man. Then I turned to a murder case.

There was a cinema close to the restaurant and I went in. The film was a Western of the worst kind and I left the cinema after half an hour of it. I had once again accustomed myself to take a good look around me. I was sure no one was following me. New York was busy preparing to celebrate New Year's Eve. I would have to celebrate alone; I still had no idea where I should go. I walked on towards Times Square. It was a dreary afternoon. There were hundreds of people hanging about in the square, people actively wanting to enjoy themselves, people who were bored or people who were out on business. On the right side of the square was a newspaper stand which carried the paper I had to see.

I walked past the stand first. I always did this when I was buying newspapers. There were a good number of people about, always three or four at the stand putting their cents in a dish and picking up the paper they wanted. A few people were standing about near by but that's something you always see by a newspaper stand. Some people just can't wait to satisfy their curiosity and stand and look at their papers in the most unsuitable places.

I walked past the stand once more. There were two teenagers behind me giggling over something that had happened at a dancing class. In front of me a wounded man in uniform was walking along on crutches. The people coming towards him looked pained and embarrassed. Cars were driving across the square in a continuous stream. A woman dropped a parcel and I picked it up for her. She thanked me with a smile. I went up to the stand. A glance to the left, and one to the right. It looked as if the coast was clear. Nowhere near could I see two men together; two men together spelled danger for me.

I had to wait a few seconds and looked meanwhile at various magazines as if I were undecided which to take. I bought two and then asked for the South American paper. The man hesitated for a moment then nodded knowingly.

"One moment, sir," he said. He riffled through a stack of papers. Then he found it.

"I don't get asked for this very often," he explained. "If you need it regularly, let me know and I'll put it on one side for you."

"I'm only a visitor here," I replied, "but thanks all the same."

I gave him a dollar.

"Haven't you anything smaller?" he asked.

"Sorry, I haven't," I replied.

He gave me twenty-five cents change, counting it out to me carefully. I unbuttoned my overcoat and dropped the change into the left breast pocket of my jacket. It was an odd habit of mine; my mother had in fact often taken me to task about it when I was a boy at home.

I put the papers in my overcoat pocket, the South American one wrapped round by the two magazines so that it could not be seen. I strolled on a few paces further. A man near me lit a cigarette. His eyes were on the match. Then he approached nearer. The crowd tossed up a group of young soldiers who passed by three abreast, making a great deal of noise.

"One moment, sir," said the man with the cigarette. In the same second another man appeared at his side as if he had been conjured out of a hat.

"Edward Green, I believe?"

"No," I said, "my name's Frank Miller."

"Well, whatever your name is," replied one of the two men, "you are under arrest."

# CHAPTER 13

## GRILLED BY THE F.B.I.

They certainly knew their job and I found myself so wedged in between them that any attempt to escape would have been suicidal; at the same time everything was done so unobtrusively that not one of the thousands who at that time were crossing Times Square could possibly have imagined that anything at all out of the ordinary was going on.

"My name is Nelson," said one of the two men. He was short and stocky, with a round head and lively eyes. He showed me his badge.

"This isn't a very good place to talk," he went on. "Come along with us."

The newspaper stand which had spelled my doom had behind it a small room. We went inside.

"I would now like to know what you want with me," I began.

"I'll tell you that straight away," replied Nelson. He lit a cigarette, smiled and indicated his colleague.

"May I introduce to you Mr. Gillies, Mr. Green."

"I told you my name is not Green."

"Show me your papers."

I produced a document bearing the name Frank Miller.

"They certainly know how to forge papers in Germany," he replied.

I realised now that I was for it and the only thing that surprised me was that the F.B.I. did not push me into a car and drive me off for interrogation at once.

"Well, Mr. Miller," said Nelson, "where do you live?"

"I come from Chicago."

"And where do you live in Chicago?"

I gave him an address which I had learned by heart. He made a note of it.

"And how long have you been in New York?"

"Ten days," I replied.

"And what are you doing here?"

"I am on business."

"Mm, mm," he said, "just think of that. Well, I've got a little message for you."

"For me?"

"From William Curtis Colepaugh, otherwise known as Billy. He's been waiting a fortnight for you already."

"I don't know him."

Gillies went to the telephone and dialled a number. He cursed quietly on finding it engaged. At the second attempt he got through.

"We've got him," he said. "Come along over. . . . No, you can be quite sure, there's absolutely no doubt about it." Then he hung up.

Nelson went on with his interrogation.

"I'll tell you something. About five weeks ago you landed in Frenchman Bay. The two of you. Then by a roundabout route you travelled to Boston. From Boston you came to New York. In New York your friend stole the suitcases. You recovered them at Grand Central Station — that was marvellous, the way you did that. You've got a quantity of money and diamonds with you and a wireless transmitter. And I'll wager that you've already sent a report through to Germany.

"Yes," he continued. "We've waited a long time for you. You've certainly held out a good while. Longer than all your colleagues; and you didn't make any mistakes." He toyed with his revolver. It was a Smith & Wesson, latest model. He took hold of it and aimed out of the window.

"To be precise, you made one solitary mistake. As soon as you landed, you should have taken your revolver and shot Billy between the eyes. No American would have held that against you."

"I'll take your advice next time," I replied.

I knew now that there was no point in pursuing the role of the indignant, wrongfully-arrested American. They had Billy, and Billy had given me away. There was no doubt about that. There was no harm in admitting to what they already knew about me, but I must at all costs keep quiet about what they did not know.

I thought of Joan, of Santi, of Brown, of my contact men in South America. All of them would be in the greatest possible danger if I did not keep my mouth shut.

"Where are you staying in New York?"

I hesitated for a moment.

"If you don't tell us, your picture will appear in every New York newspaper tomorrow morning, and I'll bet you anything that we'll have your address by seven o'clock at the latest. Do you believe me?"

"All right," I replied. "I'm staying at the Pennsylvania Hotel, room 1559."

"I'm glad you've decided to be sensible. Now I'm afraid I must search you. Would you please empty your pockets?"

I put everything on the table. A comb, a

knife, two handkerchiefs, a wallet and several bundles of banknotes. Gillies counted the money. There was more than 10,000 dollars.

"You certainly carry plenty of money around with you."

"It's an old habit of mine."

"Just have another look in your pockets and make sure you've forgotten nothing," said Nelson, "otherwise I shall get into trouble afterwards."

"I've still got my wrist-watch."

"Give it to me, please."

The door opened and a man of medium height with an intelligent face, lively eyes and a small dashing moustache came in.

"Here's the boss," explained Nelson. "Mr. Connelly, Deputy head of the F.B.I."

"I'm delighted to make your acquaintance," I said.

"Me too," he replied, and smiled.

"It's a good thing you've managed to keep your sense of humour. You'll certainly need it."

He had a pleasant voice. It was a voice I was to hear for days and weeks on end. The questions he put to me became ever more unpleasant, but the tone in which they were put remained always friendly.

Nelson was in a corner of the room

taking notes. Connelly came up to me.

"I've one request," he said. "I'd like to take a look at your hotel room."

"Go ahead," I replied.

"Not without your express permission."

"I don't understand," I replied. "If I don't give you permission you will have it searched just the same."

His smile broadened.

"Tomorrow, yes, but not today. I shan't be able to get a search warrant today."

This punctiliousness seemed so strange to me that I was at a loss to understand it. In the last year of the war the F.B.I. could still afford to abide by the strict letter of the law in respect of an enemy, a spy, a saboteur.

"Go along by all means," I said. "You'll be thrilled with what you find there."

"I've no doubt about that."

Connelly went to the telephone and gave instructions for the room to be searched.

"That's fine," he said. "I'll go on ahead now. We'll question you in my office." He nodded to me and to his two officers.

"I hate to do it," said Nelson, "but I must ask you for your arm."

I stretched out my arm and he handcuffed me to Gillies. "We have our instructions," he said by way of apology.

We got into a car. The noise and bustle on Times Square had increased. New Year's Eve! Confetti was flying above our heads. People were laughing and shouting and joking with each other. A new year was beginning, a year which was certain to bring peace. The Americans were celebrating this in advance. They clapped us on the back, smiled at us and utterly failed to notice that I was handcuffed. They were on the threshold of peace. I was at the gates of death.

Nelson drove and I sat with Gillies at the back of the car.

"It's time we had a drink," I said.

"I could do with one myself," replied Nelson.

"Well then, might I invite you two gentlemen to take a drink with me?"

"But you wouldn't want to go and have a drink like this, would you?" laughed Nelson.

"Well, you could take the handcuffs off. I certainly shan't run away from you."

"I quite believe you," answered Nelson. "But perhaps we'll find a bottle of something in my office."

Connelly was waiting for us. He was wearing a dark suit with a bright tie. He looked full of energy and enterprise.

"Welcome!" he said. It sounded facetious but not malicious.

"The whole of American rejoices at this moment," he said. "You've no idea what a job we've had to catch you. Next time don't put your change in your breast pocket. That's what gave you away."

"I'll make a note of that, Mr. Connelly," I said.

He clapped me on the back.

"He's a nice chap," he said, "our friend Gimpel." So he already knew my real name.

"Where's Billy?" I asked.

"In the next room. Are you impatient to see him?"

"By no means."

"I like you," said Connelly. "But I don't want to have anything to do with your friend. You might have saved us the trouble, but now we've got to hang him."

Connelly brought me a glass of whisky.

"Drink up," he said, "it will do you good. You've got a long night in front of you and a long day. We've got to cross-question you now, but we'll make it as pleasant as we can."

I answered in the same strain.

"Interrogations are always pleasant," I said. "They make the time pass so quickly."

Two officers returned from the Pennsylvania Hotel bringing with them my whole espionage equipment, money, diamonds, photographic apparatus, invisible ink, revolver and parts of my transmitter.

"You've got a nice collection there," said Connelly. He seated himself at his desk. Behind him hung a portrait of Roosevelt, almost life-size, in a silver frame. The picture was slightly hazy which made it look as if the President were perspiring. I gazed at him searchingly and imagined I saw him wink at me with his left eye.

Connelly turned round to the portrait and smiled.

"The President knows all about it already," he said. "He was informed half an hour ago by Mr. Hoover. Mr. Hoover is the Supreme Head of the F.B.I. You know that, of course." He offered me a cigarette and lit it for me. "You certainly cannot complain of lack of attention. Actually no German agent has ever before got as far as you did." He rose from his chair and paced up and down the room.

"Would you like another glass of whisky?" he asked.

I nodded.

"Are you hungry?"

"Yes."

"Tell me what you would like and you shall have it. Not only today either. You're in the best hands. When you've had something to eat we'll continue our conversation," he said. He motioned to an officer who led me out into another room which had been set up as a sort of provisional cell.

"I'll have some grilled steak and *pommes frites*. After that ice-cream and a glass of Bourbon. Perhaps you can also bring me some sweets and couple of packets of cigarettes."

"It shall be done," answered the officer and carefully locked the door behind him.

I sat on the bunk and listened as two men conversed *sotto voce* just outside the door. It was night. On the horizon I could see some improvised fireworks going off. Jumping crackers, rockets and Catherine wheels. The new year was on the way.

"Here's to the New Year," I said to myself and beat my fists upon my forehead. As I waited for my steak I felt only a mixture of scorn and pity for myself.

In the last analysis it was all the same to me whether I was executed with courtesy or without it. However correct the proceedings might be, the outcome was inevitable. Death is the penalty for espionage in wartime the world over. Every secret agent knows that and every secret agent has only one defence against it — not to get caught.

The *pommes frites* smelt tempting. The steak was tender and underdone as I liked it, but every mouthful stuck in my throat. Perhaps now the Third Degree was about to begin. That horribly cruel method of interrogation attributed to the F.B.I. . . . I ate slowly to kill time. They certainly allowed me plenty.

An officer poked his head around the door.

"All right?" he asked.

"First class," I replied.

I was now on the ice-cream. I was thinking of Joan and could see her before me. Her eyes, her lips, her brow. She had moist eyes, red-rimmed. She could not understand what I had done to her. She knew nothing of the work of a spy; thank God, she knew nothing of that. I must concentrate on shielding her at all costs. She and Santi, Brown and the contact men in South America who were probably at this moment trying to cross the frontier.

It was all over. I had been caught. I was lost, betrayed. Operation Elster had come to an end, but half-completed, on Times Square, right in the heart of New York. On the busiest spot of that vast metropolis.

Mr. Connelly, deputy head of the F.B.I. would probably allow me another five minutes. I lit a cigarette. . . .

Damn and blast Times Square! It had a bad name in the files of the German M.I. and it had got me now! Of the serious losses the German Secret Service had sustained on this spot I thought of the Osten case. At any rate it helped me to forget my own troubles for a while. . . .

In 1941, Major von der Osten, one of the shrewdest officers of the German M.I. was commissioned to reorganise the network of German secret agents in the U.S.A. It was a few months before Pearl Harbour, and America had not yet entered the war. The Major travelled with a Spanish passport, calling himself Lido, and reached the States via Honolulu and San Francisco. His papers were as expert as his experience, and he aroused no suspicion. He got as far as New York without the American Secret Service becoming aware of his presence in the country.

New York was the centre of the German espionage which was under the direction of a German-American whose name began with L. The results it had so far achieved were meagre and that was why the Major had been sent to New York; he was to inject some life into the proceedings. Von der Osten was tall and slim. He spoke English with an irreproachable American accent and could drink and swear with the best of them.

Von der Osten looked up L. who gave him maps, plans and a list of all the contact men, and von der Osten put the documents in a brief-case. L. and the Major took a taxi and drove through New York.

At Times Square the lights showed red, the taxi stopped and the two men took the opportunity to get out. They paid off the driver, L. stepped out on to the street and von der Osten followed. The lights changed and the traffic moved forward. A sports car, the driver of which was drunk, shot forward like lightning straight at von der Osten. The Major leapt to one side and landed right in the path of a Cadillac.

There was a crash, a scream, and a crowd began to form.

L. acted swiftly. He took the brief-case out of the hand of the seriously injured man and disappeared into the crowd. One or two people noticed him and informed the police.

They took the Major to hospital, but he died on the way. They inspected his passport and became suspicious. . . .

This grim accident in Times Square in 1941 cost the German M.I. fourteen trained agents. The F.B.I. had L.'s description, they went after him, and they found him.

L. broke down under interrogation and the F.B.I. made its swoop. One motor-car in Times Square had played a decisive part in the course of the war. It should have been a warning to me. . . .

"If you're ready. . . ." An F.B.I. official came for me. "Mr. Connelly would like to see you in his office."

"Yes, I'm ready," I replied.

I only had to go down a short passageway. Three officials were waiting for me.

"Make yourself comfortable," said Connelly. "It's going to be a long job."

I sat down and put a cigarette in my mouth. The officer threw a box of matches across the table to me; they had taken my lighter away. I had also been relieved of my braces, and my shoe laces had been removed from my shoes; my tie had likewise found its way into the property room. Precautions against suicide are the same the world over.

"You are a German?" asked Connelly.

"Yes."

"You have been going under the name of Edward Green?"

"Yes."

"You have also used the name of Frank Miller here?"

"Yes."

"You made an illegal entry into the United States five weeks ago?"

"Yes."

"By means of a German U-boat?"

"Yes."

"What was the name of the U-boat commander?"

"I don't know."

Connelly nodded.

"Do you not know or do you not wish to tell me?"

"I don't know," I replied.

Nelson laughed.

"You don't expect us to believe that, of course."

"You can do what you like with it," I replied.

"That's fine," replied Connelly.

"You are an agent of the German M.I., are you not?"

"Yes."

"You were trained for the work at the German schools?"

"Yes."

"At which schools?"

"I'm not going to tell you."

"Just as you like."

Connelly got to his feet and paced up and down in the room.

Then he said: "My job is to investigate the case, nothing more. You'll be handled decently here, you'll discover that. We're not the Gestapo. I even have a certain understanding of the fact that you should wish to shield your associates. . . . But don't get me wrong. I mean I have a certain human understanding for it; as an officer of the F.B.I. I must do my duty."

He sat down and lit a cigarette.

"I just had to make my little speech," he said. "You know, of course, that we Americans like making speeches."

"Well, I've nothing against it."

"What were your instructions in America?"

I remained silent.

"Do you deny that you intended to gather information about the American armament industry?"

"No," I replied.

"You know, of course, that that is called espionage."

"Yes."

"Therefore you don't deny that you are a spy?"

"No."

"But you will not tell us what you have been spying upon."

"Have you ever met a spy who'd tell you that?" I asked.

"Oh," said Connelly with a smile, "we've had a whole host of amateurs here."

"Well, I'm no amateur, I can tell you that."

He roared with laughter.

"I haven't much to tell you," I said. "My own story isn't of much interest to you or to me. . . . I came to America with a citizen of the States — that's no news to you. There's no one apart from him who had anything to do with this undertaking. I just had to find out what I could about the capacity of the American armament industry. I tried but I did not succeed. . . . Any questions you may care to ask me which concern me personally I will answer willingly. You know, of course, that a secret agent is only one small cog in a great machine, and that he himself is kept in the dark as far as possible about the picture as a whole."

Connelly nodded.

"But you're no ordinary secret agent," he replied. "You were working for Germany when you were in Peru. You were a layman then, of course, but after that you received your training. You served under Canaris and you did so well that you were transferred to Reich Security, a department of the S.S. There you developed into one of Germany's most dangerous spies. Then I could tell you a few things from your time in Spain. . . . Oh no, when they send a man like you across the Atlantic they know what they're doing."

We conversed politely enough but continued to talk past rather than to each other. We told each other only what we knew already. The interrogation was being conducted in an almost leisurely manner, but it was just therein that the danger lay. The F.B.I. was first of all applying the 'soft' method; when would they bring the 'hard' into play? When would they start using noise, loud music, flood lights, shouts and blows? When would they come at me with an outstretched revolver and threaten to shoot me? When would they promise me my freedom? When would they describe the execution? When would they try the sexual methods? When would they use the lever of religion? When would they get brutal?

It had to come. Perhaps not today, but

certainly tomorrow. Then it would start. They would hold a photograph of my mother before my eyes and threaten reprisals against my family. I knew exactly how everything would be done and I knew that there was small chance of my surviving these methods of torture and keeping quiet.

The officials were relieved every ten minutes. New faces appeared, new names cropped up. Some of the men looked rough and brutal but they spoke gently and courteously. No, I certainly would not fall for the 'soft' methods. . . .

They brought me coffee. I was chain-smoking and my fingers were getting quite brown. The morning mist descended on New York and I could hear the bells ringing in the New Year. The city awoke, milk churns clattered and newspaper men called out the headlines upon the morning air. The people shouted New Year greetings to each other. The post man got his tip, and those who clung to their beliefs went to church. Those who had drunk too much the night before were taking headache powders, and anyone who had a day off from work would certainly go on sleeping.

"What were the names of your contact men in America?"

"Don't lie."

"What were you doing with so much money?"

"Just tell us the names of the people with whom you had dealings and then you can sleep for two days."

They brought me ham and eggs and wonderful coffee. There were cigarettes on the tray. Nothing was spared.

Another crop of new faces. It was hot. I took my jacket off and unbuttoned my shirt. My beard was growing and my face was irritating. I passed my hand over the stubble once or twice.

"Oh, would you like to have a wash?" said one of the officers, interrupting the interrogation. "I'm so sorry. We'll pause for half an hour."

I was taken back into my cell.

"What's the time?" I asked.

"Nine o'clock," answered an official.

The interrogation had already gone on for eleven hours. That was quite enough for me but it was to continue.

At twelve o'clock Connelly appeared again.

"Just tell us what you'd like to eat, and we'll order it from the hotel. You can have whatever you like. You must be tired. I wish I could leave you in peace but you understand I have my duty. . . ."

If this consideration, this attitude of human understanding were false, Connelly must have been the best actor I had ever known. But I believe it was genuine. All the officials, whether they seemed detached or interested, whether they had any private conversation with me or declined to talk to me personally, regarded me with a look that was a mixture of shyness, pity and horror. I was to be the object of this look for weeks on end and I was finally able to define it. It was the look one gives a man who in measurable time is going to be led out to the gallows.

And so the interrogation went on. The same questions again and again, and again the same answers. When evening came we had not progressed one step. The sweat was running off my forehead, my legs were swelling and my mouth was parched although I was drinking coffee and Coca-Cola all the time. Night fell and Connelly went home for a short time.

What was happening in the background meanwhile I learned only later. On my account a special conference was called at the White House and the decision was taken to strengthen the coastal defences. The fact that a German U-boat had been

301

able to break through the defensive ring had caused painful surprise in many quarters, and those responsible were to be summoned to appear before a court-martial. They re-constructed the landing, followed the route we had taken and interrogated all the people we had spoken with, however trifling the conversation might have been. The F.B.I. had been put on its mettle. . . .

Connelly returned. He had food sent up. We ate together and discussed the proper way to grill a steak. We discovered we had the same taste. We had the wireless on while we were eating and let Harry James blow a trumpet solo at us.

"Any complaints?" asked Connelly.

"Actually, no," I replied.

"Let's have another cigarette in peace," he said when we had finished our meal. He stood up and turned the radio off. "I'll have a doctor sent in to you, if you like."

"Thank you, but I'm as sound as a bell."

"Well," he said, "that's worth a good deal. My wife is in hospital. She suddenly contracted diphtheria. Diphtheria at twenty-four. My children are with their grandparents."

"So you've children too?"

"Two," he said, "a boy and a girl."

He stubbed out his cigarette. At the

same moment the door opened and two officials entered the room. The interrogation proceeded. Connelly sat in the background. He put his feet on his desk and brandished an outsize ruler in the air. Now and again I looked over in his direction, but he appeared not to notice it. He was doing everything he could to appear indifferent to what was taking place.

It was midnight and once more the men were relieved.

"Ah well," said Connelly, "we still don't know any more than we knew at the start. You're very uncommunicative, my friend."

"Speech is silver, silence is golden."

"Is that a German saying?"

"Yes."

"You could make things much easier for yourself and for us too. You've only to name the men who are backing you up."

"There are none."

He shrugged.

"Then we shall have to institute a change in the proceedings," he said.

Once more a door opened.

Half pulled, half shoved, Billy appeared on the scene, pale, unshaven, his face swollen.

"Now come along," said Nelson, giving

him a push forward, "shake hands with your friend."

Billy remained as if rooted to the spot. You could have heard a pin drop. I lit a cigarette. Billy was incapable of speaking and could not look me in the face. He presented a picture of such complete stupidity that for one moment I had to struggle with a feeling of pity for him. It was, however, soon dispelled.

"Come on," said Connelly. "Say something, Billy. Tell us again what you know about him."

Billy was silent.

"Come along, talk!"

The official shoved him nearer to me. He had a bruise on his head. He certainly had not been handled gently, that was obvious.

"Have you lost your tongue?" asked Connelly.

"You know everything already," said Billy. He still had his eyes on the floor. "He was with the S.S. He was quite a big shot."

"Go on, Billy," said Connelly, "what else do you know?"

"He intended to blow up some factories here."

"Which factories?"

Billy was silent.

He stood there pale, hang-dog, like one paralysed. His long, ape-like arms hung limply down. His hair fell into his eyes. He looked sickly and was shaking from head to foot.

"Billy," said Connelly, "you're a swine. Get back into your cell again." He turned to me.

"You didn't pick a very good companion for your trip."

"One learns by one's mistakes, but it's always too late then," I replied.

The interrogation went on. There were days and weeks of it. The court-martial was set up. Counsel were appointed. They did their best to separate the proceedings against Colepaugh from my own case, arguing that I had been a soldier while Colepaugh was a traitor. But they did not succeed. The opening day of the trial loomed ahead. I was approaching my end with uncanny speed.

# CHAPTER 14

## IN THE SHADOW OF THE SCAFFOLD

In my prison cell in Fort Jay, New York State, to which I had been moved after the F.B.I. interrogations had been brought to a close, I became acquainted with the dull, crushing monotony of prison life and the feeling of inward rebellion against it. My cell was a sort of wire cage through the mesh of which it was just possible to push a cigarette. It was kept immaculately clean and was big enough to enable me to walk six steps forward and six steps backwards. It was lit by a 200-watt lamp which burned throughout the day and night. A camp-bed provided a minimum degree of comfort for sleeping.

I had now become a captive of the American Army. My fellow prisoners in Fort Jay, whom I saw only rarely, were American soldiers serving sentences for insubordination, cowardice and similar military delinquencies. The guards were men of the military police. The warders wore military uniform and had military rank. One of them, Corporal Kelly, used to push cigarettes through the cage for me and would stand guard so that I should not be caught enjoying my forbidden smoke.

"My brother," he explained, "is a prisoner-of-war in Germany, and I only hope he's got a warder who can carry on like a human being."

I hoped so too. I had got out of the way of recoiling at the harshness of war, but was very much affected whenever in the midst of it all I came across a man who thought and acted in a human way.

I was the pride of Fort Jay and was visited every day by high-ranking service officers. Three or four times a day the door would be opened, the sentry would call "Attention!" and I would grasp my trousers (my belt having been taken away just as my shoe-laces had been removed as a suicide precaution), and stagger towards the staff officers.

They were, without exception, friendly and chivalrous towards me. They enquired searchingly as to how I was treated, whether the quality of the food was to my satisfaction and if I had any requests. These were unfailingly granted so far as lay within their power.

It took me some time to get accustomed to this treatment. I simply could not understand why they should treat an enemy so fairly. The treatment meted out to me was quite different from that which fell to the lot of my Judas friend, Billy Colepaugh. I had already noticed with the F.B.I. that they were particularly nice to me whenever Billy was around. It went something like this:

"Is there anything you want, Mr. Gimpel?" from the warder.

"No, thank you."

"Have you any complaints?"

"No complaints either."

"Unfortunately I may not bring you whisky, but perhaps we can offer you some other form of refreshment?"

"Bring me a Coca-Cola."

Once a colonel visited me.

"How far do you walk each day?" he asked.

I looked at him uncomprehendingly.

"They do allow you exercise, don't they, Mr. Gimpel?"

"I do all my walking in my cell," I replied.

His face coloured up, and he had the officer-of-the-guard called.

"Every prisoner has the right to fresh air," he barked at him. "Can you explain why you have not allowed Mr.

Gimpel to leave his cell?"

"How can I, sir?" answered the captain. "I have strict instructions not to allow him any contact with the other prisoners."

"Then just lock the others up for the required length of time," said the colonel.

He offered me a cigarette, lit it for me and added:

"It won't do these fellows any harm."

After that, every day at dusk I was allowed to take a turn in the enormous court-yard of Fort Jay. The guards watched me at my exercise. Once they clapped as I passed them, and the cook asked me if the food he prepared was to my liking. I was, as I have said, the pride of Fort Jay. Another prisoner was the former trumpet soloist of Benny Goodman's orchestra. He performed every evening to the delight of guards and prisoners and instead of the Last Post played "Good-night, Baby." He had been sentenced on account of some military misdeed, and was soon to be released. His warders granted his every wish. They all enjoyed his music. . . .

I had been about three weeks in Fort Jay when things took a serious turn. I was told that Major Charles E. Reagin and Major John E. Haigney had come to see me. I was taken to the visitors' room. Both men were middle-aged, slim and very personable. They were extremely nice to me and introduced themselves with such perfect courtesy that we might have been meeting at the Waldorf Hotel for a business conference.

"If you are agreeable," they began, "we are prepared to take on your defence."

"I am most grateful to you," I replied. "Of course I am agreeable."

"We are familiar with your evidence," said Reagin. "From the legal point of view your case is quite clear."

"Yes," I said.

We sat down and cigarettes were handed round.

"We will conduct your defence with every means at our disposal, that we can promise you. We can also assure you that the court will in no way limit your defence. As a matter of fact, the court has just recently assembled. President Roosevelt directed the matter personally."

"And what do you think my chances are?" I asked.

The major looked me calmly in the eye.

"Legally speaking," he replied, "they're nil. You must know that as well as I do. I think it would be foolish to have any illusions on that score."

I nodded.

"However, in spite of that I do not regard your case as hopeless," continued Reagin. "If Germany capitulates, that will probably save your life, but if the war goes on, you'll be hanged. It's really a race between your life and the end of the war. It can't go on much longer. The Russians are at the Oder and our troops are in the Ruhr."

"You've certainly brought me some good news," I said.

"We must drag out the proceedings as long as we possibly can," Reagin went on. "And I'll tell you this: We will use every trick we can think up; we'll make things as difficult for the prosecution as we possibly can. In the first place we'll delay the start of the case. We've not yet completed our study of the documents. That will dispose of a week. And now listen carefully to what I have to say."

The major got to his feet and paced up and down the room. He had a fresh, healthy complexion. On his left breast he wore a row of medal ribbons. He spoke with emphasis but without raising his voice, and underlined his words with economical, unobtrusive gestures.

"They will call you into the witness box. They will ask you if you are guilty or not guilty. If you say you are guilty you are as good as dead already. Don't worry about the depositions you have already made to the F.B.I. That counts for nothing in a court of law. Just stand up there and think and do what you like — as far as I am concerned you can scratch your backside if you want to — but whatever else you do, say as loudly as you can, 'Not Guilty!' "

The two majors shook hands with me and departed. Both had a fine reputation in the Army. They were the best counsel I could have had and they went all out for me in such a way that it was hard to imagine that they belonged to a people against whom I had been sent to spy.

"It was bad luck," Major Haigney had said to me at our first meeting, "that you were caught, but you're fortunate in that you will appear before an American court. Just think what it would have been like if you'd been on the other side and had fallen into the hands of Reich Security, for instance."

The distractions which the warders did their best to provide for me, the chivalrous treatment and the businesslike conversations with my counsel could not close my eyes to the one ghastly certainty that my days were numbered.

Any court-martial in the world would sentence me to death. That was beyond all possible doubt, and there could be no appeal against this judgment. It was unalterable. I could present a plea for pardon to the American President but it would only be a waste of paper.

When you have perhaps only three or four more weeks of life in front of you, the tendency is to thrust aside all thought of the final hour. But at the end of each day the thought that you're one day nearer the grave comes home with added force. You can think of death in a manly way when you've not been sentenced to death, but heroics die a natural death of their own in the shadow of the scaffold. Before you meet your own death, the phrase 'Death for the Fatherland' dies. Those who preached it, did not, alas, die that way.

The anxiety, the fear, the horror, came ever closer and I became their prey. I counted the meshes in my wire cage — once I got to ten thousand — but while I tried to divert myself by some mechanical means, fear clawed at my back, dried up my mouth and caused the sweat to stream from my pores. Sometimes I tore up and down like a madman, racking my brains day and night for some possibility of escape from prison or some legal loophole to escape the hangman.

During this period, in the course of which my mind and my nerves were approaching breaking point, I received another visit from some senior American officers. A colonel and two majors had me called to the Interrogation Room. The colonel was tall and broad-shouldered and looked like an overfed physical training instructor. One of his companions was short and frail-looking and had a pale, pointed face with a somewhat fanatical expression; the other one wore an ashblond moustache on a completely expressionless face. I always took a good look at any visitors I had as I was glad of any break in the monotony, however meaningless.

"How do you do?" said the colonel. "Do sit down. Can I offer you a cigarette?"

"Thank you."

He pushed a whole packet of Camels across the table to me.

"We've come straight from Washington," he began. "It was a long journey, but let's hope it will prove worth while for you."

I listened carefully.

"You know what lies in front of you?"

"I'm being reminded of it half a dozen times every day," I replied.

314

He stood up and walked round the table. He held a long cigar between his fat fingers and puffed quick little clouds of blue smoke into the air.

"We are from the O.S.S.," he said, "the Office of Strategic Service. You know, of course, what that is."

"Of course," I replied. "I've already met some of your agents somewhere."

The O.S.S. was the military espionage organisation of the United States. The German M.I. had sparred with it with varying degrees of skill.

"We have a proposition to put to you. . . . You don't have to make up your mind at once, but in any case, listen carefully."

He remained standing.

"Who do you think is going to win the war?" he asked.

I remained silent.

"Come, come," he said jovially. "Let's leave hopes and fears on one side for the moment. You've got a good head — use it! Have you really any doubt that we are going to win the war?"

"No."

"Good," he said. "Germany hasn't a chance now."

"That may be so."

"It is so."

The thin major with the fanatical expression now took a hand in the conversation.

"I'll be delighted to give you details," he said. "Yesterday there was a particularly heavy air attack on Berlin. Field-Marshal Model has shot himself in the Ruhr. Eleven Gauleiters have deserted. If you like, I'll give you the names. . . . The German people, or at any rate those who have taken no part in the war crimes, want only one thing, peace. Every day by which the war is shortened means less bloodshed. And it's mostly German blood that's being shed now."

"That's true," I said.

"I'm glad you're amenable to reason," said the major. "I think we're going to get along well together."

"What actually do you want with me?"

"You are going to be hanged," said the colonel.

"Thanks to your readiness to give information, that fact is already abundantly clear to me."

There was a pause, and I looked from one officer to the other. The massive colonel appeared to be quite indifferent. The major with the fanatical expression was staring out of the window. The third officer was carefully studying his well-kept finger-nails. There was plenty of time, time for everyone, except me. For me, time had run out, or hadn't it?

"You could work for us," said the colonel.

I remained silent.

"You can, for example, sit down at your Morse keyboard and make a few transmissions to Germany which interest us."

"So you want to turn me into a double-crosser?"

"Put it that way if you must," replied the colonel.

"It would be treason."

"No," interrupted the colonel. "I believe that in present circumstances it would be the greatest service you could do your country."

"You would be preventing more bloodshed," said one major.

"And you would save your own head," put in the other. "I imagine that is an argument you won't want to dismiss out of hand."

There was another pause. My mind worked feverishly. The offer was certainly attractive. As I considered it a terrible weariness came over me. What I should most of all have liked to do at that moment was to lie down and go to sleep. Temptation, soft, insidious, temptation! Freedom! Release from the prison cage! Release from the cell, from fear of the judge, from the threat of the gallows! Back perhaps to Joan, to Joan of whom I thought day and night, whom I saw constantly before my eyes, near enough to touch, and who disappeared as soon as I stretched out my hands towards her.

The war was as good as over. Lost. Everything had been in vain. The blood that was shed in Russia, the losses in Africa, the suffering in France, all for nothing. All for a system of government that had deserved its collapse a hundred, thousand-fold. The continuance of hostilities now was pointless except for the purpose of gaining a few more months for the ruling clique before they were overtaken by their inevitable doom. During the past weeks I had had opportunity enough to ponder well on many things which formerly I had obstinately thrust away from me. It had become clear to me that in this war one could not serve Germany without at the same time becoming a tool of Hitler.

But I had realised this too late. I might have considered turning against Hitler, but against Germany — never.

"No," I answered the colonel, "I can't do

it. Just think for a moment if you were in captivity in Germany and it was suggested to you that you should work against America, what would your answer be?"

He remained silent.

"We could force you," interrupted one of the two majors.

"You might shoot me but you could never force me."

There was a painful silence. After a while the colonel took up the conversation again.

"There is no need for you to reach a decision today. We will call again tomorrow. I have this proposition to make to you, that you enter our service. I am not sure yet how we can make use of you. Perhaps you can broadcast to the German people. You have seen now what things look like in America, and you have yourself admitted that Germany will lose the war. You are the only man who could make this clear to your fellow-countrymen. When the war is over they will thank you. If you accept this proposition you are a free man, with certain conditions, of course. When the war is over you may leave America or remain here, as you wish. The decision on that rests entirely with you. You will not have to appear before a court-martial. The American newspapers know absolutely nothing about you. Do I make myself clear? There simply would be no German spy Gimpel. There would just be a German reader for Allied broadcasts to Germany for whom we should have to think up a name and a background story."

He stopped speaking, remained standing and looked me fixedly in the eyes. The two majors also looked hard at me. A few seconds passed. The electric fan was humming softly. It was warm in the room. The Americans have the unfortunate habit of overdoing the central heating. In front of the window a whistle sounded; the guard was being changed. Then I heard my fellow-prisoner from Benny Goodman's orchestra play a few bars on his trumpet. Then came laughter, and footsteps sounded outside the door. A man stopped in the corridor and then walked slowly away again. . . .

The officers were still staring at me. Once again I felt that dry feeling in my mouth. I passed my tongue over my lips a few times. They were parched. I wanted to say something but no word came. It didn't matter anyhow. What I wanted to say I could not say and what I had to say they knew already.

"It's damned hot in here," said one of

the two majors. He opened a window and looked out for a moment into the yard.

I took a cigarette from the packet of Camels the colonel had produced. He gave me a light and put his hand on my shoulder.

"You can let us have your decision tomorrow morning at ten. Your fate is in your own hands. You can be your own hangman, of course, if you want it that way."

I went back into my cage, and threw myself down on the bed. I felt a mixture of hate, fear, defiance and self-pity well up in me. What I should really have liked to do at that moment was to shriek and at the same time weep. Senselessly I beat my hands against the wire mesh.

"O.K. boy," a warder called out laughing. "I know what you want." He pushed a cigarette through for me.

My two counsel came to see me. I told them of the offer I had received from the O.S.S. They shrugged their shoulders and made no attempt to influence me, but later Major Reagin said:

"I never expected you'd do any differently, and I must say I wouldn't have been too keen on defending you if at that juncture you had wavered in your attitude. To me, you are a soldier, nothing more, nothing less. I am a soldier too. Actually the only thing that distinguishes us is the colour of our uniform, and our language, of course."

Meanwhile my counsel's manoeuvre had come off and the case was postponed for a week.

"As I see it," said Reagin, "the war will come to an end in May 1945. We are short of four weeks. How we can get over the difficulty I don't quite know. The case begins on the 6th February and will last at least a week. Sentence will be executed about four weeks after its pronouncement, that is to say, roughly in the second week in April. I reckon that the war will come to an end in the second week of May but those damned four weeks may cost you your life."

I was certainly in a strange situation. My sole chance of survival lay in the immediate capitulation of my Fatherland. It was a terrible position to be in. The annihilation of Germany was the condition for my continuing in the land of the living. I could, I should, I must speculate on total surrender. Meanwhile my brother had fallen at Stalingrad, my father had been wounded in the First World War, my closest friends had fallen in the north, the east and the west, millions had fallen for Führer and Fatherland, and the architect of all this misery was at the last moment to desert by suicide. . . .

My warders did all they could to cheer me up, but I was my own worst enemy. Strangely enough, my appetite for life increased and day and night I plagued myself with thoughts of all the things I had missed. My mind was full of fantasies which would have been good material for a psychiatrist. I drove in Cadillacs, bathed at Miami, kissed tall, slim, beautiful women, ordered expensive made-to-measure suits, ate lobster mayonnaise and counted out thousand dollar bills. I bought jewellery and drank champagne, and ate pounds of caviare which I had never actually cared for.

Then my father was there again.

I saw his drawn, lined face. I felt his hunger, his fear of the bombs, his anxiety for me — after all, I was all he had now, and he would probably have me for only three more weeks. He had no idea where I was and he could have no conception of the situation in which I now found myself.

My superiors in Berlin must of course be aware of what was happening, but they would take great care not to give away any details. When Dr. S. of Reich Security learned that I had been caught, he swore vigorously to himself.

A conference of colleagues was called and they discussed whether I would be likely to hold my tongue under F.B.I. interrogation. Most of them believed I would, and not without justification. I did, in fact, succeed in keeping secret the names of our men who were working in America or who had worked for us there, but it must be admitted that I owe my steadfastness largely to the fair treatment I received at the hands of the F.B.I. who made no serious attempt to coerce me.

My fate was naturally of no special concern to my colleagues at Reich Security. They were all very much concerned with their own affairs, preparing their get-away. Most of them were trying to find some way of slipping out to Spain. One of them started a new life for himself with the proceeds from my gold watch and other personal valuables which I had been obliged to leave behind in the safe of the Reich Security Central Office in Berlin.

My case was still being kept a close secret and I still cannot imagine how the F.B.I. and the Army authorities succeeded in keeping the high-pressure American journalists away from me. But still no Gimpel story appeared in the press. The repercussions of the landing of U-1230 in Frenchman Bay were, however, felt in innermost government circles and President Roosevelt himself ordered the convening of the court-martial which was to try me. I must say that they did one-time Agent 146 of the German M.I. every honour.

The Army order for the opening of the trial was signed by General T. A. Terry. At the judge's table sat Colonels Clinton J. Harrold, Lathrop R. Bullens and John B. Grier and in addition, one lieutenant-colonel and three majors sat with the jury. The case for the prosecution was conducted by Major Robert Carey and First-Lieutenant Kenneth F. Graf. The leading Public Prosecutor of the U.S.A. — he was entitled to be referred to as Your Honour — attended as observer and adviser. Next to him sat the leading Public Prosecutor for the State of New York.

The case was heard in a government building on Governor's Island. The general commanding the Second Army Corps also had his headquarters there. I was taken there in a closed car in handcuffs. Billy travelled in a second car. The Army had taken enormous trouble to see that we were kept apart, but in any case we had no desire for contact.

It was at this point that I saw the first reporters. They had no idea what was going on but the preparations for the court-martial had not escaped their notice and they had stationed themselves with flash-light apparatus and newsreel cameras at the entrance to the court. They were waging a desperate battle with the military police, and needless to say the military police won.

As soon as I entered the building my handcuffs were removed. I was to appear before the judges as a free man. The corridors reeked of cleanliness. It was a modern building with a pleasant atmosphere. The room in which the case was to be heard was on the ground floor. It was not very big and was filled to capacity.

Nearly all the people there were either Navy or Army officers. In the background of my own case, the Navy and the Army were conducting a private battle, trying to push the blame for my successful landing on to each other. The domestic arguments had in fact become very heated and neither arm of the American forces was disposed to spare the other. Among the many witnesses who had been summoned were several high-ranking officers who were responsible for the coastal defences of the State of Maine. They all left the witness box with red faces.

On the 6th February at 9 a.m. sharp I was led into the room. To the left and right of me walked members of the military police. Much decorated war heroes had been selected to be my guards, and everything had been done to make a good spectacle and achieve the maximum effect. On the President's table which was draped with the Stars and Stripes lay an enormous wooden gavel. An outsize portrait head of Roosevelt stared at me with icy indifference from out its wooden frame.

Everyone stared at me. I sat down between the two majors who were my counsel and they nodded to me encouragingly. One minute later Billy was brought in and one could positively feel the wave of animosity that greeted his arrival. There was much hissing and whispering.

Before the proceedings began, everyone had to stand; members of the jury, counsel for the prosecution, counsel for the defence, the court personnel and everyone present had to take the oath that they would preserve secrecy on all details of the case.

The President, Colonel Clinton J. Harrold (like all other members of the court, he was in uniform), took his wooden gavel and brought it down ceremoniously three times on the table. Harrold was tall, slim, grey-haired and fresh-complexioned. He spoke slowly and very distinctly, weighing every word. He was so soigné in both manner and appearance that he might have been a candidate for the American Presidency appearing before the television cameras.

"The Session has begun," he said.

# CHAPTER 15

## SENTENCED TO DEATH

Major Carey, counsel for the prosecution, rose briskly from his seat. He was small and wiry, had black hair, a pale, austere face and dark, staring eyes. He spoke very distinctly and very convincingly. Naturally the Army had put forward its best prosecutor.

That morning, my warder had said to me:

"Go carefully with Carey. That man's darned dangerous."

I had already met the major. The law demanded that he must serve the indictment on me personally and at the same time formally acquaint me of the fact that I was to stand trial. This formal pronouncement had to be made while I was a free citizen and that was why the handcuffs were removed.

While the major was reeling off his little speech I had noticed that he was holding his right arm bent behind his back. I thought at first that he must have been wounded in the war and had got into the habit of holding his injured hand out of the way, but I learned later that he had been holding a loaded revolver. He was so utterly convinced of the truth of his indictment, which described me as the most dangerous German spy, that he had regarded the loaded revolver as a necessary precaution.

"With the Court's permission," Carey began now — he spoke slowly in a deep voice, and mouthed his words with an almost coquettish precision — "I will open the case for the prosecution. The United States of America against Erich Gimpel and William Curtis Colepaugh."

"Please begin," said the President.

Major Carey struck a pose. His voice took on a brighter ring and he seemed to become more personally involved in what he was doing. All the same it was obvious that to him it was all a matter of routine. He had done the same thing hundreds of times before. I, on the other hand, was appearing in a court of law for the first time in my life. If there was anything which I feared as much as the sentence it was the trial itself.

I took a look at the members of the court commission, and as I glanced from one to the other I felt that there was an impenetrable veil between us.

"The prisoners, Erich Gimpel and William Curtis Colepaugh," continued Carey, "enemies of the United States, in the month of November 1944, secretly and in civilian dress and acting upon the instructions of the German Reich, an enemy nation at war, passed through the coast and land defences of the United States with the intention of carrying out espionage and other hostile activities. The prosecution is prepared to present evidence of this in the course of these proceedings."

Carey seated himself slowly. He leaned back, riffled through the files in front of him and assumed an attitude of cool boredom. The President of the court, Colonel Clinton J. Harrold, threw a glance in Carey's direction. The prosecutor rose to his feet again, walked a few paces towards me, looked me in the face and then raised his voice:

"I now ask the accused, Erich Gimpel, if he admits his guilt within the terms of the prosecution."

I stood up, but Major Haigney, one of my counsel, forestalled me.

"Before we proceed with the case," he said, addressing himself to the President, "may I, as counsel for Mr. Gimpel, make a submission?"

"Please proceed," said the President.

Haigney paused for effect.

"This court," began the major, "is trying two men, one of whom is a German and the other an American citizen. Germany and America are at war with one another. They are declared enemies. Counsel for the defence is of the opinion that it is not fitting to try a traitor, as Colepaugh is, together with a German patriot, even if he is an enemy of this country. I do not wish to anticipate events, but everyone present knows that the other prisoner, Colepaugh, is the lowest type of American ever to stand trial, and counsel for the defence is of the opinion that the justifiable indignation of the American people at what Colepaugh has done will automatically be transferred to my client, whose actions according to the evidence are to be judged by quite different standards."

The President interrupted him.

"You submit, in fact, that there should be two cases?"

"That is exactly what I wish to submit," said Haigney.

Carey was on the spot at once. He tried to nullify Haigney's proposal with legal arguments. The court evidently was undecided and there developed a vigorous legal duologue which went on over two hours, the greater part of which was beyond my comprehension. All I gathered was that my counsel maintained that the proceedings would be simplified by separating the Colepaugh and Gimpel cases, whereas counsel for the prosecution held the opposite view. The court withdrew for an hour to discuss the point. Then once again the President banged his gavel on the table.

"The submission put forward by counsel for the defence has been rejected by the court," he announced. He then turned to Major Carey.

"Please proceed," he said.

Once more the major came up to me.

"I ask the accused, Gimpel, to answer the charge, guilty, or not guilty."

I stood up. It is a strange experience to be suddenly the cynosure of several hundred eyes. I had now to follow the advice of my counsel. I knew little of the juristic background of the case. I thought only that it would sound strange when I now protested my innocence after having admitted in the course of the interrogation which preceded the case that I had come to America with the express intention of spying. I tried to conceal the uncertainty in my voice and looked straight ahead of me as I said, as I had been bidden:

"Not guilty."

The same question was now put to Colepaugh, and he too declared that he was not guilty.

The prosecutor now began to build up his case point by point, disclosing some exceptionally fine work on the part of the F.B.I. who had succeeded in tracing back practically every step we had taken on American soil. He also revealed that the American Secret Service knew details about our past lives which we found positively astonishing. Billy's strange route from Boston to Berlin was accurately reproduced in all its stages. Major Carey even knew the names of the German officials who had been in touch with him. He produced Billy's reports from the naval academy, and drew attention to the collaboration of the former American sea cadet with German diplomatic missions.

As far as my own past was concerned, Major Carey's account was a bright nosegay of the true and the false, of exaggerations and wrong imputations. Nevertheless, it was amazing with what care the F.B.I. had X-rayed my past.

The break for luncheon was not made until after midday and the President then allowed only an hour. The case for the prosecution was then resumed. It was about four in the afternoon. Carey remained noticeably detached and unmoved. He now seemed something like an over-pedantic schoolmaster lecturing about the Thirty Years' War in an institute of adult education. I could not imagine why I had been told that he was particularly fanatic and aggressive, but I was soon to learn.

At the end of our respective biographies, Carey said:

"I have shown how the two accused arrived in the United States by enemy U-boat to work against us. I have today reconstructed their route from Frenchman Bay via Portland and Boston to New York, and I have narrated their activities in New York. A whole crowd of witnesses is waiting outside, and we can start cross-examining them straight away. But before we pass on to that I should like to introduce an entirely new point into the case."

His apparent boredom, his weary indifference, his pedantic matter-of-factness suddenly fell from him. He stood there now, quiet, cynical, obviously feeling his power. He straightened himself, his voice became penetrating, his gaze wandered from one to the other, over us the accused, the defence, the court, and back to the spectators.

"It is now my duty to present proof that the two accused have in fact caused infinite suffering. The matter does not rest with the mission which they failed to fulfil." He paused. Then his voice became louder, more penetrating. His whole countenance seemed to be aflame and his eyes had a fanatical glint.

"I maintain no more and no less," he said with infuriating slowness, "than that forty-seven gallant American sailors paid with their life blood for the entry of these men into our country. I put it to you that the grain steamer s.s. *Cornwallis* was betrayed through short-wave transmission by Gimpel to U-boat 1230, and that this act of betrayal cost the lives of forty-seven men, citizens of this country."

"I protest," called my counsel, Major Haigney, in a loud voice. "This occurrence has nothing whatever to do with the substance of the prosecution."

"We will see about that," answered Carey with vigour.

"Protest rejected," said the President. He leaned back and added *sotto voce:* "The court commission has no more intention of limiting the rights of the prosecution than

336

of limiting the rights of the defence. Please proceed, Major Carey."

A fleeting smile passed across Carey's face. He was in his element. He leaned slightly forward. At that moment he looked alarmingly small and frail, but from that moment he was to drive the proceedings forward, blow for blow, remorselessly, without respite.

"I request the court to call First-Lieutenant Frank C. Gordon of the American Navy as witness."

The colonel nodded.

The man who stepped into the witness-box looked the typical American officer. He was of medium height, powerfully built and sun-tanned. He gave his replies loudly, with precision and without looking to the right or left.

Carey began his examination.

"Where are you stationed, Lieutenant?"

"In East Atlantic Coast Headquarters."

"What do you do there?"

"I am responsible for the area."

"Would you please explain your function more precisely?"

"I am responsible for seeing that all sections of the coast are evenly covered by air and sea patrols in accordance with a precisely laid plan."

"So you work in collaboration with the Air Force?"

"Yes sir, we complement each other's function."

"And what are your terms of reference from the military point of view?"

"Our instructions are to attack and destroy the enemy, to protect our own ocean traffic, and to keep the sea lanes open."

The lieutenant gave his reply smartly and automatically. It was obvious that he had repeated the words over and over again in dozens of instruction sessions.

I had no idea what Major Carey could be driving at. Actually at that moment I knew nothing of the disaster which had taken place on the high seas on the 3rd December, 1944. It was the only point in the indictment on which I was completely innocent, but the prosecutor made it his business to see that the occurrence should redound very much to my discredit, at any rate from the psychological point of view.

"So the matter of defence against U-boats is also in your sphere," continued Carey.

"Of course, sir," replied Lieutenant Gordon.

"When did you record the last U-boat attack?"

"I protest," called one of my counsel.

"This question has nothing to do with the matter under discussion."

"I would ask you to leave the matter of how I conduct the prosecution to me," replied Carey with severity.

The President took no part in this battle of words. The argument went this way and that till finally he put in the decisive word.

"The court considers that the question as to the date of the last U-boat attack is justified. The objection cannot be allowed. Please continue, Major."

Carey passed his tongue over his lips. He held out a document to the lieutenant.

"I have here a report from the few survivors of the grain steamer s.s. *Cornwallis*. Do you recognize the signature?"

"Yes, sir. It is the signature of Admiral Felix Gygax, Commander of North Group Navy."

The major turned quickly to the President, and laid the document on his table.

"I present this document as evidence."

"I protest in the strongest possible terms," called Haigney.

"Why?" asked the President.

"The prosecution is making no attempt to keep to the facts of the case. The sinking of the grain ship has nothing whatever to do with the terms of the indictment already presented. The prosecution is obviously attempting with the help of the forty-seven dead of s.s. *Cornwallis* to influence the court against my client. It is an attempt to whip up emotion and animosity which is unworthy of an American court of law."

"This document," interrupted Major Carey, "is signed by an admiral. I have selected this report from a whole pile of documents because it presents in the clearest and most concise way possible the essential facts of the case. . . . It is clear proof that a German U-boat — and we know that this U-boat was U-1230 — torpedoed a grain ship which was sailing with lights on, without any previous warning. I strongly protest that the official report of an American admiral should be described as an unworthy attempt to whip up feeling."

The atmosphere of the court-room was at fever pitch. Major Carey's dramatic revelation had not failed to gain its effect. It had still not been decided whether the document could be allowed as evidence or not, but in the course of the heated discussion which followed, the prosecutor succeeded in introducing, not without a certain relish, the most gruesome details of the death of the forty-seven sailors.

"I uphold my protest," said Haigney. "I consider it out of order to admit this document as evidence."

The President addressed him sharply:

"I should be obliged if you would leave it to the court to decide what is admissible and what is not."

Then my second counsel took a hand.

"I should like to put a few questions to the witness," said Major Reagin. "You are carrying a brief-case, Lieutenant, and I assume that it contains all the documents relevant to the sinking of s.s. *Cornwallis*."

"That's right," replied the officer.

"Please open your brief-case," said Reagin, "and take out the documents. Now, have you also got the official report of the sinking of s.s. *Cornwallis* in front of you?"

"Yes, sir."

"Will you please look at it," said Reagin, "and tell us what is given there as the reason for sinking."

"It is stated that the ship was in all probability destroyed by an enemy U-boat."

"And what is the meaning of 'in all probability'?"

"It means that the authorities can imagine no other cause."

"But that does not mean," Major Reagin continued sternly, "that there could be no other cause."

"No, of course not."

It was plain that Reagin felt a sense of achievement.

"What other reason could you suggest?"

"A mine, sir."

"But you cannot say with certainty that it was a mine?"

"No, certainly not."

"I would like to point out," said Carey, "that in this operational zone there are no enemy mines."

In his eagerness he had for the first time run straight into the trap set by my defence.

"Who said," interrupted Reagin with delight, "that it might have been an enemy mine? I ask you, Lieutenant," and he turned now to the witness, "whether in this area mines are laid for coastal defence?"

"Yes, they are," answered Gordon reluctantly.

"It would therefore be quite possible that s.s. *Cornwallis* ran into an American mine?"

"That possibility cannot be excluded."

"Thank you," said Reagin.

He turned with a bow to the President and smiled.

"I leave it to the court," he said, "to draw its own conclusions from this piece of evidence. And I should like to repeat that I consider that the way in which the prosecutor has attempted to use an unhappy accident of war which we all regret to trip up the accused, to be unfair and un-American. I request that the matter of s.s. *Cornwallis* be excluded from the case."

The President nodded.

"The court will have to decide upon that when they are considering their verdict. The court is now adjourned until to-morrow."

The case proceeded with nerve-racking slowness. The court investigated everything so thoroughly that I could no longer be in any doubt as to the outcome of the case. For hours on end my counsel battled with Major Carey. Victory and defeat followed on one another in tantalising sequence, but my counsel were really defending a hopeless case, and displaying their forensic skill on a dead horse.

My case had by now appeared in the press, without comment. On the first day of the proceedings a press photographer had caught me and my picture had appeared with the caption "An Enemy Spy."

The newspapers did not know the details of the case, and I cannot say that the photograph they reproduced was particularly flattering. Anyhow I attached no special importance to it at the time. But this photograph was to bring about a situation which — I think it was on the fifth day of the case — was to leave me shattered and helpless.

The President opened the session as usual with cool, gentlemanly detachment.

I think it was the thirtieth witness who was being cross-examined. Everyone who in any way had come in contact with me, the first taxi-driver, the sausage salesman, the man at the newspaper stand, the hotel porters, even the charwomen, all were questioned.

The President, consulting a small scrap of paper in his hand, announced:

"Another witness has reported. She is waiting outside. We could hear her now."

"I attach no importance to her," Carey said at once.

"The defence is of the opinion that no possibility of establishing the true facts should be excluded," said Reagin.

"Then the court will hear her," said the

colonel. He motioned to the bullet-headed sergeant at the door. The man went out. For just a minute subdued conversation could be heard in the court-room. Then the door opened slowly. I did not at once look in that direction. It was only when everyone else had turned round that I took a look at the witness.

I got the shock of my life. I wanted to jump up, run towards her and rush her away. I wanted to scream, to implore, to threaten, but I remained seated in my chair as if rooted to the spot.

"Your name?" asked the President.

She walked up to him confidently. She was tall, slim and lovely. She looked straight ahead. Only as she passed me did she throw a quick glance in my direction. It was a sad, an infinitely sad look.

"My name is Joan Kenneth," she said. "I am an American citizen. I live in New York and run a small fashion shop."

She gave her personal details.

"You know the accused?"

"Yes," she replied.

"Where did you meet him?"

"In the apartment of a mutual friend."

"When?"

"Six weeks ago."

"Did you know," asked Major Carey,

345

"that the accused was a German spy?"

"No," answered Joan quietly.

Carey turned to the President. "I cannot see how this witness is relevant to the case," he said.

The President hesitated for a moment.

"But I can!" Reagin broke in before I could stop him. "I should like to put a few questions to you, Miss Kenneth, with the court's permission."

"Allowed," said Colonel Harrold.

Joan turned towards me. She looked at me. Her face was pale, she tried to smile at me but somehow the smile went astray. She made a helpless gesture with her hand as if she wanted to come to me and comfort me. She ignored all the men who were staring at her, the strained surprise on the faces of the court, the lurking hatred of the prosecutor.

"Why have you offered yourself as a witness?" asked Major Reagin with caution.

"Because I have a close relationship with the accused."

"What am I to understand by that?"

"I love him," said Joan simply.

For a few seconds there was a complete silence in the court-room.

"You may be surprised to hear me say that," continued Joan, "in view of the fact that the accused is an enemy of our country. I do not know if the work he did here was bad or harmful . . . the war is to blame for everything, and everyone who is in the service of war is also its victim. I am a woman and a woman knows a man far better than men can ever know him, and as a woman there is something I must tell you."

She paused for a while. The words came with difficulty. She swallowed. No one but Reagin attempted to meet her half-way, but it seemed she did not need this.

I could not take my eyes off her. Until this moment I had followed the case with a sort of numb indifference. Now I felt worked up. Pain, excitement, and a feeling of suffocation came over me. I felt like shouting: "Leave her alone. Tell her she must be quiet. All this is our affair, ours alone. It's nothing to do with anyone else, the court, the defence or the prosecution. Hang me, hang me if you like, but leave her alone!"

I forgot time and place. I saw and heard nothing more. Everything was spinning in front of my eyes. Faster, louder, faster, faster! It was suddenly as if a roundabout was there, with figures with human faces, evil, mocking faces. And in the midst of them stood Joan, and everything was dancing around her. They all wanted to get hold of her, to drag her into the mud. But she smiled and looked through the roundabout at me, looked me straight in the face, and once more I was standing beside her just as I had stood on Christmas Eve. . . .

We had opened the window because the room was too hot. We were standing close together and I put my arm round her. The cool night air fanned our faces. We stood there without saying a word. We already knew all there was to say to each other. I drew her to me more closely and we kissed. Our nearness took on a new beauty as time, war, fear, everything fell away from us. The future and the past fused into the present, into this one hour which was ours alone. No power in the world, no state, no country, no war, no court of justice could rob us of our golden hour.

"It's just as if I had always known you," said Joan. "I've been waiting for you always, only for you, and I've always known what you would be like."

I forgot everything, I looked into her eyes and we kissed again. To me it was a painful happiness . . .

And then came the end, the morning,

flight. It was all over. It had to be all over, for Joan's sake. And Joan would always hate me.

But she didn't! She understood! She understood the incomprehensible. She knew why I had left her. If I had not left her I would have gone away with her, fled into happiness, happiness that knew no frontiers, no tears, no wars. If only I had put everything behind me. What a fool I had been. . . .

"The accused is a man, a human being," Joan said quietly. "He feels as a man, he thinks as a man, he lives as a man. I do not know in what light he has been presented here, but if this man has done anything which is punishable by law I must ask you to remember that you are not sitting in judgment on a barbarian but on a man who is loved by a woman, a woman who is a citizen of this country."

The court-room was silent. No one said a word. All eyes were on Joan, on her dear face, her lovely hair, her graceful figure, her elegant fur coat. The President turned to Major Carey.

"Do you wish to cross-examine the witness?"

"No, thank you," said the prosecutor.

"Does the defence wish to put any questions?" asked the colonel.

"No, thank you," said Reagin quickly.

He looked round the room. Joan had really had no evidence to give, but no one had remained unaffected by what she had said, and in an American court feeling counts for a good deal. The dead of the *Cornwallis* were being weighed against the love of a young American woman.

"You are dismissed," the President told Joan.

For a second she hesitated, and once more she turned to me. We looked at each other, our lips tightly compressed. Then she tightened her grip on her handbag and walked calmly and confidently to the door. Each one of her retreating footsteps was like a pain in my heart. The wound had been torn wide open, for I had glimpsed once more the happiness which was to be denied to me for ever.

Joan was an important psychological factor in my defence, but what had the matter of my defence to do with our love?

The case went on, endlessly, relentlessly. I followed it with something akin to apathy, as witness followed witness, gave evidence, took the oath and went. The arraignment of the officers of the American coastal defences was a nice little titbit of military scandal for those who could extract any enjoyment from the situation. They certainly got a severe handling. The witnesses entered the court-room as pale as if they had been the accused. Every bit of negligence and carelessness was censured in the harshest terms. My judges were all military men who were very much at home on matters of defence.

When the fifteen-year-old scout, Johnny Miller, stepped into the witness-box, the lamentable spectacle reached its climax. The boy, a bright lad who seemed much older than his years, described how he had discovered our footprints but had tried in vain to apprise the American authorities of our arrival. Perhaps it was only my impression, but it seemed to me that both the prosecution and the President cross-examined Miller with special thoroughness. Finally, Colonel Harrold said:

"You have shown courage and foresight, my boy, and I feel it is my duty on behalf of the American people to thank you for your action. You have demonstrated a greater feeling of responsibility than many a grown man and indeed many an officer who was explicitly entrusted with the task of guarding his homeland."

The hearing of the evidence was concluded. For six whole days there had been a tug-of-war between prosecution and defence and there was no doubt that the prosecution was winning. But that went without saying. Anyhow, the rope they were tugging at was to become a rope for my neck . . .

The seventh day brought the final pleadings. This, of course, produced nothing new, but Major Carey, the prosecutor, who at the start of the proceedings had so firmly refused to recognise any distinction between my case and Billy's, suddenly changed his tactics. He could see which way the wind was blowing and he did it for effect. He abandoned the attitude of contempt and constant accusation and became almost chivalrous. He knew he had led me up to the noose and thought it superfluous to dance about on the corpse.

Mr. Tom C. Clark, the Chief Public Prosecutor, who so far had functioned only as an observer, spoke at the end:

"I have not a great deal to say about Gimpel, the accused. He stood before us and told us that he had nothing to say. I am sure he realised what lay in store for him when he left his homeland. He will see his own situation as the American national hero, Nathan Hale, saw his when he said before his execution: 'I regret that I have only one life to lay down for my country.'

"The case of Colepaugh is quite different. He is a traitor, a liar and a deserter. In the first place he betrayed his country, then he betrayed Germany and then he betrayed his comrade Gimpel. There is only one thing for him, the rope."

The court withdrew to consider its verdict. Another forty-eight hours passed. Then they took me back into the courtroom. There was a deathly silence. Everyone knew what was coming. The court commission entered the room, and we stood up. The President called my name and I walked up to the judge's table.

"Erich Gimpel, as President of this Court it is my duty to inform you of the sentence which has been passed upon you. You have been found guilty on all charges . . ."

The Judge stood up. He did not look at me as he spoke the words which I shall never forget. ". . . to be hanged by the neck until dead."

# CHAPTER 16

## SIZED UP BY THE HANGMAN

In four days, the rope, thirteen times knotted in accordance with the grim rules of hanging, would encircle my neck. I had ninety-six hours left in which to think and breathe, and then the horror of the night, the waiting in the cell, the choking sensation in the throat, all that would be over.

I paced my wire cage at Fort Jay like a madman. The hours, the minutes lay upon me heavily as lead, now oppressing me, now rushing away from me, now standing still, now stretching themselves like some grim accompaniment to my fear of imminent death.

My forehead streamed with sweat, my tongue was as dry as a piece of old leather. I drank indiscriminately everything I was given, and I was given everything I asked for. The prison officials viewed me either with timid side-long glances or with grinning embarrassment. They nearly all felt sorry for me, but with Americans sympathy often shows itself in strange guises.

I was an exhibition piece. Everyone was brought to see me before I was hanged, everyone, that is, who was on good terms with Fort Jay and its commandant, everyone who counted for something in the Army. I was seldom alone. Nearly all my visitors shook me feelingly by the hand, told me things which I did not understand and wanted me to tell them things which I did not know. They asked me how I was and it sounded facetious, but it was worse than that, it was just a habit.

The sun rose as on every other day, the hour had sixty minutes and the minutes had sixty seconds. The children played, the mothers laughed and the men went to work as they always did. The typists arrived at their offices just as usual and told each other about their little adventures of the previous night. The lift boys said their 'good mornings,' and the recruits were marched up and down on the barrack squares. The world went its normal way, but for me everything was abnormal. In four days' time I would know no more.

The verdict had been given just five weeks before. The judgment was clear. There could be no appeal. My counsel shook hands with me. Major Reagin said:

"It was a privilege to represent you, Mr. Gimpel."

He gave me a cigarette and offered me a light. My hands were already in chains. Just twenty seconds after the verdict had been made known a military policeman had clapped the handcuffs on me. It appeared that they were to accompany me through the days which still remained to me.

"You made a good impression in court," continued Reagin. "If there's one thing I can't stand it's an abject defendant. You can't imagine some of the cases I've had to handle."

I nodded.

"Keep your chin up," said Reagin, "at any rate while you can. The verdict will now go to the Supreme Court and will be examined to see if there have been any faults in the procedure, but I'm afraid they won't find anything."

"And then?" I asked.

"There's still the possibility of a petition to the President."

"But there wouldn't be much point in that?"

"As good as none at all," replied Reagin, "at any rate while the war's still on. But a petition has at least one advantage — it

shows you're not a dyed-in-the-wool Nazi.
. . . Many men who've been sentenced could perhaps have saved their lives if they had not been too proud to petition the President."

"Would you please prepare the petition?" I asked. I tried to smile but I don't know if I succeeded.

"I'll keep in touch with you," said Reagin, "and let you know what's happening. I'll visit you every week. Let me know if you have any complaints about the way you are treated. I can always have anything like that put right at once."

We shook hands.

"I should have liked to spare you the handcuffs," he said, "but I'm afraid that's not possible. That's a rule that can't be changed."

A week passed, then a second week, then a third and a fourth. I had now reached the point when an official came to me for the address of my next-of-kin in Germany. I knew what that meant. The chef enquired what I wished to eat during the next few days. I knew what that meant. The Army chaplain enquired whether he could visit me, and I knew what that meant, too. . . .

When I gave them my father's address I had to pause for a few seconds to remember where my father was living. How far, how long, how hopelessly all my past life seemed to lie behind me.

I called to mind the man whose face, bearing, eyes and nose I had inherited, together with a liking for forbidden things. When I was three years old I had stood beside my mother's coffin, still too young to realise what was happening, and I had grown up at Father's side, in that silent, matter-of-fact comradeship which is often brought into being between father and son by the early death of the mother. As a boy I had done all the things I ought not to have done. Once when I was playing football in the street I scored a goal and the ball went right through a café window. I quickly retrieved my ball from the heap of broken glass before the proprietress shooed me off with her broom. I was two hours late getting home, and was full of the darkest forebodings. But when I arrived back, my father had already paid for the damage.

"You're not frightened, are you?" he asked.

"Yes," I admitted in a small voice.

"Don't be silly," continued Father. "Do you imagine I never did anything like that when I was a boy?"

What would he be doing now? Would he

be thinking about me? He had never questioned me about my work.

"I just don't want to know," he said once. "You know what you're doing and there's only one thing I want. When the war is over I want you back, sound and healthy."

When the war is over. . . .

Johnny, my warder, arrived and pushed a lighted cigarette through the wire mesh.

"Hurry," he said. "With you, you never know who might be coming along."

"Edward," he called after a while — all the men called me by my assumed name — "things aren't nearly so bad as you imagine."

"I'm sure they're not," I replied.

"I read a book recently," continued Johnny, "written by a schoolmaster. It was about the American War of Independence."

"Very interesting," I replied.

"But listen," said Johnny. "A man was condemned to death and they hung him on a tree. He was already strung up when the pardon came through. They cut him off the rope again."

"Do you think that's what might happen with me?"

"I must admit it's improbable," answered Johnny, "but I'm telling you about it for this reason: afterwards the man wrote a book on what it felt like to be hanged. He said that you feel terribly afraid at first and then suddenly you don't feel anything more. Suddenly everything becomes soft and gentle and easy and you feel you're already in another world and that the last moments of your life are far more beautiful than you've ever imagined . . . Only," continued Johnny, "when they cut him off the rope and tried artificial respiration on him he suffered the most terrible pain."

I tried not to listen to any more. Johnny was a fool, but he was harmless and good natured. He really was trying to comfort me, but his comfort was horrifying. He had a frank, youthful face. One finger of his left hand was paralysed through an injury which had got him his cushy job at Fort Jay. He wrote letters to all his friends and relatives, telling them about me. I was the adventure of his life. But the adventure was to come to an end in ninety-six hours.

I felt I would go mad at the thought of it.

A sergeant entered my cell. I had never seen him before. He was a frail-looking fellow with a sharp little face and a certain nonchalance about his dress that you could almost call slovenliness. He shook hands with me, at the same time looking past me out of the window. He had small, dark eyes which could not keep still. He came just about up to my shoulder.

"Is there anything you want, Mr. Gimpel?" he asked.

"No," I replied.

"Is the food to your liking?"

"Yes."

"Would you like a cigarette?"

"Yes."

I took it. The man observed me from the side. He looked at me in a sort of business-like way, carefully sizing me up. I took one or two quick draws at the cigarette, wishing the fellow would go to the devil. "He's had his look at me now," I thought. "And he's had a word with me. Now he can go and write his postcard to his girl-friend."

But he stayed on and walked all round me. When I took my eyes off him his stealthy sideways glance was there again. I felt instinctively that he wanted something of me, something uncanny, something horrible, something shudderingly frightful.

"Unfortunately I'm not allowed to give you anything to read," he said. "That's a very strict rule here. That is, nothing but the Bible."

"I have the Bible already."

"Well, so long," he said. He shook hands with me, looked past me once again and walked off.

"Hi, you!" called Johnny. "Do you know who that was?"

"Of course I don't."

Johnny was all excitement.

"That was the hangman," he said. "He came to get an idea of your weight and measurements so that he'll know what he's got to do. He's taken your measurements for sure. Didn't you notice him? Didn't you know that everyone in here gets a new rope? Money's no object here."

He laughed. He just couldn't keep his mouth shut. He kept pushing cigarettes through the wire to me, just blabbing out whatever came into his mind. He was a fool, such a fool, but an honest, well-meaning fellow.

"Johnny," I said. "How much longer have I got to live?"

"I don't know," he replied. "You never know the exact time until one night before, but I think they're coming for you on April 15th. I heard something of the sort."

At eleven o'clock they called me to the Commandant. For a moment I was relieved of my handcuffs.

"Mr. Gimpel," he said. "I have something to tell you. The President has rejected your petition for pardon. That means that the death sentence can now be carried out. You will be told twelve hours before execution when it is to be."

He had a small mouth, a straight nose and a round head. I kept repeating this description to myself so as not to lose my grip.

"So far you have borne yourself like a man. Keep it up. Good morning."

I was back in my cell again, alone once more. Once more a prey to time and idle chatter.

What was my life? Would it not be all to the good for it to be brought to an end? A saying came to my mind and I kept repeating it aloud to myself:

"Better an end with fear than a fear without end."

It would soon be all over. They would carry me out in a simple wooden coffin and my body would be used for purposes of anatomical research.

"Here, gentlemen, you see the liver, the spleen and the gall bladder," the professor would lecture. "The heart was quite sound. How does one reach that conclusion, Mr. Miller?"

Never again would I see the cherry trees in bloom, never again would I hold a woman in my arms, never again would I sit at the wheel of a car, never again would I hear the trumpet of Louis Armstrong or the trombone of Tommy Dorsey. Never again . . . never again . . . never again. . . .

The women in my life passed through my mind. I stood at the rail of the *Drottningholm* — it was 1940 — and at my side stood the blonde Swedish girl, Karen S., in a wispy summer dress, the wind playing with her hair.

"Come with me. I know my father will like you. He likes your type. We can get married. I'm not badly off and the war will then be over for you. If you love me, come with me."

"I do love you," I replied.

"You don't love me."

I kissed her.

Later I said: "When the war's over."

When the war's over. What nonsense. . . .

And then I saw Margarete, my pert little Berliner.

"Don't be crazy," she said. "Stay here. Don't go to America. Everyone says you'll never come back. You're mad to go. Just look at this Billy, look at his ape-like arms, look at his shifty eyes. He'll give you away, you can be sure of that. A woman feels these things. Stay here in Germany, stay with me."

How many of fate's warning lights had I ignored!

And then Joan; Joan, tall, slim, graceful.

"It's odd," she said, "I've a feeling that we've known each other for such a long time. . . . I always seem to know in advance what you're going to say and what you're thinking. Men like you always say what they think and they think straight."

She put her arms round me and I looked into her eyes. Time stood still. Dare I kiss her? Dare I love her? Dare I bind her life to the curse that clung to my life as a spy? Heart and head were at variance. We laughed, we whispered, we kissed. Then in a few hours it was all over and I had to leave her.

Was an hour then the same length as an hour now? Now, as I waited for the sergeant with the sharp little face who was expertly to tie the thirteen knots about my neck? I threw myself on to my cell bed only to jerk myself up again in the same moment.

Once again I was bathed in sweat, once more there was the dryness in my mouth, my tongue like a piece of leather. "No, don't think about it! Keep away from it!" I told myself. "Think of something else! Think of the good things of life! Keep off this thrice-damned war! Keep off your own accursed end! Best of all, make your mind a blank!"

And then I saw the motto of Reich Security in front of me and heard one of my chiefs say:

"Leave thinking to horses; they've got bigger heads."

It was now ten o'clock and Johnny was relieved. He'd be back again at twelve. His colleague immediately offered me a cigarette. It was odd how at Fort Jay all the regulations were punctiliously observed except that concerning smoking. All the prison officers made an exception of smoking.

A G.I. from the kitchen brought me a mid-morning snack, coffee, rolls, butter and marmalade.

"Now eat up today," he said, putting the food on the small cell table. "You can't go on like this, you know. You left half your food yesterday. Take a cue from the others, they eat like horses."

"I don't want anything."

"You're only making matters worse," he said. "Keep your stomach full and the world takes on a different look."

He grinned.

"You need a good square meal," he said.

"Oh, shut up!" I said.

We weren't exactly refined at Fort Jay but we understood each other.

"The chef wants to know what you'd like to eat tomorrow," continued the soldier from the kitchen. "He says he knows how to do a goose in the European way with chestnut puree. He'll roast one for you, if you like."

"No, thank you," I said. "It doesn't appeal to me at all. All I want is to be left in peace. Now shut the door from the outside, will you?"

"Right you are," he replied, and went on: "I don't know, the others always seem to be in better spirits when I visit them."

"Well, the others aren't going to be hanged the day after tomorrow."

"True enough," he agreed, and finally took himself off.

For a quarter of an hour everything was quiet. I lay on the bed and tried to sleep, but of course it was hopeless.

There was still today. And tomorrow. And the next day. Then, I told myself for the hundredth time, it would be all over. They would come for me at five o'clock in the morning. They would offer me a last cigarette. The death sentence would once more be read out to me. It was short enough and it would not take long. Then they would put me in a black jacket, with a hood, and I would have to put the hood on my head. Then they would take me to the place of execution. It was a little outside Fort Jay. As a rule no one was executed in Fort Jay. Fort Jay was military territory, and the military was not the competent body for executions, not at any rate in the ordinary course of events. Prisoners under sentence of death were sent to Sing Sing in New York State and there put in the electric chair.

But I had been expressly sentenced to death by hanging and Sing Sing was not the place for that. Therefore the matter of execution had been left within the province of Fort Jay. That was why there had been all the excitement, the constant visits, the care for me personally. It was only the attraction of something novel — my execution was something out of the ordinary for Fort Jay.

Until now I had never thought much about death. Who does think of death when he's young and healthy? To me dying had always been something that lay a long time off. When I was seventy or eighty perhaps, or even later. When you're old and tired, when you've lost all interest in food, when your eyesight's failing and your hands are shaking, then you might perhaps give a thought to the eternal sleep, and in the circumstances the thought may not be unpleasant. Then one day you close your eyes for good and people say:

"Well, well, poor old Erich. He lived to a good old age; it was time for him to pop off."

But I wasn't old, damn it, I didn't want to die. Damn it again, I wanted to live, to live like everyone else who was young and healthy.

I looked in the mirror. I was certainly rather paler and thinner than I had been, but apart from that I looked just about the same. And yet I was to be in the land of the living for only a few more days, a few more days, another ninety-four hours and a few minutes and then a notice would be posted at the gate of Fort Jay:

"For espionage, sabotage and conspiracy against the United States of America, the German citizen Erich Gimpel, alias Edward Green, was hanged by the rope this morning at 5:13. According to the results of the medical examination, death occurred seventy seconds after execution. Gimpel was found guilty by court martial. The Supreme Court of the United States confirmed the death sentence. A petition from the German spy for mercy was refused by the President."

It was now twelve o'clock and Johnny had come back.

"Here I am again," he called.

"So I see," I replied.

This time I was glad he was on duty again. His chatter was preferable to my own thoughts. But I could not stop my thoughts from straying constantly to the grim scene in the half-light of dawn. I could not help thinking of the unthinkable. Years before I had seen a film about Mata Hari. It was a piece of sentimental trash with a tragic end. Practically everyone in the cinema was in tears, but I was laughing. I think Margarete was with me and she too had tears in her eyes. The woman spy wore a dark dress and had a face well suited to the tragedy of execution. She wore a silver cross round her neck, and this she kissed and presented to her wardress. The wardress wept. A soldier in a steel helmet entered, his face twitching. He was a young French lieutenant.

"My duty, Madam," he said.

Any who had so far restrained themselves now finally gave way to tears, but I laughed even louder. The lieutenant's voice sounded hoarse.

"I can't think why she's being executed if she's so noble," I said to my companion.

A woman behind me told me angrily to keep quiet.

Mata Hari was led down a seemingly endless corridor. One saw her from the front, the back, the side. Above all one saw her face. From every angle it looked equally beautiful and noble and sad and lost.

Then at last the corridor came to an end and she stepped out into the open air. There was a dense mist. Suddenly a group of soldiers appeared. They were all wearing a funereal expression for the occasion. "Wonderful," I thought. "Soldiers can usually think of something better to do with a beautiful woman than shoot her." Then the salvo was heard and Mata Hari died slowly and photogenically.

How would I die? Would I call out? Would I try to tear myself free? Would I scream for help? What's left of the photogenic, heroic approach to death when the hangman is close upon one's heels?

371

"Hi, Edward!" called Johnny. "Would you like to have a word with the chaplain?"

"No," I replied.

"Don't be a fool," he said. "He's a nice chap. I can thoroughly recommend him."

The parson wore the uniform of an Army captain. He was tall, slim and broad shouldered, and somehow combined the figure of a baseball player with the nobility of a gentleman rider. And he didn't seem a bit pious. That was why I took to him immediately.

"This is a terrible business," he began. He walked up and down. "We can speak about it quite openly. It's easier to talk about death than to die. That's where you've got the advantage of me straight away."

"Well said, Captain," I replied.

He smiled.

"I am only a captain as a side-line," he said. "You know of course that I'm a priest. The uniform is just camouflage."

"There's no need for you to camouflage yourself," I replied.

We shook hands. For the first time in days I felt relaxed. For the first time I forgot what lay in front of me.

"I don't want to get on your nerves," said the priest, "and don't worry, I'm not going to preach a sermon to you. Unfortunately, everything that's coming is your own affair. Somehow you've got to come to terms with it yourself. I only wish I could help you a little." He looked at his finger-nails. "Easy to talk, isn't it?"

"But you talk well, Captain."

We then went on to talk about baseball and gangster films. After half an hour he made to go but I asked him to stay. The soldier from the kitchen brought my midday meal.

"I could eat a second portion," I said smiling.

"Well, look now, at last he's seeing reason," he said.

We ate together. The priest told me his name and where he came from. He had in fact been a baseball player at the university and was a well-known member of the team. He had wanted to become an engineer.

"And why did you become a priest?"

"That's a long story," he said, "and you probably won't understand it. I was not what you might call a friend of the Church."

"What happened?"

"I became a priest in spite of that. My young sister died. How shall I explain it to you? I loved her more than anything else in the world. I used to cut lectures and go for walks with her. At five she was a real little lady. She had real charm. I just don't know how to explain it to you. You can't imagine how sweet she was."

"And then?"

"She was run over by a lorry. Seven years ago. I think I lost my reason for a while. My parents had been dead a long time and I had been alone in the world with my sister. There was no consolation for me. Not a glimmer of understanding. To this day I don't know how I survived that period. It took me months, years even, to get over it."

I had kept my eyes averted and now I looked at his face. Every word he spoke was genuine, direct, convincing. He got to his feet and paced up and down. His face, which for a few moments had looked rigid, became animated again.

"Then you see," he said, "I became a priest. For just that reason, really. Just to be able to stand by people who have to get through something like I had been through, to help them keep their grip."

"Yes," I replied.

"You see," he continued, "you're one of those who've somehow got to get through a spot like that."

"I think I'll manage," I replied. "And even if I don't, it won't do anyone else any harm."

He was quiet. We smoked away, sitting together on the bed, so closely that our shoulders touched.

"Have you ever prayed?" he asked me.

"Yes, of course. But it's a long time ago now, when I was a child. When I grew up I forgot how to pray."

"That's how it is with so many people," he said. "They just forget. But it often comes back to them again." He stood up.

"I'll come again tomorrow. That is, if it's all right with you. I'll come any time you want to see me."

We shook hands.

Prayer. . . . Could I pray? Should I pray? Ought I to pray?

I tried to remember how it had been when I was a child, the organ playing in church and the parson giving the blessing. I was wearing my first dark blue suit with long trousers, and the burning candles were giving off that holy fragrance which all my life I had avoided. . . .

I tried to remember the words of the prayer, but it was a long time before I could recall them, and then I could not get them past my lips. All the same, I determined I would try to pray.

"Our Father," I said to myself, "which art in Heaven."

I said it again and again, mechanically, dully, until it began to take on some meaning.

Who had thought of prayer in the terrible time just past? Reich Security had abolished all such things — God, Heaven, the work of Christ. There was only one thing which it was unable to abolish: death, dying, the end. Death took no account of Reich Security.

It was now two o'clock in the afternoon. Once more Johnny was relieved. There was a good deal of scurrying about in the cell block of Fort Jay today and I could hear the soft thudding of rubber boots in the corridor all the time. My new warder was very correct. I wanted to smoke, but I had no matches. I called him. He did not answer. Perhaps he was afraid of reprimand.

At about three o'clock in the afternoon the officer-of-the-guard came to see me.

"Everything all right?" he asked.

"Yes, so far," I said.

"Good."

"I could do with a glass of whisky," I said.

"Apart from your freedom that's the only thing I can't give you, but," he reflected for a moment, "perhaps we can just go along to my office for one. I know what it's like without a drink." He sat down on my bed. "Have you had a word with the chaplain?"

"Yes."

"I'm glad."

A G.I. ran excitedly along the corridor. Suddenly I heard shouts. I strained to hear what was happening but I couldn't gather what it was all about.

The Captain got up with a sigh. A G.I., red in the face, rushed into the cell. He was just about to blurt out something but the officer motioned to him and they withdrew into a corner.

I had got into the way of lip-reading and I kept my eyes on the mouths of the soldier and the officer as they spoke. Something quite extraordinary must have happened, something which had cut right across the normal routine of Fort Jay.

I watched the G.I.'s lips and I thought I had grasped what he was saying. Yes, I did understand, but surely . . . it couldn't be true!

The G.I. had said: "Roosevelt is dead."

The whole of America heard this same

piece of news at that moment . . . Roosevelt is dead. The man in the White House had died, from a haemorrhage of the brain. Roosevelt was dead. . . .

The officer came up to me and put his hand on my shoulder.

"This is a bit of luck for you," he said.

"Why?" I asked.

"The President is dead. That means that there will be four weeks' state mourning."

"And what's the use of that to me?" I asked.

"During the period of state mourning no death sentences will be carried out."

The officer left. I could hardly believe my ears. Franklin Delano Roosevelt had done me a good turn. . . .

# CHAPTER 17

## GERMANY'S CAPITULATION
## SAVES MY LIFE

The truth of what the officer had said was confirmed on the morning appointed for my execution. It did not take place. A few hours later, relayed by all American radio stations, the ceremonial obsequies for Franklin Delano Roosevelt began. I listened to everything and understood nothing. I had to get used to the idea that I was still alive, I had to thank pure chance that I was not already hanged, and adjustment to the new situation came slowly. The congratulations of my warders were almost overwhelming. They all wanted to shake me by the hand. A sergeant said laughing:

"We'd rather have you alive than dead."

"That goes for me too," I replied. No one took it amiss that I preferred Roosevelt's death to my own.

Four weeks' postponement! What an eternity it seemed, and at the same time how short a respite! The war in Europe was approaching its end by leaps and bounds. You could almost work it out on your fingers when the last bomb would be dropped. Capitulation was imminent. But how imminent? Days? Weeks? My counsel were confident. All America was confident. I wanted to be confident, too, but one day I ran into my hangman in the yard at Fort Jay, and once more I became anxious and unsettled. . . .

Germany's capitulation happened, so to speak, with the utmost punctuality, and once more I received congratulations from every side. I waited impatiently for my final pardon, but it did not come. Still, there was no talk about hanging. It seemed as if they had simply forgotten all about me.

Then I was moved. In American style. I was dragged through half America in handcuffs, the handcuffs being required by the regulations, for which my escorts apologised at least three times a day. There were some remarkable scenes: people stared at me, schoolboys ran after me, and shoppers in the streets stood to watch me go by.

My journey took me by long-distance express train through the States of New York, via Pennsylvania, Ohio, Indiana and Illinois to Missouri. At St. Louis we had to leave our comfortable train for a six-hour wait. My escorting officer said:

"I want to look up some friends here, and I can't take you around with me, so I'll put you in the city gaol for a few hours."

"All right," I said.

"I don't know what the food's like there," he continued, "so I think we'd better eat out."

We stayed in the station restaurant and never in my life have I eaten in such strange circumstances. There was a private dining-room there, but this was occupied by a choral society, so we had to go into the main part of the restaurant.

My handcuffs were now removed, but my guard was not going to miss an opportunity for a piece of real American showmanship and he placed four tall military policemen around the table with their machine guns trained straight on to my plate. They looked very war-like standing with their arms at the ready while I ate my steak.

The table next to us was occupied by some members of the American Women's Army Corps, the WACS, and they kept looking over at me. They evidently thought that I was an American soldier who was being punished for some military misdeed and kept making rude noises at my guards and sticking their tongues out. One of them, a tall slim blonde, went up to the officer in charge and said:

"Don't make such heavy weather of it, boys, or are you afraid of him?"

The officer kept a straight face and the girls went on making fun of him.

I ate my ice-cream and then they took me to the city gaol in a jeep.

"You'll survive a few hours here," said my escort.

I was taken in charge by a tough-looking warder. While the formalities of introduction were taking their course I had to put my hands on the table as everything was taken out of my pockets and listed. This did not amount to a great deal. Above the desk of the guard on duty I read in large letters:

"If you don't like it, tell us. If you do like it, tell your friends."

I had to laugh out loud.

"There's no need to put you in a cell," said the warder, who was much nicer after my guard had withdrawn. "You look such a good boy. What have you been up to? Are you hungry?"

"No," I replied.

"You'll soon get used to eating," he replied. "None of them are hungry when they first come in, but when they go they're all eating like horses."

I was put in a cell for a few hours, after all, and then I was fetched. My journey continued by car right across Missouri to Kansas. I was then delivered to Leavenworth prison and my escorts took friendly leave of me.

I was put into the Fort at the outset. I was later to be transferred to the civilian penitentiary, but during those first few days I came into contact with death in the most horrible way.

Five German soldiers were executed. It was all quite senseless. Just because they had declined to petition the American President for pardon.

They had been prisoners-of-war. Two opposing factions had come into being in their camp, one of which co-operated with the Americans, the other working against them. Certain denunciations had been made and men were continually being betrayed to the camp authorities.

The prisoner responsible for these betrayals lost a letter and this led to his being found out. There was a skirmish and in the course of it he was lynched. In the heat of the moment the camp authorities grabbed five men as scapegoats. Whether they were in any way guilty in fact no one knew, but they were sentenced to death for murder. The sentence would immediately have been set aside if they had agreed to present a petition for pardon, but one of the five, a fanatical Nazi, declared:

"As a German soldier I refuse to petition an American President."

The five condemned men remained obdurate to all pleas, threats or arguments and just let themselves be hanged in Fort Leavenworth. I saw them a few hours before their end, their faces pale and distorted with hatred. They were the war's last fanatics. . . .

The Leavenworth penitentiary houses more than 2,400 prisoners. I was given number 62008. I was now among the men who were to be my constant companions for the next ten years of my life — murderers, procurers, thieves and bank-robbers. They all had their criminal records and were proud of them. Prisons have their own quite rigid hierarchy. At the top of the tree are the bank-robbers, but murderers are outsiders. Petty thieves rank as small fry while burglars and housebreakers are well regarded. As for the procurers, no one can abide them.

Spies occupied no clearly defined place in the criminal hierarchy. They were assessed according to the way in which they conducted themselves in captivity. The same applied to the élite of the American communists who were my fellow-prisoners for a while. They and I succeeded in achieving good rank and high prestige.

But I am anticipating. First I entered the quarantine block where I had to stay for four weeks. Quarantine must have been an invention of the devil. Everyone concerned seemed to take a positive delight in my discomfiture. I, for my part, thought it would be a matter of taking certain hygienic measures but it was in fact a sort of novitiate training to accustom the prisoner to the discipline, the drill and the change-over to a new way of life with a number and striped clothing.

The warders wore uniform. Some of them were men, some were machines, and I was to have some interesting experiences with them, to say the least. I did not at all like the man who received me at the quarantine block. He had a coarse, florid face, shouted louder than was necessary and used insulting and offensive forms of expression to tease and torment me. It was just as well that he did only six hours duty at a time and was then relieved. The man who took over from him was more tolerable, but even he was by no means as good natured as he looked.

"Oh, ho," he said, "so your name's Gimpel. Funny name. Now what have you been up to? Oh, espionage! Well, you should have left that alone. You'll realise that. You'll have plenty of time to think about it."

The prisoners called him the Pumpkin. All the warders had nicknames. All their peculiarities, their habits, their gestures were very keenly observed by the prisoners, and many of them were almost completely in the prisoners' hands. The Pumpkin pursued a middle path. Working in the quarantine block he had an easier time than his colleagues outside. After all, he was occupied with beginners and could always fall back on having the regulations tightened up.

There were twenty of us and we were isolated. Our course of instruction was to begin on the following morning, in the lecture room to start with. The Inspector appeared in person.

"Smoking is not allowed," he said. "Anyone found smoking will be sent to the 'house.'"

The 'house.' That was solitary, close

confinement with bread and water and no exercise.

"We want no laughing here. No walking; everything at the double. If a warder speaks to you, you must stand to attention at once and answer 'yes' or 'no.' If there is any answering back you will be sent to the 'house.' The same applies for any rudeness, or carelessness."

He went on barking out his lecture. He had given it every month for twenty years. His face was grey and drawn. He had trouble with his stomach, and dyspeptic prison overseers are never very popular.

"You may go to church if you wish every Sunday. You may have your hair cut once a month. You may take a shower twice a week. If you behave yourselves you can go to the cinema once a week, but there won't be any crime films or love films. You already know how criminals carry on and you don't need love in here. If you work you get paid and you can buy chocolate, biscuits, sweets, shaving soap and cigarettes in the canteen. You can have two packets of cigarettes a week, that's enough for you." He ran his eyes over us. Then he continued.

"Anyone who won't listen to instructions must take the consequences. Anyone who doesn't shave will be sent to the 'house.' Likewise anyone who leaves his jacket buttons undone. The 'house' is always ready for you. Remember that. We've plenty of single cells."

Some of us laughed while he was delivering his lecture, but laughter was soon to desert us. At bedmaking, for instance. The edges of the pillows had to be damped so that they did not slip. There were the most trifling regulations. An American prison has a devilish resemblance to a German barracks.

We had to learn our rights and duties by heart.

"What are you allowed?" I was asked.

"Two razor blades a week."

"A month, you fool."

"And what else?"

"Earphones for the radio."

"How long for?"

"Till nine at night, sir."

The Pumpkin grinned.

"When you get outside again you can listen longer," he remarked. "But for the present you're staying here. And don't forget the 'house.' It's lonely there. Not at all nice. You'll see."

Every day we were taken last into the dining hall. We had to sit down without speaking and take our soup in silence. Once we had to get under the tables because of disobedience. Our tin plates were overturned and the meat fell on the floor. It was not replaced. After that I made a practice of eating my meat first and have retained the habit to this day.

At first my fellow convicts were very reserved in their attitude towards me. I was an outsider. It was true that I had the distinction of a life-sentence, but the deeds of a spy were appraised with some discrimination in the penitentiary.

One day, however, I succeeded in gaining the full acclaim of my fellow prisoners. For twenty-four hours on end I was the sole topic of conversation in Leavenworth and was thereafter received into the society of old lags.

We were sitting in the dining hall as on every other day. Everyone had his own place at table. The chef, himself a prisoner, came along and ladled out the food. He spoke German. He bent over me.

"There are two packets of Camels under the table," he whispered. "Don't forget to take them with you."

I thought he was joking. The tables had no drawers and their under-surfaces were quite flat. Surreptitiously I felt about underneath and discovered that the chef had cleverly wedged a fork there and had impaled the cigarettes on to the fork. I pushed them into my pocket, feeling not too happy about the situation, for fellow prisoners at the same table must have noticed something and the warders always noticed any disturbance, however slight.

"Right!" shouted the 'Rat,' the most unpopular of our overseers, when the meal was over. "Stand up!"

We all jumped up from our chairs like automatons and the march out of the room proceeded in precise order. In due course it was the turn of our table to file out. We went silently, one after the other.

"Halt!" called the Rat. Then: "Hands up!"

Our pockets were searched as we left the dining hall. It all went very rapidly as prisoner after prisoner left the room.

I flung my arms up. I had the two packets of cigarettes wedged between my fingers. The Rat stood in front of me, small, puny, suspicious. If he had pulled himself to his full height, his head would just have reached to my shoulder. He tapped my pockets, got impatient, and then thrust both hands into them. Meanwhile the other prisoners were standing around. He found nothing. His face turned scarlet. He had made a fool of himself. The prisoners were all grinning now.

I went on standing there with my hands in the air, the cigarettes between my fingers. Everyone could see them except the Rat.

"Get on, back to your work!" he shouted. Then he barked at me: "Be off with you! What are you hanging about for?"

I let my hands drop and shoved the cigarettes into my pocket as quickly as I could. Then I ran off as fast as my legs would carry me. My trick had won me my spurs.

I managed to get through the four weeks quarantine period without a visit to the 'house.' I was promoted to the rank of a 'proper' convict, was moved to the main section of the prison and became eligible for the usual privileges.

I was amazed at how many Germans there were among my fellow convicts. Most of them had been sentenced as recalcitrant prisoners-of-war or as associates of the German M.I. I met Hermann Lang, said to have been responsible for the leakage of information to Germany about a bomb-directing device. I also got to know an American of German descent who had been a prison guard and had allowed German prisoners-of-war to escape. I found myself in contact with some remarkable types and learned some extraordinary histories.

The cell I occupied was the one in which Cook, the self-styled North Pole explorer, had done remission for his ludicrous imposture. Cook had declared that he had reached the North Pole and his success had been acclaimed all over the world until it was revealed that he had never been there. America never forgave him for having made a fool of his country and he remained in prison until he died.

My fate remained uncertain. Technically I was still under sentence of death. My counsel had presented a second petition to Mr. Truman. Actually this was unconstitutional as the decision to reject it had already been made by Truman's predecessor.

The war in Europe had now been over for several months, and I had become an accomplished coal-heaver. I had to shift forty tons each day, with no Sundays off. I could not manage this formidable quota alone, and was assisted by two hefty Negroes. In other respects, and inside the prison, coloured men and whites were strictly segregated, but in regard to the most despised form of labour, coal-heaving, no race distinction was observed. I had to thank the governor of Leavenworth for this edifying job. He detested me. Contrary to all regulations, he had neither been present to receive me nor was he to appear to take leave of me. However, my departure was to take place a few years later in strange circumstances. . . .

My fellow convicts, and particularly the Germans among them, were most friendly towards me. Immediately upon my arrival there, a former prisoner-of-war presented me with a packet containing sweets, soap and cigarettes to the value of ten dollars. To a prisoner this represented a veritable fortune. They all worked together to help to make things bearable for me. At first, when I returned to my cell from my coal-heaving activities, I fell literally flat with exhaustion; gradually, however, my biceps developed until I had muscles like a prize-fighter. Once I got into an argument with an ex-housebreaker and knocked him out. From that moment I became a member of the ruling class of Leavenworth.

One September evening in 1945, I was listening to my favourite band (Tommy Dorsey) on the radio. The programme came to an end at eight o'clock and the news followed on. I felt like tugging the earphones off with annoyance, but for some reason left them there.

There were political reports from all over the world and I listened desultorily to the account of some sort of disagreement with the Russians. Then came the news from Washington. Suddenly I sprang from my bed as if electrified. I had heard my own name quite plainly, without a shadow of doubt. The news reader went on slowly and carefully. He could not know, of course, what his words meant to me:

"President Truman has today commuted the death sentence of the German spy, Erich Gimpel, to one of life imprisonment. Gimpel made an illegal entry into the United States at the end of last year on board a German U-boat, to spy out atomic secrets. The F.B.I. succeeded in catching him. An American court-martial sentenced him to death by hanging. Execution was postponed indefinitely after the sudden death of Mr. Roosevelt."

My companions congratulated me excitedly. A warder came, stuck his head in the window, and said:

"Did you hear, Gimpel? So you can keep your head. Some people are lucky."

The American President had held a press conference at the White House that afternoon and the time had been taken up with political questions. The session had already lasted nearly two and a half hours when Mr. Truman read out my pardon. About a hundred American journalists were present. I got the details from the newspaper the following day.

"Why have you pardoned Gimpel?" President Truman was asked.

"Gimpel was a spy," replied Truman, "and a spy is a man who fights for his country. No country in the world fights a war without spies. We, of course, had our own spies in Germany. It is customary to hang spies during a war, but it is also customary to pardon them when the war is over."

The President had smiled woodenly into the flash-lights of the press cameras.

"For that reason I decided to commute the death sentence to one of life imprisonment."

I was to feel the influence of the invisible governor of Leavenworth for some time yet. I heaved coal for four years. The monotony of the work at first dulled all thought, but later my anxieties became ever more insistent.

Was my father still alive? What was it like in Germany now? Would I ever leave prison? Would this eternal waiting, this unchanging hopelessness, this life in which a few cigarettes or a bit of chocolate could be of paramount importance, would this ever come to an end? Would I ever again speak with men who neither boasted about crime nor protested innocence? Would I ever again hold a woman in my arms? Would I ever again enter a restaurant as a free man and choose what I wanted to eat?

One day I was taken off coal-heaving and drafted to some excavation work. At first I could not imagine why. Then suddenly I realised. I took a closer look at the man who was digging opposite me and I recognised him.

It was Dasch.

Dasch the traitor, the murderer of his comrades, the man who was responsible for the fact that the six German agents who had regarded him as a colleague, had died on the electric chair.

He shovelled away slowly. No one talked to him. He was despised by all prisoners alike, whether German or American. He looked deliberately right past me. Very rarely did he make any attempt to talk, for he knew well enough that no one would answer him.

Out of the 2,400 men in Leavenworth who between them had broken all the ten commandments, the traitors alone were singled out for ostracism. Even among this company of pimps, robbers and murderers, a traitor was always an outsider.

We were exactly facing each other, separated only by a ridiculously shallow ditch about six feet wide. The prison governor had seen to it that we were placed like this. Each of us had a spade handy, a good solid American spade. I would only have to give him a blow. No doubt that is what everyone in Leavenworth was waiting for. But they waited in vain. The man who worked facing me was a prisoner of his own thoughts. He was on the martyr's pile of his own conscience, pilloried by his own crime. He had been a Judas-friend, and he knew it.

I got used to Dasch. I looked past him as he looked past me. Later I mastered myself sufficiently to exchange a few trifling words with him. He was small and seedy-looking. He was obviously frightened, and looked as if he never had enough sleep. Perhaps the last desperate cries of his victims still sounded in his ears. Perhaps he could see them before him, dying with a curse on their lips, one slowly, another quickly, according to how their bodies reacted to the electric charge. Perhaps he saw before him the simple cheap wooden coffins in which the bodies of his comrades were taken away for medical dissection. I didn't know and I couldn't worry my head about him. Our respective backgrounds were known in Leavenworth and the men were surprised that my spade didn't some day somehow slip out of my hand. . . .

"Of course you know what's the matter with Dasch, don't you?" a fellow prisoner asked me one day.

"Of course," I replied.

"You know, don't you, that he's got your pals on his conscience?"

"What are you getting at?"

"Fellows like him deserve to be rubbed out," he went on. "They've no right to go on living."

I nodded.

He grinned.

"If you'd like to give me ten packets of cigarettes I'll see to it that Dasch quits the land of the living."

"How do you propose to do it?"

"Quite simple," he replied. "A slight accident, you know. I'm working up there on the scaffolding. Tomorrow when Dasch

398

passes by I'll let a two hundredweight girder drop on his head. See?"

"Yes," I replied.

He stretched out his hand.

"That's a bargain then. Ten packets of cigarettes. You needn't give them all to me at once."

"I haven't got any," I said, and left him standing.

Dasch is still alive today. He was pardoned long before me and sent back to Germany.

One thought, one project, one fixed idea now became rooted in my mind. Day and night I thought of only one thing — escape! I wanted to try it, however hopeless it seemed, and slowly, patiently, surreptitiously I went about my preparations.

I was now able to move much more freely within the prison walls and I knew my way about. It was clear to me that on three sides escape was quite impossible. On the fourth side the cell block formed a natural wall which was supplemented a few feet away by a fence of steel mesh. There were watch towers all round, occupied by guards armed with machine-guns; the guards, however, often took a nap. The wire fence was illuminated at night, and no escape that way had been attempted for years. There were, after all, plenty of other opportunities, in the course of the day's work outside, for instance, which was where the privileged prisoners, among others, made their attempts to get away. Two or three times a month the Leavenworth sirens would wail, giving the alarm that a convict had escaped. The farmers in the neighbourhood would then band together and take part in the hunt. For every escaped convict they intercepted they got a reward of fifty dollars. Some of them had made it into quite a profitable side line and were highly skilled in the technique of pursuit.

I wanted to try another method. Anyhow, I was not allowed to work outside. The governor saw to that too. Once the coal elevator in the engine-room went wrong and the whole heating system threatened to break down. A crisis seemed imminent, for in Kansas the winters are extremely cold. The chief engineer of the prison tried desperately to put things right but was unsuccessful. Then he remembered me and the two of us managed it together. But the governor was not to know that I had helped. . . .

After that the engineer suggested that I would be useful to him as an assistant and he made a great deal of my expert knowledge to the governor. But no luck. I went on digging, dreaming day and night of escape.

My first task was to discover how I could get out of the cell block, which at night was locked up. To this end I made a tool with which the iron bars could be prised apart so that I could slip through them. "Necessity can break iron bars. . . ."

I told no one of my plans.

Then one day all was ready.

I waited until midnight. Then I put my levering tool to work and was successful at the first attempt. I jumped out of the cell block into the open — the narrow no-man's-land between the cell block and the wire fence. I could still keep in the shadow of the main building. Now I had to make a quick leap across the brightly lit space between. If I was seen I wouldn't have a chance. It was just a matter of luck. Once I reached the wire fence the first step would have been completed, and the second, and more difficult, would begin. Perhaps the machine-guns of the guards would be trained upon just that spot at which I intended to work my way through the wire.

I flattened myself against the wall of the

cell block. Then I crouched, ready to spring. "Now," I said to myself, "keep calm." Then I bounded forward.

# CHAPTER 18

## MY YEARS IN ALCATRAZ

In the same moment the beam of a searchlight swept the wall of the cell block. It moved about slowly and rather casually two or three yards away from me. Then it moved further away; then came nearer. And nearer. I flung myself to the ground; the beam passed over me and then was lowered, capturing me in its cone of light. And there I was, as exposed as if I had been in broad daylight. Within the next second, the first warning shots were heard. I jumped from the ground, raised my arms and waited. I had been caught.

On the following morning I appeared before the vice-governor of Leavenworth for questioning.

"Do you admit that you attempted to escape?" he asked me.

"I have no alternative but to admit it."

He nodded.

"Perhaps in your place I would have done the same," he said, "but you realise, don't you, that you must pay the penalty. I sentence you to fourteen days close arrest with bread and water." He nodded again. "Well, that's all, thank you."

I got through those fourteen days pretty well. When you know that the punishment will come to an end on a definite date, it is not so bad, and I had meanwhile become a hardened prison inmate, well able to stand up to such passing afflictions.

But there was a fly in the ointment, and that was the governor himself, who, as I have said, could not stand me. When I had got through the period of close arrest with bread and water, I was put into solitary confinement for eight months 'on silence,' that is to say, I was forbidden to speak. Every day before lunch, in accordance with the terms of my punishment, prison service cadets appeared, in front of whom I had to strip completely. This burdensome performance, which was designed ostensibly to prevent any further attempt at escape, was only another means of causing me annoyance. Fresh air and any chance of exercise outside the few square feet of my cell were denied me. When I was taken out into the corridor for the daily roll-call I occasionally succeeded in communicating with my fellow sufferers by means of sign language.

It is a terrible thing not to hear the sound of your own voice for eight months, to see no ray of sunshine, to breathe no fresh air and have no idea of what is happening in the world outside. Time stands still, and memories come crowding in, memories of things long ago and far away, things that can never come again. Among these memories was Joan, whom I could see standing before me smiling and talking, only to disappear when I put out my hand to touch her.

I don't know how I managed to get through this period. Many prisoners before and after me have taken their own lives during spells of solitary confinement. I actually never entertained the idea, although it did seem as if all hope had departed from my life.

When after eight months I was allowed to leave the cell, I was unable to walk. I should have fallen downstairs if the warder who escorted me had not seized me by the arm.

"Don't be in such a hurry, old chap," he said. "You've got to learn to walk again. It's the same with all of them when they first come out. You've got to get your balance back."

My days in Leavenworth were numbered. My attempt at escape had been reported to Washington, and the supreme authorities thereupon took a decision which made my blood run cold.

I was to be transferred to Alcatraz, the Devil's Island in the Bay of San Francisco, the safest prison in the world, the gaol of living corpses, the penitentiary which only the dead or dying had been known to leave.

Two of us in handcuffs and ankle chains were rushed across America in a prison car. The man who was attached to me like a Siamese twin was called W. Kingdom de Norman, and was the right-hand man of the celebrated gangster king, Dutch Schultz, who had been shot in the street by the machine-gun of a rival gang. The nature of his past was indicated by half a dozen bullet scars. He was a nice fellow with a touch of gaiety about him and he had pleasant manners. We behaved like gentlemen, as befitted the circumstances, for we had to stay together even when we ate or went to the lavatory. The honour of ranking as an intrepid gaol-breaker had to be paid for by many discomforts.

After several days' driving we landed in Alcatraz, having sailed from San Francisco in a motor-boat belonging to the prison. In

Alcatraz, which is a rock two miles from the mainland, there is a warder to every prisoner. There are never more than 2,000 prisoners on this Devil's Island. I was the smallest fry among them. With only one sentence of life imprisonment I had to display a certain diffidence. One of my fellow prisoners had been sentenced to 600 years' imprisonment, many had sentences of life imprisonment plus one day, and many more 199 years. Others had had three life imprisonments plus one day. It was here that Al Capone, one of the most famous of American gangsters, had spent the last years of his life. The most celebrated inhabitant of my time was Machine-gun Kelly, so called because he could shoot his name on a wall with a machine-gun. It was estimated that he had thirty murders on his conscience. A prisoner by the name of Straub had started prison life at the age of seventeen, and had celebrated his fiftieth year in prison in Alcatraz. Straub's hair was snow-white, and his face had an unnatural ruddy colour.

I was received by the captain of the prison guards. In Alcatraz there are only single cells, but they are so arranged that one can talk with one's neighbours. They are iron cages running the length of a long corridor. One can also see one's neighbours if one uses a mirror, and every inmate was well equipped with mirrors which were used mostly to keep an eye on the movements of the guards. The man in the next cell to me was a Negro. He grinned at me in a friendly way and gave me a newspaper as a welcoming present. The light was very bad and I could hardly read. A man wearing civilian clothes surprised me while I was peering busily at the paper.

"You'll ruin your eyes," he remarked.

"I'm sure you're right," I replied.

"I'll see that you get a light," he said.

My first thought was that I was going to be punished again with bread and water, but five minutes later the electric bulb in my cell was actually turned on. The man who had ordered this was called Edward B. Swope, governor of the prison island.

Strangely enough, Alcatraz represented an improvement for me. The island is one of the sights of America and nearly every week senators, foreign journalists and police experts come to view it and admire the model way in which it is run. It is, among other things, the only prison in the world from which a convict has never escaped. Four prisoners were once successful in breaking out over the rocks but they were shot in the water.

In fine weather, excursion boats circled our rocks and we could hear the voice of the guide coming over the ship's loud-speakers:

"Ladies and gentlemen, at the top, left, of the long building you see the cell which Al Capone occupied until his death from a tumour on the brain. If you look lower down and a little further to the right you can see the cell of Machine-gun Kelly. So far it has proved impossible to convict him of the thirty murders he has committed. If he had a machine-gun now he could pick each one of you off even from this distance."

The guide related in full detail the crimes which the inmates of Alcatraz had committed. On one occasion my name was mentioned too; the wind carried a few words into my cell:

"Gimpel, that's the man whom the death of President Roosevelt saved from the hangman's rope."

Sometimes the excursion ships came too near to the island and our warders fired warning shots into the air while the prisoners glued themselves to the tiny spy holes to get a look out into the world. They saw pretty women and ugly women, slim women and fat women clad in light summer clothes, and well-groomed men who enjoyed their coffee while they were regaled with hair-raising stories about Devil's Island. When the weather was fine and if one had good eyes one could pick out every detail on the ships. One could see how the holiday-makers had themselves photographed with Alcatraz as a background. One could see women indulging in the rather poor joke of blowing kisses to the invisible prisoners, while the cruel rock of the island was constantly being committed to the tourists' ciné-cameras.

At dusk the ships would sail back, their passengers having got a little nervous titillation for the price of a few dollars. In the evening we could see the lights of San Francisco and the Golden Gate Bridge, the longest suspension bridge in the world. With hungry eyes we would cling to the neon light advertisements, while the wind would blow scraps of dance music into our cells as the members of the various golf clubs and yachting clubs took their evening's pleasure.

The prisoner in Alcatraz is written off for good. The utter hopelessness of the situation led to a bloody revolt in 1946, in which five men died and fifteen were seriously wounded.

The rising began on the 2nd May, 1946, and it lasted forty-eight hours. The warders were helpless, for the prisoners had armed themselves to the teeth. The American marines landed on the island in force. . . . The American public did not learn what had happened on Alcatraz until some days later.

Two convicts had attacked and overcome a warder, taken his bunch of keys from him and locked him in the 'bloody cell,' that is, cell 403. The two prisoners then succeeded in reaching the armaments gallery. A second warder was relieved of his revolver. The other prisoners were then freed and shouted as one man:

"Now Alcatraz is ours. Let's clear out."

But this first fine careless rapture did not last long.

The rebels did not have the keys to the massive steel doors which shut off the cell blocks from the outside world. A few prisoners returned voluntarily to their cells but three officers who were trying to restore the prisoners to a reasonable frame of mind, were overpowered and locked into cell 403. The rebels also shot at the watch-towers.

"Keep your heads!" called Captain Weinhold from cell 403. "You won't be able to hold out like this for long and you'll have to pay dearly."

One of the prisoners replied:

"If someone's got to die, you can be first!"

The sirens wailed. Alarm! In a sudden access of rage Convict Kretzer fired his gun into cell 403. The governor of Alcatraz had to summon help from outside. The rebels barricaded themselves into the armament gallery. It was like a Wild West film. The battle lasted two days. The marines worked their way up as far as the ventilators, then they dropped gas grenades, but even then the revolt was not crushed. The soldiers took off the roof and threw hand grenades into the armament gallery. The last prisoners to hold out barricaded themselves in a tunnel below the cell block and they died fighting. . . .

Alcatraz was almost completely destroyed and had to be re-built. I was convict number 866 in this gaol with the bloody past.

Although every form of organisation was officially prohibited, prisoners were nowhere so closely organised as in Alcatraz. The bank robbers and kidnappers were the ring-leaders. While rope-making was supposed to be in progress, alcoholic liquor was being brewed from sugar, yeast and raisins stolen from the kitchens. Specialists in the art brewed a mixture of high alcohol percentage and this was distributed among those prisoners whom the 'leaders' favoured. For a long time I was quite ignorant about all this, but one day one of the prisoners called over to me:

"Hey, Dutch, come over here! You can have some, too."

I drank a whole mug of the stuff and couldn't walk straight afterwards. From then onwards I received my daily ration. Alcohol makes everything more tolerable. Our supplies of liquor were discovered and confiscated, but we retained our primitive distillery. The warders, of course, observed that we were drinking, but there was a sort of tacit agreement that it should not be ruled out entirely.

One fellow convict, Kenny Palmer, drank too much one day and lay on the ground in a state of semi-consciousness. When we had finished our day's work and were ready to be taken back to our cells, he, to our horror, staggered over to the captain of the prison guards and blurted out:

"You're really not a bad bloke, Captain, but I don't know how I'm going to get up those stairs."

The captain put his arm round him and dragged him into his cell.

"Have a good sleep," he said. "You're not well. See that you soon get better again."

He did not report the matter, a fact which put him right on top in the prisoners' estimation. Since the bloody uprising of 1946, prisoners and guards had learned a good deal from each other.

Although Alcatraz is known as the toughest of American gaols it also has its pleasant aspects; the dining hall, for instance, which was so appetising and almost comfortable, that you might easily have imagined yourself in a hotel. The tables were of walnut, and we sat in groups as we wished. The menus were well balanced and the food tastily prepared. Of all the American prisons in which I have been obliged to spend nearly eleven years of my life, Devil's Island had the best cuisine.

That was typical of the spirit of the penal system: as none of the prisoners had any chance of ever being free again, the authorities tried to mitigate the desperate monotony of their existence by allowing certain essential reliefs within the framework of the otherwise severe routine. Here, too, I was allowed to go to the cinema twice a month. Once a year, each prisoner appeared before a disciplinary commission of which the captain of the prison guards, the governor of the prison, the block warders and the prison chaplain were members. Although this commission was competent to grant only trifling privileges, the fact that one could appeal to them was in itself of great psychological importance.

For instance, one official said to me:

"Actually, Gimpel, I have no idea why you are still here. After all, you are a prisoner-of-war. I will see if anything can be done for you."

And the governor said:

"Your conduct is excellent, and apart from that you work voluntarily, which is another very good point in your favour. Of all the prisoners here I like you best."

The hope that I might some day be allowed to leave Alcatraz was naturally nourished by these words, although after what I had already been through, it was really foolish of me to cherish any hopes at all.

My sixth year of imprisonment had meanwhile come round. I knew nothing of what was going on in the world outside apart from what I could gather now and then from newspapers which were smuggled into the prison. Every link with my homeland had been broken. I received no letters, and when a warder came to me one day and said: "There's a visitor for you, Gimpel. Get yourself ready," I thought I must have been confused with another prisoner.

But no, he was right.

I was taken into the visitors' room, one of the most remarkable affairs in Alcatraz. Visitors and 'hosts' were separated from each other by a wall in which were spy-holes of thick glass. You could see the other person but you couldn't hear what he was saying, so telephones had been installed on either side of the wall, and you talked to your visitor by telephone. A warder was there to listen to what was said, and if the conversation took a turn which was considered unsuitable for some reason, he pressed a button and cut off all communication.

I entered the visitors' room like a sleep-walker. My escort showed me a spy-hole and I looked through it. On the other side stood a middle-aged man in a well-cut suit. He smiled at me and I picked up the receiver.

"Good morning, Herr Gimpel," he said in German. "You will be surprised to receive a visit. I have been wanting to come to see you for a long time, but I have only just been given permission. I am the German Consul-General in San Francisco, Dr. Schönbach."

"I am delighted to meet you," I stammered.

"I just wanted to tell you that we have not forgotten you. We are doing everything we can to get you out of here. You will understand that we have to proceed carefully. You must have patience and yet more patience."

"I'm quite used to being patient," I replied. "Thank you very much, Consul. You can have no idea what it means to me to be able to speak to someone other than a warder or a convict."

"That I can imagine. I should like to offer you some comfort, but it's easy to talk. I have not come alone," he added. "I have brought with me the chaplain of the German colony in San Francisco." He smiled at me again and a man wearing the typical dress of a pastor stood before the spy-hole. We talked for twenty minutes. Both men promised me that they would come again, and they kept their word. On

the second visit, the governor made a quite unusual concession. I was allowed to meet my visitors in an ordinary room, that is to say, without spy-hole and telephone.

During this time when I began once more to have hope, I was involved, quite without meaning to be, in a small-scale convict revolt. We had come into the dining hall as on every other day. The menu was spaghetti with meat sauce, that is to say, the prisoners' dinner was much more frugal than usual. While we were eating there was an unnatural quiet in the room; not a word was exchanged at any table. Evidently something had been arranged, something I knew nothing about. Then it started. As if at a word of command, the prisoners jumped from their chairs, threw the tables over and smashed everything within reach.

"Meat! meat!" they roared. "Where's the meat? We don't want your filthy sauces, we want meat!"

The guards' machine-guns were thrust through the dining hall windows and we flung ourselves to the ground. The shooting might start at any moment now. After the bloody uprising of 1946, the guards were in no mood to trifle and the prisoners of Alcatraz were not regarded as men to be reasoned or reckoned with;

some of them were, in fact, nothing more or less than beasts.

The captain entered the dining hall and the men whistled at him. Then the governor appeared in person, and the room was suddenly as quiet as it had been before the outbreak.

"What's the matter?" he asked. "Have you all gone mad?" No answer. "I request you to leave the dining hall singly, do you understand? Anyone who does not obey my instructions will be treated as a mutineer. Just remember that."

No one moved.

"I will give you another sixty seconds," continued Mr. Swope, "another fifty-five, another fifty, another forty-five. . . ."

A prisoner stood up hesitantly, looking neither to the left nor to the right. The others whistled at him. But some more men followed him. Most of us were more afraid of the instigators of the revolt than of any punitive measures the governor might take. It was a tricky thing to decide when it might be too soon to leave the room or too late to stay there. Then one of the prisoners stood up and said:

"If we don't get any meat tomorrow, it will happen again. We have every right to have meat, we need meat as part of our diet."

"I will have the matter investigated," said the governor.

The speaker, Pinszky, was as ring-leader removed to Block D, the silent block, for his punishment. He stuck it out for six months, then he committed suicide — on Christmas Eve. He had somehow managed to get hold of a razor blade and severed his main artery. How he succeeded in doing this was never explained, for on Alcatraz the distribution of razor blades was attended by great ceremony. Twice a week, a privileged prisoner appeared with a tray on which were arrayed a number of razor blades, spaced according to a precise layout. Each prisoner was allowed to use a blade for three minutes and had then to replace it on the tray. The blades were changed every week. The prison authorities were anxious to prevent other prisoners going the same way as Mr. Pinszky.

The safety system on Alcatraz worked with all the latest technical refinements. Anyone who had reported for work, had on leaving and entering the cell block, to walk past a device which registered the tiniest piece of metal. If the apparatus buzzed the prisoner had to strip completely and submit to a thorough search. It was therefore quite impossible to smuggle any sort of escape tool into one's cell.

In contrast to other prisons work was not compulsory in Alcatraz. Nor could one buy anything with the few dollars one earned. The so-called 'canteen goods' were not sold but distributed. Everyone got three packets of cigarettes a week. Shaving soap was free, also fruit. A certain amount of chocolate was also distributed.

I was three and a half years in Alcatraz and came into contact there with the most incredible men with the most incredible histories. I was there when an oil millionaire struggled in vain for the freedom of the man who had kidnapped him. And practically every day I met Machine-gun Kelly, who had extracted 200,000 dollars from another oil magnate. He died in Alcatraz on his fifty-ninth birthday from a heart attack.

I had acquired a certain dexterity with rope-making and a few hundred dollars with which I could do nothing stood to my credit. I had gained the confidence both of my fellow convicts and of the prison authorities. I went to work every day and lay every evening disconsolately in bed. I had become a part of the barren monotony of prison life.

Then one night I was suddenly awakened. I looked at the clock. It was three in the morning.

"Has something happened?" I enquired sleepily.

"Yes," replied the warder, "something has happened. Come on, guess what!"

"I know nothing about it," I answered surlily. "Leave me to my sleep or I'll complain in the morning. You've no right to come and disturb me."

"Pack your things, you dolt," said the warder. "Would you believe that a chap could sleep away his own release?"

"Release?" I asked.

"I'll come back for you in five minutes. You've been transferred to Atlanta, Georgia."

I thought I was dreaming. A miracle had happened! I was to leave the Devil's Island of Alcatraz alive and well. It was a sensation which was to appear in all the newspapers, a piece of news which seemed incredible. Transferred to Atlanta! That might be the ante-room to freedom.

# CHAPTER 19

## PROMOTED FROM CONVICT TO MISTER

My hopes soared, but the American legal machine moved slowly. The Atlanta penitentiary to which I was transferred was in the State of Georgia on the east coast of America, that is to say, exactly at the opposite side of the States from Alcatraz. I entered the prison feeling strangely detached from all that was going on around me. But I was once more to learn the meaning of waiting — hopeful, stupid, resigned waiting.

For the second time my sentence had been reduced. I was now to serve thirty years' detention. A good conduct prisoner can, according to American usage, apply for release within the framework of 'parole procedure' when he has served a third of his sentence. Prisoners who are released on these terms must report every day to a certain police station, they must also be indoors at a certain time, and they may drink no alcohol. They have, in fact, still one foot in prison.

I applied for 'release on parole' and was

allocated to a parole officer, Mr. Boone, a coloured man. He was tall, slim, and sported a little moustache, and he proved that a prison overseer can conduct himself with all the considerate good manners of a gentleman. He was a human being and I owe it to him that I am today a free man.

My first application for parole was rejected. I was in despair, hope alternating with apathy. I ate hardly anything, could not sleep and lapsed into a state of dull resentment.

A prisoner could appear before the parole panel only once a year. I had therefore to spend another three hundred and sixty-five days in Atlanta before my case could be reconsidered. Mr. Boone did all he could to banish my mood of resignation. On his advice I took up weaving on the prison looms and became expert at the work. There is no doubt that work does distract one. It was at this time that I completed my first decade in prison, blown with the wind to Atlanta, the scene of the famous novel, *Gone with the Wind*. Ten years among crooks and murderers, in the company of hate-filled prisoners and indifferent overseers, ten years with a number on my arm, three thousand six hundred and fifty nights in a prison cell, nights full of longing, full of hope, full of unshed tears, full of imagined kisses, full of angry curses.

I may have been coal-heaving on the day my father died. I didn't know, I didn't know anything. I didn't want to know anything. East-West relations, the war in Korea, the conflict in Indo-China, none of these things interested me in the slightest.

Nothing but eating, sleeping and once a week the cinema. Then I was joined in my cell by the man who had murdered his wife. It was strange how good-looking a murderer could be. He was young, fair and handsome. He laughed heartily and had a pleasant manner. Apart from the fact that he had killed his wife there was nothing about him to which I could take exception. He had been in Germany, in Munich. He had got to know his girlfriend in the street, and then the thing had happened. The psychiatrist had saved him from the gallows. They sent him from Munich to Atlanta under a life sentence. He told stories of Germany, and as I listened I nearly choked with revulsion.

There were six of us in the cell, including another German, also a spy.

"You can have any woman in Germany," said the murderer. "Sometimes I had to

give ten cigarettes, sometimes twenty, occasionally a bar of chocolate as well perhaps."

"Keep your mouth shut," I said.

"But I'm serious," the murderer continued. "They're easier to get than French
women."

"Don't be an ass," said my German co-
prisoner. "You could get an American
woman and a packet of cigarettes thrown
in."

I felt sick and walked over to the
window. It was of course shut. Nothing all
day but dry stale prison air, coarse talk, the
old jokes, hideous laughter and the morose
faces of the overseers.

Once again I was called away from my
work. Mr. Boone, the coloured parole officer, took me on one side.

"Now pull yourself together," he said. "I
have arranged that you are to appear again
today before the parole judge. Ahead of
your time. See that you leave him with a
good impression."

The man at the judge's table looked
pleasant enough, the typical American petit-
bourgeois. He was neither indifferent nor
sympathetic. He was simply the
mouthpiece of the Washington bureau-
cracy. He could hardly be aware that he

held the fate of men in his hands.

"So you are Gimpel?"

"Yes, sir."

He pushed his spectacles up on to his forehead. I hadn't even had time to wash my hands, my clothes were grubby and I felt awkward and inhibited.

"Now what have you got to say to me?" asked the judge encouragingly.

I couldn't get a word out.

"Is there something you wanted to ask me?" he continued.

"I want my freedom, sir."

He fiddled about with his pencil.

"Well?"

Mr. Boone now took a hand.

"The prisoner has just come straight from his work, sir. He had no idea that he was going to be called before the parole panel today. I would ask you to take that into consideration."

The judge hesitated for a moment, then he became just a shade more friendly.

"I know that your conduct here has been good, but . . . but" — he cleared his throat a few times — "espionage against the United States. That's no trifle, you know." He paused for a while, then he said: "If we sent you back to Germany, would you go to East Germany or West Germany?" He looked at me expectantly.

"To West Germany, sir."

He nodded, satisfied.

"Well, I'll see what I can do for you."

I went back to my work. I heard no more from him for weeks, and months, not a word. Once more Mr. Boone talked to me and tried to keep my spirits up, but prison psychosis, attacks of which I had so far happily escaped, finally got a grip on me and I vacillated all the time between complete numbness and intense excitability. The crisis was reached when I was transferred to another cell.

They were an unappetising lot of men with whom I found myself now, and I wanted to have nothing to do with them. When I had finished my work, I spoke to my warder.

"I'm not going back into that cell any more," I said.

"That's insubordination, and you know what the penalty for that is."

"I don't care."

"I shall have to report you," he said.

I was put into solitary confinement. That was nothing new for me. Bread and water again. By the tenth day I had lost forty pounds and was as thin as a rake. I never answered when I was spoken to and the prison authorities began to get worried about me.

One day I was summoned to the presence of the deputy-governor. The man who took me to him was called Mr. Lowe. He was a human being, too.

"Pull yourself together," he said. "Don't be so obstinate. They're all quite well-disposed towards you here, but you mustn't kick against the regulations."

I made no reply.

The vice-governor looked me over from head to foot.

"Well, Gimpel," he began, "are you still obdurate?"

"Yes, sir."

"I will give you one minute to reconsider your answer," he said. He got to his feet and paced up and down the room. "You're not a child, you know. Think well what you are saying."

He remained standing.

"Are you going back into your cell?"

"No, sir."

"Take him away," said the vice-governor reluctantly.

Mr. Lowe walked by my side. He stopped in the corridor.

"Listen," he said. "You know me, don't you?"

"Yes."

"You know, don't you, that I don't wish you any harm?"

"Yes."

"Well then, just go back to the governor, and tell him that you will obey orders. I dare not tell you what is at stake, but I beg you to go back to him. If you don't, you'll bitterly regret it."

My obstinacy knew no bounds, but I had a high regard for Mr. Lowe and I liked him. He was an elderly man and often talked to me about his family. So I turned back just to please him. Beaming with pleasure he told the vice-governor that I wished to speak to him again.

"Have you thought it over again?" he asked.

"Yes, sir."

"You realise that you acted wrongly?"

"Yes, sir."

"Very well, you will be released tomorrow morning. Your parole has been granted."

I could hardly believe my ears. I had waited for my freedom for nearly eleven years and when it was granted me I could not realise what it meant. I looked into the beaming face of Mr. Lowe.

"You see now what I meant, don't you?" he asked.

"Yes."

"I couldn't tell you, but if you hadn't gone back just now your pardon would have been withdrawn because of insubordination. It's a good thing I was there to advise you."

I grasped his hand and pressed myself against the wall. I was on the point of breaking down.

Things moved forward at great speed. I chose a suit and a shirt. I received personal documents and a cheque for a few hundred dollars. I was just able to shake hands with a few of the men and then I was taken out of the prison. I was free. I was wearing ordinary clothes. I was a man among men. A person with a name and without a number. I was accompanied by an official of the emigration authority, a nice chap.

We drove off at high speed to the Atlanta airfield. The *Italia*, the ship which was to take me back to Germany, was leaving New York harbour the following day.

Then there I was at the airport, with my ticket in my pocket. I laughed, I breathed and looked at everybody and all the everyday happenings around me with radiant eyes. And still I could not fully realise what was happening. I walked over the runway to the four-engined machine. A stewardess in a smart blue costume was standing on the steps of the aircraft. She was slim, blonde and beautiful, and she was smiling. For a few seconds I stood there as if rooted to the spot, staring at her and trying to smile, but the smile failed to come off. My escort gave me a friendly thump on the shoulder.

"Go on," he said.

I sat down, took a piece of chewing gum and tightened my belt. 3,000 feet. 4,500 feet. One hour, two hours. We landed in Washington and then flew on to New York. I was met at the airport by a coloured police official.

"Are you Gimpel?"

My escort answered for me.

The Negro nonchalantly produced some handcuffs from his pocket and clasped them on to me.

"Are you crazy?" said my escort. "He's free."

"I've got my instructions," replied the Negro coldly and in front of all the aircraft passengers he led me away as if I were a criminal. The pretty blonde stewardess looked at me dumbfounded. The emigration authority official apologised to me for his colleague and went away shaking his head.

We drove through New York, the city in

which I had been hunted down, the city in which I had loved and left Joan. Joan . . . the memory was like a pain in my heart, even after ten years.

In the city prison I was torn out of my melancholy dreams and became the convict once more, to be photographed and registered.

"Come on, don't fool about," said the warder. "Stick your paws in the ink."

For the last time my finger-prints were taken.

I could not sleep a wink. In a few hours my ship would be leaving harbour; without me perhaps. Perhaps it had all been a misunderstanding. Perhaps they had heard about my insubordination and had withdrawn the parole. Theoretically I was free. But when a free man is locked up on his last night in the country with murderers, thieves and robbers and is himself treated as if he were a thief or a robber, then something must be wrong somewhere.

At a quarter to six there was a shaking on my cell door.

"Get dressed!" The words were bawled at me harshly. Then a cup of coffee and two slices of white bread were pushed through the cell window.

I was taken to the interrogation room.

Then the procedure of the previous day began for the second time. Photographing, registration, finger-prints, handcuffs. A car drove up.

The official who had the day before fetched me from the airport seated himself beside me. He looked out of the window and didn't say a word. I suppose he was thinking of his instructions.

The *Italia* was to leave within the hour and friends and relatives of the passengers were standing at the pier, laughing and joking, some with tears in their eyes. It was hot, oppressively hot and the women were wearing light summer dresses.

The curious among them formed a lane for me as, still in handcuffs, I crossed the gangway and was taken on board. The press photographers were on the spot and I was 'shot' from every angle.

It seemed as if my escort must have delivered prisoners on to the *Italia* many times before, for he certainly knew the ropes. Without asking anyone he piloted me towards the children's playroom. Then he removed my handcuffs, threw my papers on to a table and shoved a piece of chewing gum into his mouth.

"Sit down," he said. It was the first time he had said anything at all. He looked at his watch. Evidently he was in a hurry.

I looked round at the gay murals of Snow White and the Seven Dwarfs.

My guardian consulted his watch once more and then stood up.

"O.K.," he said, and casually raised his index finger to his cap. That was my leave-taking from America.

He locked the door from the outside and exchanged a few words with one of the stewards. The ship left harbour, for Germany, my homeland, and freedom. I was sailing into the greatest adventure of my life.

When we had passed beyond the three-mile zone, the steward came and unlocked the playroom.

"It's all a lot of red tape," he said. "Just a lot of nonsense."

He showed me the printed passenger list. My name was right at the bottom, added at the last moment.

"Mr. Erich Gimpel," I read.

Mister.

I looked at this word again and again. Promoted from Convict to Mister!

It took me days, weeks, months to understand the miracle of freedom. It was a long time before I could look people in the face without embarrassment, before I could eat just what I liked once more, before my palate learned again to distinguish a Moselle from a Rhine wine. It was a long time before I shook off the habit of avoiding women, before I dared to make enquiries about my relations. . . .

I was now forty-five years, seven months and six days old and had 424 dollars and 24 cents in my pocket. I had been free for six days. Released from prison, expelled from the U.S.A. On parole. I still owed the U.S.A. more than nineteen years detention. To the American authorities I was a spy; to the German a late repatriate. I should in fact have been dead nine years and eleven days.

I avoided going on deck until it was dark. I had forgotten how to speak to people. I had first to get used to the world again. To time. To fresh air. To money. To laughter.

In the long dreary years of captivity I had become unsure of myself and had to force myself to go to the bar. I ordered a whisky and it came. Whisky's cheap when you're free. The bartender smiled. The people near me were talking about me and made no attempt to hide their curiosity. Rumour is the quickest, cheapest and most irresponsible newspaper in the world. A woman was sitting next to me at the bar. I had no idea what she looked like. I had accustomed myself not to look at women any more. She spoke to me, but I did not grasp what she was saying; I was much too agitated. I would never have dared to start a conversation with a woman myself. Women are dead to you when you're living in a cell.

We went on deck together. The *Italia* was now on the high seas. A light breeze blew up and the clouds slowly blew away and revealed the stars. The crests of the little waves danced in changing colours in the moonlight. The ship's engines were working almost silently. The wind was playing with my companion's hair, and as we stood there in the dark, I dared for the first time to look at her. She was good to look at. I was actually standing in the company of a woman at the ship's rail. I was seeing the stars. A fresh breeze was blowing. Suddenly, everything was changed. It was as if all the old imaginings and anxieties had been blown away. For minutes, for hours, I forgot the unforgettable. I forgot that I had been measured by the hangman. I ceased to see the face of the judge as he murmured quietly:

"Death by hanging"; I no longer remembered how my two counsel, having done their best for me, shook me silently by the hand and, embarrassed, quickly turned away. I no longer felt I was Agent 146 who had sailed for forty-six days with U-1230 through depth charges and air attack to land in Frenchman Bay, North America, and carry out the most fantastic task the war could command.

"You look ill," said my companion.

"I am ill," I answered.

"Is it serious?"

"I hope not."

"I noticed at once that there was something wrong with you," she continued. "I think you must be very lonely."

"Yes," I said.

We went back to the bar. My companion was wearing a red cocktail dress and she had thrown a mink wrap round her shoulders. She looked fresh, young and well-off. She smiled. How lovely it was to see a woman smile. A woman who looked young and pretty and rich. That same morning I had still been in the hands of the New York Criminal Investigation Department together with thieves, murderers, and pimps; that evening I realised for the first time all it meant to be free. Free! And alive! And going home! Home to Germany.

"Do you dance?" asked the lady.

"No," I answered. I wanted to tell her why but I couldn't bring myself to it.

"Just as I thought," she said.

We sat together for another half-hour, then I went to my cabin. I could not sleep, although I knew I wouldn't be wakened here every two hours for roll-call.

In the morning I realised that I wasn't a convict any more. I forced myself to stay in bed. Free men don't get up at a quarter to six. I tried to fix my tie, but I couldn't manage it and had to appear at breakfast with an open-neck shirt. My companion of the previous evening was waiting for me. Red seemed to be her favourite colour. She was wearing a woollen dress. She stretched out her hand to me as I approached her.

"I didn't know who you were yesterday, but I do now. Do forgive my tactless questions."

"I was only too happy to have you talking to me," I replied. I wanted to tell her how helpless I still felt but I couldn't find the right words. People were still staring at me. The papers had got quickly to work and were after the Gimpel story like a pack of hounds. So long as I was in captivity no one knew anything about me, but now . . . A hundred and fifty American reporters had waited at the wrong gangway at New York docks. The cables were piling up now. Offers were coming in from all over the world. I had had no experience with newspapers and publishers, and although I didn't know what to do with myself, I wanted to be left in peace.

"Shall we go on deck?" asked the lady whose name I still did not know.

"Yes," I answered.

I doubt if she could possibly have realised what it meant for me to walk on deck with a woman, to talk with her, to see her smile, to breathe her fragrance, to feel the pressure of her hand. That morning I had looked in the mirror. I had grown old. My hair was snow-white. My face was pale, the skin was taut and leathern. According to my birth certificate, I was forty-five but the mirror told a different story.

"Are you Mr. Gimpel?" An officer of the *Italia* had come up to me. "We're putting into Plymouth this afternoon. The English newspapers are bombarding us for an interview with you. Are you willing?"

"Must I?" I asked.

He shrugged his shoulders.

"All right," I said.

There was not much prospect of my

being able to avoid the reporters for long.

I met them in the smoking-room. The officers of the *Italia* didn't at all mind these press conferences. It would be reported that I had travelled back to Europe in their ship. The United States government had paid for my passage — tourist class. I had first of all been placed in a cabin with people who were a bit too noisy for me. I had gone to the purser to ask him if I could change quarters. I had made a slip of the tongue, and said: "Would it be possible for you to give me a different cell, sir?"

He had smiled.

"We haven't any cells, but perhaps a cabin will suit you." We shook hands and had a drink together.

The British reporters were not so persistent as their American colleagues.

"Have you had a good journey?"

"Oh yes," I replied.

"Have you been in England before?"

"Oh yes."

"What do you think of England?"

"It's a very lovely country."

"What do you think of English people?"

"They are very nice people."

"Do you hate America?"

"No, by no means."

I didn't want to say more than a few com-
mon-place courtesies. I still didn't know
whether I should keep silence or whether I
should speak, and so long as I was unsure
the cleverest reporter would not have got
anything out of me. But now the German
press men were after me. One who had
flown to Plymouth to meet me was observing my every movement. I was constantly being called into the wireless room to
talk on the radio-telephone. This was a fore-
taste of what was to await me in Hamburg.

"Did you enjoy being a spy?"

"No, not at all."

"Were you a member of the Party?"

"No."

"Did you know Hitler well?"

I had to smile. What ideas these people
did have about spies! I had been a soldier
like any other man, but on a specially
tricky sector. I had not volunteered for it
any more than ordinary soldiers volunteered for any special posting. We were the
servants of the most unyielding master the
world has ever known. War.

"Have you parents waiting for you at
home?"

"No."

"No wife?"

"No."

"Where will you go?"

"I don't know."

"All the best," said the reporters.

"All the best," I replied.

I was now only a few hours from Hamburg. I wished to leave the ship unrecognized and to this end secured the cooperation of the ship's officers and the German Red Cross. They asked a German exchange student if she would care to be Frau Gimpel for ten minutes and with her I left the *Italia* through a side exit, just above the water-line. We made a somewhat ill-assorted married couple but excited no attention. One woman photographer penetrated the ruse and released her shutter, but I escaped the main hustle and bustle. I climbed into a Red Cross car and was taken to the Friedland camp. I was home again. I was given a gratuity and a late repatriate's passport, and so that I could remain undisturbed for a while they sent me to the Black Forest for a few weeks, to the Marxzell Convalescent Home for Mothers.

It was late summer and the sun smiled on me. I went for walks in the woods at six in the morning. People greeted me in friendly fashion. In the evenings I sat in the Marxzeller Mühle eating trout and drinking Moselle. My digestion was not proving as resilient as my tongue. There was peace here and quiet. Most of the summer visitors had already gone. There was a lady from Karlsruhe recovering from an operation; a hotel-keeper and a master hairdresser from Bonn were taking a few days' holiday; a builders' foreman was killing time between contracts. I was with human beings, gradually getting used to human society. It was peacetime. The war was over. Over. The War. . . .

Then I suddenly knew that I must write my story. I knew that I must draw the veil from an aspect of the war which no one knew about. I must tell of the silent war which I had fought for years and which became my murderer. I wanted to place on record what it had been like. How mean. How cold. How merciless. Over here as over there, in the east as in the west, how men had suffered and died and how men had been tortured to death.

I have spent a few months writing my reminiscences. I have tried to present them in a deliberately unsentimental way and I have not glossed anything over. There is not, there was not, and there never will be any glamour in the metier of spy. The silent battle the secret agent fights is a dirty battle, merciless and cold. It is the dirtiest side of war.

And I hate war. And I hate the job of a spy — I always shall. . . .